120 GROUNDS FOR DIVORCE
BY MARK SAVAGE

Preface

The book is a journey of my life over 40 years much of which has been dedicated to supporting Crewe Alexandra and an ambition to visit all 92 grounds, a complicated affair with so many new grounds and automatic promotions and relegations. While nearly completing this I have been growing up, enjoying music and falling in and out of love, subjects that have all had an influence on the memories of ground visits.

The book also includes memories of supporting Everton in my early years and many non league grounds where 'The Alex' have often come unstuck.

A memory of car trips, train journeys and coach excursions around the length and breadth of the country.

Just as many songs evoke memories; this book is about how grounds bring back nostalgic views on people, music and childhood.

I am not claiming to be as loyal as those that make many or every away game, I just want to share my handful of games every season (although that first year in the Championship meant only a handful of away games were missed) and hope you can relate to at least some of my memories.

It is no coincidence that the book is called 'Grounds for Divorce' because to me and many

they will always be grounds and not stadiums.
GRESTY ROAD not the Alexandra Stadium.

 @markanthonysav

1964 born Bloxwich Walsall
1972 Moved to Crewe
1980 Leave school and work at the Post Office
1986 Leave Post Office
1987 Go to Hope University Liverpool
1990 Marry Kate in Kidderminster
1991 Teach in Birmingham
1992 Teach in Bilston
1993 Becky born
1996 Separate from Kate
1996-2001 Live in Crewe, Kidderminster, Cannock and Wolverhampton and meet Jackie and marry her in 2000.
2001 Back in Crewe Dylan is born.
2002 Get a job in Nantwich.
2003 Becky comes to live in Crewe, staying two and a half years
2004 Reuben is born.
2012 Teach part time and start part time casual work as a Health
Care Assistant

Accrington Stanley

It was an official coach excursion for this night game; it was made with Pete and his lad Tom Newton. I have built a good friendship with Pete after bumping into him at a Half Man Half Biscuit gig in Shrewsbury. He was a lad I knew from the 'Alex', in a nodding "eh up mate" kind of way, but our love of HMHB has meant we often meet up for their gigs and now at the Alex. His lad is now very matey with my 'Alex' mad nephew Rob. It is one of those rarer bonds/friendships that don't happen as much when you get older, and one that you appreciate even more - as you can sometimes become less tolerant and more antisocial in your vintage years!

We went straight to the ground and treated ourselves to a cup of tea in the away end, where the milk and tea was served at a table in the open. The ground had a homely/non league feel to it.

Despite a low crowd, the home support was incredible with lots of "different" football songs sung - the ones that were old Slade and Sex Pistols songs were particularly appealing to me. The Accrington banners were also more creative than the normal predictable banners, which I also found quite refreshing.

The Away End was being extended a few steps and in a few weeks the Open End capacity was going to be extended.

Out on the sandy pitch, my main memory of the game was a heated disagreement between our skipper David Artell and on loan keeper Rhys Taylor. This was right in front of the away fans - talk about washing your dirty linen in public!

I came away enjoying the new ground, relieved that in the open end it remained dry (I had my Docs on prepared for adverse weather conditions) and looking forward to a return fixture on a Saturday with more time to explore.

For more Accrington action, see also "Blackburn".

AFC Bournemouth

This is a bit of a journey and in many ways I'm glad I did it when I was on holiday. I was only 13, so I would like to return again soon.

My main memory was that the ground was surrounded by trees and large detached houses, that made it one of the most untypical football grounds I had ever visited (which still applies after visiting many more grounds over recent decades)

I visited the Dean Court twice that week. There was an open day at the club on one of the days and I enjoyed a leisurely morning greeting some of the players and gaining some autographs. We were allowed to take a leisurely walk around the ground and watch some of the players train before they mingled with the fans. I was quietly chuffed with the day and was looking forward to the match later on in the week.

The game was on a mid-week night in the league cup against Hereford United. I stood in the Home End with my dad and sister and was impressed with the end - which seemed larger than recent pictures suggest. The atmosphere was excellent (in the Home End), but I was surprised to find no visible or vocal Hereford fans in the ground. Hereford is very accessible to Crewe on the train and it is not unknown to be a fixture with some friction over several years, some of which is discussed at a later date. I presume the lack of away fans was due to the midweek factor that often deters travelling fans. I have often been thwarted by new grounds due to midweek fixtures; Middlesbrough away always springs to mind with me (if I wasn't working in Birmingham….)

While in our second week on holiday Elvis Presley died, the only other memory that was on par with the trip to Dean Court.

Aldershot

This was a long time in coming as I had never been to the Recreation ground till Aldershot had returned to the Football League and we were back in the lowest division in 2011.

I went on the official coach with Pete Johnson. Stopping at a service station in Oxfordshire, by the water feature we spoke to a couple of Asian Wolves fans that had their own coach on the way to Fulham. I thought this was brilliant, as for many years Asian faces have been missing from Molyneux, despite a large Indian population. Maybe the "Kick it Out" campaign was making progress.

We arrived early on what was a lovely day. We were meeting up with Pete Wraith who now lived in Sutton. We walked down the hill from the ground and turned right and went for a drink in a pub with a large beer garden. It was in this garden that we met up with Pete. It was a pub where the locals were keen to talk to you and I also met an old punk lad, John Cornes who used to work in Spin Inn Records in Crewe around 1979, he was now living down South.

It was interesting to go through a park to the turnstiles; it reminded us of the different types of grounds that we were now visiting again, but for me I found it homely and enjoyable.

We were situated in the corner of the covered terrace that goes around to an open side. I thought we could have made some noise in the covered bit, but everyone seemed to prefer standing in the open side on this lovely day. It was the Aldershot fans that made a great atmosphere on the day, another team who seemed to be enjoying their time in the football league with lots of great flags, banners and songs. You wouldn't have guessed that this ground only has 3 sides with such a great atmosphere.

It was nice to see Pete Wraith again, showing how visiting the new grounds can help friends to be reunited.

Altrincham

This 1979 cup tie, as the cup did in those days, attracted lots of interest at school. It was easy to get a straight train to the town before that stretch became a tram, so many travelled this way - although I went in the car with my mom and dad. They stood on the side, and I joined lots of Crewe fans in the covered end. We seemed to have taken the end successfully and peacefully, although near my mom and dad at the side some donkey jacketed "Alex" youths fought with some Altrincham "Perry" boys - punk rock battling with the new post punk phenomena.

Altrincham were a better outfit than they are currently, but nothing should explain an awful performance on the pitch on the day. Our 3-0 defeat was just one of many during the 1970's and early 1980's. There was some talk that some of the players were out drinking on the night before that game.

I didn't make our return to Altrincham in the FA Cup in 1995 but rest assured it was a much more professional team that went there 16 years later.

Arsenal

I'm still hoping for that ideal away cup draw to North London, having never visited the old or new ground. I should have taken the opportunity to have visited when the "Alex" had a great run in the youth cup twenty years ago. It is getting to the stage where I may have to visit with a friend from another club, something I would prefer not to do.

This wouldn't be an ideal situation; the guilt can play upon betraying your own side. I did miss a York away game to watch a Coventry/ Arsenal with Mick, my best mate from Coventry. I was in need of a chat over my ex-wife who didn't seem to want me anymore and I was increasingly unhappy with her. Mick was my soul mate and best man and an ideal bloke to listen to my woes. The Wannadies "You and Me" was increasingly irrelevant but hard to get out of my head.

So after admiring ex-player David Platt, the Arsenal defence and a 0-0 draw, we tried to solve my problems over a several jars of ale.
It could have been that I was too obsessed with footy to give her the attention she deserved or perhaps she just loved the attention of other men! Inevitably sex is something that you consider. Maybe I had become a bit complacent and lazy in the bedroom? Perhaps I should have put as much effort in as Arsenal did on a solid back four in those days. If only relationships were as straightforward as football.

Teaching in the West Midlands at the time, it seemed that Arsenal were a very popular team amongst many of the kids - black, Asian and white seemed keen on them at the expense of West Midlands clubs - something I found sad. Maybe it was the pull of success or Ian Wright in the 1990's?

The "Alex" did play Arsenal in a friendly in the late 1970's; a fight in the Railway end between two opposing fans and a 3-1 defeat are my only memories of another meaningless friendly in the summer sunshine.

Aston Villa

This was one of my first ever grounds at the age of 6! I travelled on a coach for the first time as a Walsall fan (we lived in Great Wyrley between Walsall and Cannock).This was a massive game in the old division 3 with a crowd of over 50,000. It was 0-0 but I was absorbed by the massive open away terrace at the Witton End. I remember thinking at the time how many people were in that end? As is often the case at an early age, it was the people and their comments that were of more interest than the game.

By the early 70's I had moved to Crewe, but I never made the mid 1970's League Cup replay to Villa Park. In the first game at Crewe we made a 2-2 draw in front of 12,000 instead of 1,200. At school the next day I remember being proud to say I was in the Gresty End despite the Villa taking it - well walking right into it really!

At 16, I returned to Villa Park having just started work as a postal cadet/telegram lad/postman. All my wages were based around trips to record shops and football matches. I could now live in relative luxury and not have to scrape for weeks to get that crucial album or train fare.

I was still into Everton and the "Alex" and made the trip with my mate Tap. Unlike me, Tap had left the punk scene for a scooter and parka although he also had an attraction to the new casual/ Perry boy look. He had a great 'flickhead fringe' which was even more impressive when he smoked and continually fiddled with his fringe. His new attire also made us look less woolly back at Everton games .Tap convinced me I should flatten my hair and buy some Lois jeans just for Everton games - something I did for a few months before giving up. I didn't feel as comfortable with the look and we still didn't really fit in which led to be drifting more towards the "Alex" eventually..

The worst/best thing about living in Crewe and following Everton was that the biggest scallies were able to bunk the train to Crewe (and some all the way). We often used to get suspicious questions and more often than not, a new packet of 20 would disappear with the help of some nicotine starved Evertonians! Occasionally, we might be asked to give them a nudge when the ticket collector was coming so they could hide in the area reserved for suitcases in between the sets of seats.

Despite our woolly back attire we must have still looked different enough to attract the attention of some Villa skins in Fred Perry t-shirts. Luckily, the bridge by Witton station was heavily policed and we were left un-scathed before the match. Everton actually won the game 2-0 in a period when their form was pretty appalling.

After the game, Tap and I got on the wrong side of the platform, on the side for Walsall. When we realised we joined the platform for New Street, some Evertonians thought we were Villa fans trying to infiltrate them: "Have you got the time mate?"

Eventually we persuaded them we were Everton woolly backs with the help of some more ciggies, but did I really need such hassle off my own fans? I was starting to have my doubts about supporting a club who weren't my local side. For years I had been desperate to follow the Toffeeman and now I could afford it I was now veering back to the "Alex".

Barnet

This is one of the few grounds where the memory of the game is the most noteworthy part. It was Barnet's first game as a football league club and we were treated with a 7-4 thriller with the "Alex" coming out on top. I drove down from Kidderminster and met Phil - an "Alex" exile who was working at the NME in London at the time.

We met up with Pete J and drank at a nearby pub in the sunshine. I can remember a group of lads having a mess around to the "I'm too sexy for my shirt" song that was top of the hit parade at the time! There was a good atmosphere in the "Alex" section, we were housed in covered terracing at the side and we had a party in the sun.

At half time we were treated to a Jimmy Greaves appearance who had to endure some good natured banter!

It was an incredibly warm day, a common feature with some Saturday games in August. It's nice to enjoy it as you know the days of woolly hats and layers of tops aren't far away!

Barnsley

The trip was on the official "Alex" coach. It avoided the motorway and picked an interesting route through Hyde, via reservoirs and the Peak District. Many of the villages were lovely limestone that give the area some character and romanticise the area that suffers perennially from adverse weather conditions. The villages reminded me of the ones featured in the League of Gentlemen TV series.

On the coach I met up with an old mate from the Post Office. Austin and I were pointed in the direction of the new leisure centre for a drink. On arrival we walked into a cloud of smoke in a bar full of people getting drunk while looking through a big window where families were having fun in a big fun pool. It was surreal to see two different lifestyles either side of some glass. It also seemed a little wrong to be staring at a lot of people with very little on, which was exacerbated by the fact that everyone was getting tanked up.

As we left, the clouds hinted that the water theme wouldn't end there. After a few moments the heavens opened at the open end where we were generously offered to buy some plastic macks (bin liners).We had been warned on the ticket and it was February so it wasn't a complete surprise. However, the stewards seemed particularly aggressive all of the game. They were paranoid that everyone would shelter under the police surveillance/tea shop shelter, menacingly asking where you were going when you were in the vicinity. They had been aggressive before the game when a wayward ball had gone into the crowd; it was being passed around in a humorous way when the stewards unnecessarily confiscated it in a belligerent way.

The "Alex" made quite a noise in the rain, especially for an open end. If anything quietens fans down in an open end, rain normally does, but throwing away a 2-0 lead in 2 minutes doesn't help!

One of the funniest moments came at a loo stop in the second half. In the port-a-loos a drenched middle aged "Alex" fan was refusing to leave the toilet so he could dry out. The stewards were telling him he couldn't stay there in a no-nonsense manner. The right to stay in the toilet and miss a match, I cant see civil liberties taking it on board but the memory will always be there!

I did return to Oakwell when the "Alex" was on the verge of being relegated from the Championship. I again frequented the sports centre and this time it was a lovely day and we were in the side of the ground, the oldest part of the ground as ground development had taken place in most of the other ends and sides. It was a joyous day with Hulse and Ashton on fire and a 2-0 win assured we stayed up and partied.

Bilston Town

This was one that made those long, cold, after school matches worthwhile. I'm not saying that taking a football team as a teacher isn't always rewarding, they just tend to be fleeting moments. Yes, you do build up a good relationship with fifteen lads over 5 years. Yes, it can sometimes help turn a discontented delinquent to respect you in class. Yes, one day one of them may, just may, go on to play as a professional but here is my reality.

You have a nightmare afternoon teaching two difficult classes (most afternoon lessons can be a real battle, ask any teacher- who isn't a super teacher!) before boarding a coach to some school for an away game. You haven't had a drink, food or fag since 12.30 and will not get one till you get home about 7 o'clock. You will probably have some school work to do afterwards. Some kids will inevitably mess around and you have to keep turning around, walking to the back of the coach saying "keep it down.......... Sit down" for what seems like the thousandth time in your teaching career (and you fear there might be another 90,000 times to go – 21st century teachers will obviously have lots of non confrontational strategies to cope with this! See Jason Bangbala)

The weather is generally dominated by a howling, biting wind and the pitch often resembles a quagmire (as a non PE teacher you are still in your now filthy suit). The game is quite enjoyable if you haven't been forced to be linesman or referee. Decisions are hard enough to make when reffing, but at this time of day you are buggered, with pressure from students and parents and staff to give the right decision.

If you're very lucky you don't have some squabble/fight/racism/decision to solve/to break up at the end before returning to deal with similar incidents on the coach on the way home. Each year group will compare results on the coach and each year group will then take pleasure in a defeat for another year group (NB: this will probably be stronger between staff managers)

My advice to fellow teachers is managing it with another member of staff; it is less isolating, less stressful and more fun! I co- managed a team with one of my best mates, Graham Collins - he is one of those rare people you really click with and although we are at different schools now, we are still really close. We both shared a love of football, music and politics and his place was my bed and breakfast for nights out in Wolverhampton. Many thanks for that - especially during my divorce year when it wasn't unknown to have one or two too many (Apologies for being sick on your patio but at least I made the bedroom window and I cleared it up before you got up in the morning)

So with the team we took on, Graham was the more competitive - but I like to think we both made a good partnership in spotting and coaxing talent. We took pleasure in having a successful team with a good influx of Asian players - something the other school years seemed to have less of.

It was the first time our school had reached the West Midlands Cup Final. I was excited at the prospect of doing a new ground as well as the chance of winning the cup. Bilston Town FC was located near the Lunt Estate, an estate with some reputation for some of the worst and best pupils (Chris Adams) but on the night they did us proud. A good crowd turned up with support, songs and banners to create a superb atmosphere. A decent stand and perimeter fencing made it a real occasion. With a dressing room and dug out, players and managers alike both felt they had made the big time.

Unfortunately we were beaten by a strong Solihull side, 3-0 but the last one flattered them as we were pushing forward and they hit us on the break. The charismatic Mr Hughes called an offside decision on a possible goal to dent any real chance of victory. Inevitably the winning team always seem older than your team and this is a gripe that players and staff can moan about afterwards.

Overall, it was a brilliant occasion and one that makes the bread and butter games year in and year out worth it.

Scott Finch, Dave Richards, Seymour McConell, Amit Sharma, Lee Moss, Chris Everett, Richard Cartwright, Rajesh Bashal, Andy Clarke, Wayne Lavender, Dipesh Patel and Scott Sandlan were just some of the lovely lads who went on the journey with us.

Birmingham City

Being a big fan of older grounds this was a ground that I have enjoyed visiting. On my first visit it had vast terraces, good cover and four very different sides that made it attractive for those that like their grounds vintage (yes, I know it has updated but like an old house that has kept its original distinctive features).

It is one of the few grounds that I have sat or stood on every side of the ground. This is partly due to me having a friend who is a Blues fan and ground changes which have meant that the away section has been moved around.

My first trip to St Andrews coincided with my student time at college in Liverpool. Rita became a good friend at college and I spent a few days there in the August of 1988, between year 1 and 2 of my degree. The family lived in Acocks Green. Of Irish, catholic origin, the whole family were Blues fans and were very welcoming - I don't think I have eaten that much food in my life (and I can put food away). Drink was also plentiful and a good time was had with a few days in Brum and Malvern.

The trip gave me an opportunity for my first trip to Small Heath on the bus from Acocks Green, catching the bus on the roundabout with the shopping centre and pub on the Coventry Road (The Swan).I didn't know at the time, but 3 years later I would do my first year teaching at Cockshut Hill In Yardley just a mile away. The year was a far less happy one than the 10 happy years I spent in Bilston.

The encounter was a league cup 2nd leg first round match with Wolves. Both clubs would have probably not wanted to be involved in the competition at this stage but both were now in a downward spiral in the football league, although with Bull and Mutch Wolves were starting to emerge again.

We got off the bus near the extensive dilapidated terrace at the side; I was impressed and excited at the prospect of intruding this Midlands derby. The crowd turnout was disappointing, but the atmosphere on the Kop at the side of the ground was witty, passionate and exciting, I soon wanted to join in and sing the Blues.

My second trip was with the "Alex" playing our first game in the old Third Division since the late 60's. Dario has brought us to another division, a first in my memory and a game that had captured the imagination of the town with 3,000 making the trip to the Tilton End. I met up with Rita on this hot August day, passing 'The Wrexham' pub with trepidation where hundreds of blues fans sang outside the pub in the sunshine. They'd just been relegated, what would it be like if they had success?

The 3,000 fans were incredible, especially when you've travelled on a coach to Bury with 17 fans on it in the early 1980's. Unfortunately, it didn't seem to have attracted the most pleasant fans. Monkey noises were in abundance when

Birmingham players touched the ball; songs about 'Pakis' were vociferous and some fought with stewards at half time. Top this off with a 3-0 defeat and I wasn't as proud as Crewe as I had been earlier in the day. I was almost quite pleased to hear that some racist "Alex" fans had had a kickin' on the way to back to New Street by black and white Blues fans.

Despite the (deserved?) bad reputation of Birmingham City fans; fans like Mal and lots of others I have met through Rita, I have always found modest and able to talk about their club in a humorous way. In my opinion Midland people are some of the friendliest in the country; this has been reflected in many conversations with people on numerous trips to Mid and North Wales on holiday.

My next visit to St Andrews took place on a midweek night. I left school in Bilston and picked up Garf from Wolverhampton railway station, having travelled down from Stoke. I'm not a big fan of night games, you tend to be too tired and drained , especially as I had forgot a change of clothes. Watching The "Alex" in a suit, wow, Garf didn't half take the mick! Things were not helped by some appalling traffic on the traffic light infested Birmingham New Road - why we didn't go on the train I don't know? Accordingly, it was all a bit rushed in the pub where we met up with Potty. Drinking by the ground is not good; the pubs are all very full or for home fans only. We did get a couple of pints but I remember wishing it had been a more relaxing weekend trip. Didn't I have some school stuff to do? I never do marking and preparation on a Saturday.

We had been beaten 7-1 on Saturday so it wasn't going to get worse! We lost 5-0. Bizarrely we made the play offs that year as well. This season the following was in the hundreds and we were housed in the lower tier of the main stand where the cameras are on TV. No racism this time, but very little to sing about. The two new sides were built and looked good in the familiar surroundings of Bordsley Green. For me staying on the same site keeps the character of a ground.

The game was a real carnival for the Birmingham fans. Not only had they won 5-0 but the Villa got knocked out of Europe. Word soon got around and it with such euphoria we knew there would be no problems on the way out tonight.

I returned again on a Saturday, the visit to St Andrews coincided with a night out in Wolverhampton. I drove to Graham's house off the Cannock Road and he gave me a lift to the railway station. Getting to New Street is easy - the trains are so frequent and quick. I met Rita and her boyfriend Vaughan and we had a convivial drink in one of the lovely new bars alongside the renovated canal area. Birmingham really does have the feel of a European city nowadays.

After some good banter, we got a lift to the ground, then we went our separate ways. This time we were in the upper tier of the Railway End. It may be old but it gave us a great view and a cover to make plenty of noise - it was the opposite of the last visit - The "Alex" making a right racket while the rest of the ground was silent watching us win 1-0.

I walked back to New Street and on to Wolvcrhampton. At the time, Wolverhampton town centre was increasing in popularity and we had a cracking night finishing up at the Cheeky Monkey night at the Civic. I drank away from my recently found new love, next door neighbour Jackie.

Premiership failure and a new mad drama teacher who supported Blues means more trips to St Andrews were on the on the cards. Unfortunately, he couldn't make it for the 1999 trip in the modernised Railway end. I met up with Rita before the game at her new home in leafy Hall Green. I arrived early and parked on their drive. With nobody in I presumed they'd popped to the shop so I checked my oil and stopped and sat on the wall basking in the August sunshine. Incredibly Rita appeared from the house opposite, apparently she lived at 69 and not 64! Boy was I glad the people at 64 hadn't come back! Rita informed me that two of our college friends are pregnant and that Rita and Vaughan were 'trying.' Even my younger friends were having babies, I must be getting older!

We took the lead after 3 minutes but were the victims of some excellent crosses and lost 5-1 in the end. Still we kept on singing throughout, despite a sparse following for this midweek game. The Blues fans sang an amusing song about not being able to fill a fridge, which was a subtle hint that we hadn't bought a great following!

Like many football fans it's your connections with people you know who can make certain games more memorable and more likely to visit. I'm sure this will always be the case for me with St Andrews.

Blackburn Rovers

This was an unexpected pleasure. Drawn away to Accrington Stanley the game was too much of an interest and switched to Ewood Park! This was Accrington's first FA Cup encounter for years after several years in the doldrums. It also gave me an opportunity to visit an old pal of mine from college, Alison from Preston. I had shared a student house with the girl with a mass of orange curls. She was a good laugh and a good mate.

The trip was made by car, an unusual bunch travelled on this occasion. Damon came for the night out in Preston; an occasional armchair fan who was more interested in Echo and The Bunnymen. He was a bit short on resources, so he wandered around the town after a dinner time drink. He had copped off with Alison on a weekend visit when I was a student and was intrigued by another chance meeting. Damon's lovely - a bit daft in a nice way, heart of gold and a bit of a looker. He would often get women giving them the eye, but he rarely took up such opportunities. He had to be really interested, unlike myself who would take up any half chances on offer!

Garf brought his girlfriend to this one. In the early romantic years there are some who will enjoy the football with their partner. Gill was one that didn't keep going although his present partner Jane was/is an avid "Alex" fan and goes as much as Garf. "Oh you know that I'd do anything for you" I wonder if Robert Smith of The Cure had football in mind when he sung this song.

Garf and Gill were good for each other at the time. Neither was superficial and enjoyed the pleasures of life. Garf is a great laugh and loved trips like this; he would keep you amused with beer and nostalgic memories of trips, sessions and gigs. His dad used to teach at our school and used to keep the kids similarly amused with little anecdotes and stories.

There was a good atmosphere in the pub before the game. On a hill overlooking the ground both fans sung and mingled together. Coming out of the pub after a few beers the ground looked superb from the higher ground. Two of the sides had been modernised, but The "Alex" fans were in the old away end which had character, even with the posts in the way. With a cover, the 3,000 away fans made plenty of noise. The crowd was over 10,000 and surprisingly there was no FA cup shame for us that day!

After the game we headed for Preston to try and find Alison's house. It was a two bedroomed terrace in a dimly lit multicultural area of the town. She was sharing with a mate and the six of us went into town for a session in the pubs and an alternative club where we danced to 'She sells Sanctuary' and other such anthems from the indie /rock disco.

Alison was particularly flirty that evening with me, while Damon was keen on her mate, being unusually eager to take such a good opportunity. Later, when Alison asked me to sit on the floor beneath where she sat, with my head in between her tight jeans I was starting to think of being unfaithful for the first time. If the opportunity arose I was considering it. Could I sacrifice the possibility of breaking a friendship? Of course I could.

The bedroom scenario helped my lusty thoughts resume. Damon paired off with Alison's mate downstairs, Garf and Gill went in one bedroom, leaving Alison and I to share the last bedroom with one bed. On arrival it became quickly clear that it had been friendly flirting rather than something more intimate. It was still a first for me, in my mind I knew I would have slept with her - in itself a big issue to admit to. We did SLEEP together, arm in arm, it was nice, talking for ages until Alison, drunk fell asleep. My mind was active and the house with no central heating was cold. I found sleep impossible until I made myself come in the bathroom.

Next morning driving home Garf kept hinting about last night and couldn't believe we had spent a platonic evening in bed. I couldn't blame him; I had read the signs similarly during and after the club. To this day I'm not sure if he believes me; Gill got on well with my wife and may have thought I was covering myself. It was the first time I seriously considered straying in my topsy turvy relationship. My pregnant wife had her suspicions about sleeping arrangements. I pleaded innocently, seeing her view as hypocritical anyway. She ripped Alison's number and address out of the phone book in a frenzy. On this I occasion maybe I deserved it?

Blackpool

The journey to Blackpool is one that most fans will relish, not because of a superb stadium or team, but because of the possibility of a cracking day trip or weekend away. On my first three trips I have been lucky in that most have been in the summer or autumn. Winter visits are more windswept and out of the holiday season you are more obvious to home fans, making it harder to be anonymous with the holiday makers.

On my first trip to Bloomfield Road, the away end was half of a large open terrace with a segregation barrier down the middle. Despite this end being dilapidated, I did love the walk from the turnstile up to the top of the crumbling open terrace, especially if you'd had a skinful. The top gave a wonderful panoramic view of the town, almost as good as the view from the tower!

I drove to this one, not long after passing my driving test. A car full of drunks and my first trip on the motorway meant the passengers arrived bleary eyed and relieved to be alive, I think my driving still had room for improvement, even in those days.

We arrived and relaxed ourselves further with a drink in Yates' Wine Bar, The Clifton and The Manchester. Near the ground there were a few skirmishes at the side of their covered terrace which owed more to bravado and chase than actual fisticuffs. I will always remember Mick G being picked up by a charging police horse during one near fray with his feet disappearing into mid air like magic.

After the game had finished, the "Alex" fans stood on top of the vast open terrace that overlooks the massive coach park, observing the pockets of Blackpool fans waiting outside the ground. I remember feeling like some kind of soldier or king many centuries ago, anticipating the threat of the growing army outside, wondering like everybody else what the best strategy would be.

When everybody got to the bottom, a charge was made at a small mob that, to my relief, scattered towards the street that led to the sea front. Chases like that are often easier as an away fan, the mob tend to be more unified and compact. The move to the front was a good strategic move by Blackpool. As we moved ahead we moved into splinter groups, either for a bed and breakfast, the station, pubs, cars or coaches. Suddenly, the tables were turned, a walk along the front meant hidden gangs in the arcades and the previous rush of fear and excitement led to fear and anguish although for us the journey back was safe.

My second trip to Bloomfield Road saw four of us stay in a B and B on a Friday night: Strainy, Tony Farrell and Faz. We had a cracking Friday night but on the Saturday Faz was feeling really rough, he would be the first to admit he is a light weight on a session. So as we headed for a dinner time drink and the game, Faz decided he would sleep in the car rather than go to the match - which was fortunate as he was woken as some young lads tried to pinch my old Maxi. They were shocked and moved on when a green looking Faz appeared from under some jackets.

In my first three visits to Blackpool the "Alex" have never scored and conceded ten goals, so it's a good job a visit to Blackpool has other interest.

The third visit deliberately coincided with the annual post office lads piss up. On a coach I was encouraged to dress up so that we could all end up in the 'dressy' nightclubs in Blackpool where the bouncers could often be stroppy on whom they let in. You certainly didn't own up to being from the town who were playing the Seasiders that day as that would make entry nigh impossible. Rather than look more acceptable I always find a gang of lads dressed up more intimidating. Still, rules are rules on these kinds of days and this was a day I decided to conform to the smart casual code of the other lads, much to their amusement.

I remember getting a horse and carriage from Blackpool North to the end near the ground when drinking at dinner time clashed with the match time. Many of us decided to go in their paddock and keep quiet as we wanted to avoid a possible escort after the game because our coach wasn't leaving till 3 am Sunday morning. This got complicated as we paid and ended up being in the terrace in their end rather than in the quieter paddock to the left. Dressed up we stuck out like sore thumbs, so we decided to walk around the covered terrace on the right which was now half home/half visitors and join the "Alex" fans. We were met by taunts when the coppers let us through and huge cheers by the "Alex" fans who thought we had deliberately tried to infiltrate their end. I certainly didn't dismiss their original thoughts.

After the game many people split up. I stuck with Swinny, a lad who had just started at the post office after me. I remember that we spent the early evening on the pier at the North End. We spent a while at the end of the pier, gazing at the Irish Sea and chatting on what was a beautiful evening. The sea breeze was lovely, on hot days inland it is often humid and stuffy, but this was lovely. I love early mornings and evenings when it is hot. We had several pints in the bar on the pier and spending lots of money on the jukebox. I remember putting on 'Keep on Running to you Burn' by the UK Subs, an unusual UK Subs song and even more unusually on the pier bar which was dominated by older people. I swear by the 8th play of this song some of the old people were beginning to tap their feet!

Swinn was a good lad and we had a good chat on about all kinds of things. We knew each other well, Swin had hung around with some 'rum' lads from the Royal Scott pub estate but he was different, despite getting into some scrapes. He has now got an excellent managerial job and proved many 'knockers'. He had a rough start in his life and has done well, but unlike some similar people he isn't trying to be somebody else; he enjoys his work and gives you time of day when you want it.

We have shared similar hassles, both going through divorce with daughters at the same age. As a result we have shared nightmares over our ex-wives, money and child access, with such exchanges helping to keep you fairly sane through a difficult period.

We ended in a club and had a good laugh. "Papa's got a new Pigbag" by Pigbag was one of the few records that stood out from the usual dross you got in such discos in the early 80's. We danced around madly to Pigbag and the odd record that we wouldn't to normally, breaking conventions as we were on a day trip to Blackpool, and you could stop being musically pretentious for the day.

We got chatting to a couple of girls from Cardiff and for a change I got the best looking and the most success. Swinn had 'skanked' me on other occasions - in particularly with an auburn haired beauty from Ostend on a short winter break. I really fancied her and we spent the night chatting in a group. The next night he steamed in and I was not too pleased. I probably dithered too long at that age, I was at my most confident in my thirties after my divorce, despite my hair receding! Strange really, I think you have more confidence on what to say and I think it then hits home why teenage girls sometimes go for older men. I remember hating girls my age going for older men when I was a teenager, not being able to comprehend it. If you use your mistakes and experiences wisely you become a far more eligible partner later I told myself. All I know is that at 18 I would eye somebody up for weeks and when I was ready for a move, somebody else would already have. At 32 I would listen and flatter, get rejected or get a really good night between the sheets. I think I had learnt this more calculated side from this screwed up period of my life on the rebound, that dithering was no good, any rejection should be met with "I get knocked down but I get up again" If you get success you have the ultimate drug rush, the catch, the cop off and the possibility of some fantastic scx with someone you barely know and maybe spending the rest of your life with them. Being a romantic, love was always in the back of my mind as well during this transitional period.

I digress. The Cardiff girl had lovely dark hair in a bob with blue eyes and that lovely South Wales accent, in my opinion. It was all fairly innocent - but some snogging at the end of the night is always a lovely end of the night. It gives you a real buzz, making a walk home or an enormous taxi queue bearable.

On the way back to the coach, we got lost and the 3am coach deadline was drawing near. Out of our heads we thought we had spotted the football ground but arrived at the nearby rugby ground only on the roadside, not the car park side. With 10 minutes to 3am, we climbed into the rugby ground, invaded the empty pitch and climbed over to the other end which backed on to the coach park where the coach was just about to go we made it in the 'nick' of time. It was hilarious! We were laughing our heads off on a real pitch at 3 in the morning! We got back to the coach with snared clothes and fast food down our once smart attire.

We needn't have worried and hurried, people still arrived after us and the atmosphere of drunkenness was apparent everywhere.

People shared tales of drinking and debauchery. It was riotous and sometimes ugly. Before we set off, one lad from Warrington who had missed his coach home tried to get a lift was told in an aggressive way to 'Fuck off' when there was plenty of room on the coach This nearly ended up in gratuitous violence. The same lad is so mellow now that I'm sure he would be embarrassed if he saw the events again.
As the coach started off late, people calmed down and many slept off the effects of drinking, sea air, dancing and singing.

It is a great trip; thank god we weren't in the top flight. Blackpool (apologies I know Blackpool have recently been in there) is a great away trip as I am sure many will agree. I did this trip 3 years on the trot and all were great, although looking back they were so close together that they all blur together into a strange memory of my late teens, a time when responsibilities seemed far away.

In my last year at the Post Office I took a non postman friend along on the annual trip and we ended up in the excellent "My Fathers Moustache" alternative night. I think it has been bulldozed down now.

I attend The Blackpool rebellion Punk festival annually now in August. Unfortunately it often means I miss the first game of the season, but for Garf and Andy and I, we have a great nostalgic night, a good drink and a jump around to some bands that still mean and say a lot to us.

I did return To Blackpool just before the old home end was destroyed. At this time the terracing and seats were now reserved for away fans. The side to our right had been bulldozed and the new home end at the other end had been complete with some of the seats on the left hand side nearly being complete.

I have made the trip with my daughter Becky. We ate chips on the front, had a few games on the pier and chilled on the beach before the game. There was no alcohol this year. We were on the front row of the seats just above the terracing. As usual the away fans were a bit intoxicated. I remember that a steward who looked like somebody famous was greeted with amusing chants all through the game. This showed fans at their humorous drunken best and long may this continue.

Bolton Wanderers

My visit to Burnden Park was a sunny day, first match of the "Alex's" 1987 season. I drove and Damon, Phil and Keith joined me. Damon came up for the evening activities and spent the afternoon walking around Bolton. Keith was a Liverpool fan and used to go home and away, but was now far more into music .This was a time when football wasn't in vogue; the game attracted less than 5,000. Keith was more interested in the trip to Sefton Park music festival after the game, he was still interested in the game but was now more of an armchair fan - he had visited Paris for the European final in the past.

He was also at Heysel with the other passenger Phil. At the time both worked at Crewe railway works and several went to Belgium on free passes - an excellent perk of the job even though some like Phil supported the "Alex" and Leeds. They left before the game started when the news of the deaths circulated the ground. They often talk about the incident, about the great atmosphere before the game and the dirty looks off the police and ferry staff as they made their premature way home.

Phil was another good friend, at the time we often confided in each other about personal matters. We also shared a love of music, left wing politics and an ambition to visit all 92 grounds. We both loved to explore and walk around the grounds - but in those days a trip to Bolton was best done by going straight in the ground.

These were still our 'pre-success days' and a following of 150 was at the time seen as pretty decent. We were situated in the corner with a bit of cover or some open terrace in between the Co-op. We opted for some cover, positioning wise, the side where we were seemed similar to the old Hull ground but smaller; neither atmosphere nor game were remarkable.

We found Liverpool for six, parking on the bohemian, but rundown Lark Lane. The trip to Liverpool had added interest for me - I fancied going to college there and this was another chance to see if the city was going to entice me. We bought some food and some cans from the 'offy' for the festival in the park. The security shutters with a small gap to buy goods was a shock for 4 wooly backs from Crewe! We felt like children at Christmas picking out toys we wanted when picking out various beers to the staff. Red Stripe was fashionable at the time and the choice of the lager drinkers.

There weren't vast amounts of people but it was pleasant; people relaxing on the bank while the bands played on the other side of the lake. We met up with the Train Set, the indie band from Crewe who had recently had single of the week in NME. The drummer Adam from Winsford talked the band up and was a bit cocky while the others often played down their talents. Clive was a night owl, a great talker and eternally unemployed at the time (ironically he now works, trying to get the unemployed back to work) the two guitarists Shig and Booty were both ex-postman and really good lads. We thought they were the best band on and although we were probably biased I believe they were much better than Benny Profane who headlined. The summer evening and atmosphere made up for some of the mediocre bands. At the festival I also remember buying a lovely fried egg sandwich which in itself is a little strange; I suppose it may have had something to do with soaking up the beer and the journey home to Crewe.

On the way back we called at a party in the Haslington area of Crewe we had heard about. The party was being hosted by somebody I knew from CND; she was the secretary of the party
I remember chatting to a girl who was clearly into CND and music. She was impressed to find that I had been to the festival but seemed nearly horrified to hear that we had been to the footy as well. This seemed to ruin any possible romantic intentions (well that's my excuse); such were the days when people into music hated football. Ten years later they seemed to go hand in hand.
I seemed to be in the minority in thinking that you could be a socialist, in CND, like punk, indie and football. I think this one of the reasons why I got on so well with Phil.

It was in very different circumstances that I visited the Reebok stadium in the 1998/9 season. We went in the car, this time with my friend Faz. Faz had lived in Bolton till he was 13 due to his dad swopping a railway job in Horwich for Crewe. I was one who tried to intimidate him on his first day of school in Crewe for looking a bit punk, being new and for being from Bolton. We immediately became friends and like a good wine our friendship is even better today. He is one of the Sunday crowd who meet up in The Duke of Bridgwater every week. Faz was going steady on our previous visit to Bolton and very into clothes and vintage furniture. He now combined the above, football and a lovely wife and 3 children. Faz and his son Eliot (who has grown up to be as lovely as his dad in attitude and looks) were season ticket holders living in Crewe. We travelled with both scarves out of the window which caused some confusion to drivers on the M6. Phil joined Faz and his lad. Phil had recently become a dad and lived in Reading at the time. This was Phil's first footy trip of the season and it was like the old days (apart from Faz's son was 12 and nearly as old as us in the old days!) It was a new added bonus to the trip and our changing lives.

We all went in the New Orleans pub near the ground. The new ground was quite impressive for a new ground, although I still have a dislike for this new football/out of town shopping complexes despite them now being aimed at the family audience that the 3 of us had now become part of. Although we enjoyed the drink in New Orleans I would prefer it if we didn't have the American diner experience before a game. Maybe it's me that is the dinosaur.

We were bottom and Wanderers nearly top but I did feel strangely hopeful. So did many others - about 1,500 made the trip and we were in great singing form. Lots of new and older were in the crowd. We were 3-0 up at the start of the second half and the game took a real carnival atmosphere. It was probably the best away trip of the year (although it wasn't shared by everybody in the car).

Boston United

A bit of a long journey to the East coast, I went with some fellow postman to this first round cup tie in 1982. Danny drove the car. Danny was a popular bloke at work, somebody who arranged football and cricket matches against other firms or colleges. The team was affectionately known at the post office as Danny's dirty dozen. His charisma meant that he could easily get a group of both older but mainly young lads to play; Danny had respect without being a hard man, a massive drinker or a great sportsman. He was one of those blokes who was miserable but had a great dry sense of humour. If Jack Dee had been a postman he would have been Danny.

He took his girlfriend to this match (which was unusual, it must have been serious!) He knew my liking for punky attire and told me to tone it down for the trip. At the time I was into Chron Gen, Anti Pasti and Blitz as well as loving the Jam and Wah Heat.

The other passenger was ST who was an unusual passenger in the car. One of the first people in Crewe to take up the Perry boy/casual attire and a follower of Manchester City,   we made up a rather strange foursome. ST was a little older than me and he had been and done the punk and mod style before the designer clothing.

When in Boston we split up. ST and I thought we'd get a pint. I don't know if we were unlucky or if the first round of the FA cup brings out a more undesirable fan than usual in the lower leagues, but we quickly attracted the attention of the whole pub. The bar staff seemed to be ignoring us and we decided to make a sharp exit. We were out safely, but within a hundred yards a gang came across the road at us in a menacing manner and we were lucky to reach the ground without a big kick in'.

On entering the ground I was aware that the non league ground was better than ours. We were situated in a decent, large, covered terrace. The humiliation was furthered with another exit to a non-league club.

Bradford City

This was a midweek "Alex" game over Easter while I was a student. My dad offered to take me and my friends Rick and Phil and was one of those trips where very little stands out. The ground was difficult to find and my dad's presence meant behaviour was more sombre - although Phil and Rick got on very well with my dad. All my friends seemed to, although this wasn't always the case with me in my teens, not unusually. However, as I have got older I have found that we have got increasingly closer and his remaining optimism for life has been immense in helping me through dark times.

The ground was more modern than most at the time, rebuilding after the tragic fire. Recently, I have been doing some casual work as a Health Care Assistant and as part of the training on fire safety we watched the you tube clip of the coverage as it went out live on Yorkshire TV. It is still one of the most compelling moments in football history as reflected in the engaged audience of health workers. The disgusting comments by some Crewe youth at a recent City game with regards to the fire was shocking and I will use this opportunity to apologise for a tiny minority.

Valley Parade has kept its character with the houses in close proximity to the ground. We were situated in a covered terrace behind the goal, but the recent poor form, being a midweek match and a 2-0 defeat, meant one of those trips that won't be thought about with much fondness. But I was pleased that I had managed to notch up a ground in a season that meant away games were a rare novelty.

A deeper memory of Bradford was when I was 11 at Gresty Road. Bradford was top of the old 4th division and brought about 600 fans on a Tuesday night. My dad usually went with me - although he stood in the pop side, so I was given some freedom, but was more confined than my other friends. He rarely came over to me, but did embarrass/protect me by coming over when there was serious trouble, usually somebody like Stockport or Northampton who were the bad boys of the mid 1970's. This was the first game on my own and I promised to be careful but was looking forward to the freedom.

Bradford had taken the Gresty End, and me and my school mates were in the Railway End. My mates usually ran on the pitch at the end and I was going to take this opportunity to join them - just as several hundred Bradford fans, surprisingly, decided to join the pitch and run over towards us. I remember running, probably faster than most of the 1975 "Alex" team, across the pitch, clambering over the pop side wall and stopping running half way down Nantwich Road. The laughter and the speedy heart beat at the end of the chase reflected what was exciting and frightening at the same time. When I was at High School, and up until the point where I had been caught and hurt ,such chases were exciting and a major talking point at an all boys school, the running and singing were just as important as collecting the football cards.

I now work with a top guy who is a deputy head, Mr Falamarzi who is a big Bradford fan; I hope to visit Valley Parade again with him soon, something that is long overdue.

Brentford

A game with Brentford doesn't really excite either fans, but there have been some talking points to make Brentford games eventful.

This trip to Brentford was made on the "Alex" coach with Phil in Easter 1991. As per usual, we were catching up with football, left wing politics, music and women, and the trip to west London flew by. We arrived early and strolled around the ground. Hemmed in by terraced houses and a pub on every corner of the ground, I immediately liked it - even the open end where we were situated looked good in the sunshine. The covered terrace on the side was spacious and noisy, and the end with terraces and seats (now the away end) was impressive. We tried the pub on the corner of the away end /singing terrace and felt welcome, making the most of the early arrival on the official coach.

A disappointing game led to defeat in front of a fairly quiet and meagre away following. It was brought to life by a bizarre incident. Apparently some fan had been barracking "Deano", Dean Greygoose, our goalkeeper. Somebody took offence to the criticism and fists were thrown in the ensuing argument which must have puzzled the Brentford fans.

During this period there was trouble when Brentford came to Gresty Road, fighting with the stewards and invading the pitch spring to mind in one season. I was going to omit this bit but in 2014 there was trouble with the stewards again so I decided it was still relevant. This was in stark contrast to the good behaviour of Will, who followed Brentford rather than Chelsea in John King's book 'Headhunters'. He was often the well behaved one of the lads. On our visit we felt very comfortable and relaxed at the friendly ground.

 I always feel uncomfortable when passing through London on a coach, you hear comments that would make Phil and I squirm like "spot the white man "and much worse. Another amusing one was "shit around here" I think London may have a few places that are of interest!

Brentford has other memories for Crewe fans - Shaun Smith scoring from the half way line; winning the play off final to get into the championship for the first time; the sale of Gary Blissett and Clayton Donaldson **and** a crazy 6-4 defeat in the 1970's. Maybe the Brentford game does excite after all!

Brighton Hove Albion

This away game was fortunate, falling in the February half term holiday. Kate was up for this weekend away in winter, Becky was nearly two making going away a bit easier and I could visit the Goldstone ground for the first time. It was a win/win situation. We looked forward to this immensely, as vegetarians, Brighton appealed with it having a vegetarian shoe shop and many vegetarian restaurants. As a "Levellers" and "Peter and the Test Tube Babies" fan, the town also had an added interest for me. We had pre-booked at the Butlins hotel, not the ideal option but when you have children the situation changes.

When we arrived after a long journey on Friday night we quickly realised that it was a 60's weekend which was reflected in the age of the people, the dress of some of them and the music. I was left pondering if they will have such weekends for punk and new romantics in the future?

20 years on I look forward to and attend similar events at the Rebellion Festival in Blackpool. Still, you don't feel uncomfortable with a baby at Butlins although northern accents do stand out a bit down there.

The next day, the three of us ventured into Brighton by bus and explored early in the morning. The Lanes were interesting and there were plenty of shops to please the three of us. I bought a pair of boots from Vegetarian Shoes, the main quality non leather shop in Britain! Good, non-leather boots are especially hard to get so I took the opportunity with enthusiasm, it was nice not having to do the usual perusal around shops looking for 'man made upper, man made sole.' Trainers and pumps are easier if you are looking for non leather products.

I left Becky and Kate about 1.30 and made the small journey from Brighton to Hove. On the station I spoke to a lad who was going to protest about live animal exports nearby, this was the big media event at the time in nearby Shoreham. I'm more active to footy than protesting at animal events, although I am a committed veggie which is easier and involves no hassle once you have initially made the decision. Vegetarianism is a personal thing for me; I have no problem cooking meat or eating with people eating meat. I am not a preacher!

On the train to Hove I met Steely, the "Alex" fan from the South West, by chance; it was good to see him and we had a couple of pints at a boozer between Hove station and the ground. There was a good atmosphere in there with a fair few "Alex" fans in there. The ground was interesting, every side being different. The open side was strange, it was empty apart from a small section at the back near the centre which was full and with the tightly packed fans stood in the February sunshine it looked like the Albion fans were away fans isolated from an intimidating home crowd.

We were behind the goal in a seated section partly covered. We shared it with the Albion fans that who had most of the end. It seemed a small away end with the "Alex" having a few hundred there and nearly filling it. Many others seemed to have made a weekend of it, obviously not to the same scale as Blackpool, but it was an opportunity for fans to have a good winter break, which was even better after Robbie Savage got the only goal of the game.

After the game, I joined Steely for a couple of hours drinking in a pub near Brighton station. This was an unusual time for me to have a drink. I much prefer to go home and listen to the radio and go out later, but this made a nice change, especially as I didn't see Steely that often. We both now had children and wives which added to our other common interests.

The next day was wet, so we visited the eastern influenced Pavilion, which looked and was spectacular (although Becky was a bit young to appreciate the finer details!) However, there was plenty for her to engage in on the promenade where I recognised one or two "Alex" faces. The stony beach was too cold today but I had seen enough to tempt all of us for another visit.

That visit came under very different circumstances, I was no longer with Kate, and Brighton was now playing at the athletics stadium the Withdean Stadium. I drove down on the Saturday with Pete Johnson to see an old friend Pete Wraith who now lived in Sutton in Surrey/South London (depending on the spin you want to put on it). Monica treated us to a lovely meal and we were astonished to see how their children had grown up. We met up with Tony Fox who had also moved to London and had a civilised and enjoyable night out in Sutton. Tony was an eccentric guy, and it would be this that would sometimes lead us into scrapes - but tonight wasn't one of them.

The next day the lads went with the kids to the park before dropping them off and venturing into Sussex. The ground is on the outskirts of the town in a wealthy area on the outskirts of the town that wasn't very car parking friendly. We were situated in an open end with about 300 others. The Brighton fans amused us with a few humorous songs about how we were only here for the sun and on the pitch; the "Alex" put four past the Albion.

On the way back we listened to the Brighton fans moaning on the local radio. One of us decided to ring in and I was nominated to speak live. I wittered on how we had been slaughtered at home last week and our local radio had been similar, suggesting that the reactions were knee jerk and that football can change very quickly and many radio callers can be very fickle. In fact I heard some "Alex" fans moaning in the game and we had won easily.

I have yet to visit the new ground, if I do I will make a weekend of it, I could do with some new boots!

Bristol City

This first trip was made during Easter of my second year at college in Liverpool. I was currently into the 3rd month of a whirlwind relationship with Kate who was to be my wife at a later date.
She lived in Kidderminster, on the way to the South West, so during a stay there we both decided to make the visit. As she had been lazy with her Art coursework, she wanted to stop at some rural spot for some inspiration with the brush. As it was an evening game we made an early start, Kate had provided a great picnic and she did a bit of sketching in Gloucestershire, we had deliberately chosen this rural route for this purpose. We made our way towards to Bristol for early afternoon, busy touching each other on this journey as happens in relationships that move forward in an exciting way very quickly. Unfortunately, they are often the ones that fizzle out as quickly as they started.

Arriving in my mum's car I was horrified by how astronomical the car park prices were. Hence we did some window shopping in a lively and large shopping centre.

We had problems finding the ground, it was one of the worst signposted grounds I have been to. We eventually stopped at a pub for a pint and some food before getting further directions. We found some street parking with some difficulty and then found Ashton Gate.

At the time the Robins were top of the Fourth Division and there was an unbelievable 17,000 in the ground against the "Alex" who were pushing for promotion. Bristol City doesn't get that many in the championship very often, proving that supporters love success at any level.

We were in a small section of the old open end, squeezed in between the houses at the back. Despite the reputation of the City fans, I have never had hassle there, home or away. One memory that does stand out was the one 'class conscious' song of the City fans "you can stick your fucking poll tax up your arse- sideways" This was the same month of the poll tax riot in London and the nations feelings had obviously reached the terraces. I did like this ground, despite my antagonism to an away end with no cover (perhaps because it was dry and warm). Their end was compact, similar to the old Trent end at Forest. The high stand at the side with the steps down was unique and a distinctive element that football ground enthusiasts would clearly recognise as Ashton Gate.

About 500 made the trip for this evening game. This really was the season where our following took off due to our increased success under Dario. Unfortunately, not all stayed as we were 4 down in half an hour and ended up losing 4-1.

I returned to a different and even better Ashton Gate while living In Kidderminster with my wife when we were both in the old Third Division in the mid 1990's. I met Phil (who was living in Cardiff at the time, and had travelled by train) at Bristol

Temple Meads Station in the car. It is a lovely station that from the outside looks like an elegant town hall.

This time we were situated in the old home end although it is now seats, it is deceptively large and I think I changed my mind with the Forest comparison. The old away end looked impressive, now covered and even though the steps going up to the stand had disappeared, the replacement had made the ground even more compact.

The following game was a bit disappointing but the singing was much easier under cover, with some quite amusing chants despite a disappointing defeat.

The journey from the station to the ground was far easier this time; parking was by a ring road. This park was a memory on both visits to the ground, thriving with many games involving local youngsters of all races. I hope the park is still there today, I know Bristol is known for its radical politics; I would be surprised if its proud citizens would let this park that seems at the centre of its community disappear.

Bristol Rovers

This was the year of the "Alex's" first play off in the old Third Division.

I first made my trip to Twerton Park Bath in the league. I had passed the old ground in Bristol when lost in Bristol although I had never visited it for a game.

I travelled from Kidderminster and parked on the Bristol Road walking up towards the ground. I enjoy trips to the South West because I usually meet up with an old friend who now lived in the area. I met him on this day, on a bright sunny winter day which was fortunate as you are in an open end. Steely and I were brought together by a love of the Undertones and this was reinforced by a love of the "Alex". We were still friends despite an embarrassing period when he had a brief fling with my sister who wanted it to be more than that.

The ground was interesting if not a little adequate for a club of Rovers' stature. Lots of different stands a long the side kept its unique non-league feel which I find quite romantic but it is usually disappointing to be in an open end.

During the game one stand kept many fans fascinated in a macabre way - somebody had had a heart attack and for about 15 minutes (and what seemed a lot longer) paramedics tried to revive him by pushing up and down on his chest. The game quickly became a meaningless sideshow for the second half.

Making the play-offs meant a quick return to Twerton Park. A sell out crowd and 1,500 tickets taken by the "Alex" meant a great atmosphere for the first leg Sunday fixture. The "Alex" end looked great boosted by lots of European club football flags being waved about by some of our 'boys' It reminded me of the Kop at Anfield on some of their great European nights, Maybe this was the nearest we would get to it!

The "Alex" got a credible 0-0, which didn't go down with the home fans. A pitch invasion by Rovers greeted the final whistle and only the presence of dogs and horses kept them from our pen where we were kept in after the game. After the game I remember feeling the most nervous I had been for several years. As you walk past the shops, the path is raised above the road with a kind of barrier along it, like the old terraces. As everybody filtered out down the road, the Rovers fans leaned over intimidating and picking out some "Alex" fans who were met with fists and kicks. Play-off semis do seem to intensify rivalry (unlike finals which seem to be friendlier) and this game certainly reflected this.

Rovers scraped a 1-1 draw in the second leg and went through in the 2nd leg on away goals. Their fans were really cocky - forget local rivalries, I personally put the Pirates near the top of my "don't like" list.

This didn't change much when I returned to see the "Alex" play at the Memorial ground back in North Bristol. I made the trip in the car with Pete and Tony Gebbard, an old friend from the Post Office. I was back in Crewe then, and we stopped at Kidderminster on the way to pick up my teenage daughter, she was coming up to Crewe for a few days so I was treating her to the added bonus of an away game. She was really pleased!

When we arrived, we parked near a park and went for a drink to be told it was home fans only and we didn't even have colours. We did find a pub eventually, but it wasn't the type of pub where you got into a friendly chat with the opposing fans where you share tales of teams and previous meetings.

I did like the Memorial Ground; we were in a terrace on the side with stand behind us. There was a good covered terrace to our right and a small stand behind the other goal. Some might call it a mish mash, but for me it was an interesting ground with some originality. It was another dry day against Rovers which made it ideal for Becky to sit on the terrace and fiddle with her mobile phone, a far more interesting activity than the game!

I have mellowed my opinions to Rovers, accepting that a play-off doesn't bring the best out of fans, but for me I take a bit more pleasure with a win against Rovers than most teams.

Burnley

My first trip to Turf Moor was one that whetted the appetite, we were eternally in the fourth Division and this was a prestigious ground and club in 1983.They were in the Third Division which at the time was well below their 'station' in social class terms.

It was a second leg League Cup game and we had won the first tie 1-0. It had engaged the town so much that 3 coach loads made the visit for this on a weekday night, daring to sing the Hovis tune from the safety of our coach as we travelled through the outskirts of Burnley. We parked near the ground and were met by a large police presence.

On television, Turf Moor seemed to have a great atmosphere, with a great view of the moors behind the open end. The large covered terrace at the side that accommodated home and away fans seemed brimming with energy and noise and it didn't disappoint - there was a huge amount of noise from the Burnley side even though it probably wasn't one of their most attractive games of the season. I remember that they sold beer in the ground which was very unusual in those days, perhaps that explains why the atmosphere was so good! The view from the side was also superb and made this terrace in the 1980's one of my all time favourites.

The "Alex" part must have looked fairly empty, but the 200 or so of us made a fair bit of noise and boy did we have plenty to cheer about, winning 4-

3 and going through to the next round! This was the early 80's, a time of little cheer and this stands in my memory as one of our greatest moments on a big stage.

I returned to Turf Moor in 1997 during my divorce period. The game clashed with a time when I had got over the trauma and was beginning to build my confidence. Ironically, it was Kate wanting and sleeping with me when we met up to sign the divorce papers that gave me confidence to look elsewhere with higher esteem. I felt that I must have meant something, even if she just wanted to say goodbye in an intimate way.

The night before I had stumbled into 'Gregs' night club in Nantwich and had a brief encounter with a girl who worked in Safeway's in Sandbach, going home with a phone number in my pocket. I remember feeling rough on the coach but quite chuffed. This was early days in rebuilding my life so any good interaction was a tonic. I knew I was going out with Mick in Liverpool that night so I took the tea option in the ground This time we were behind the goal in the enormous and impressive old stand.

What a contrast in 14 years. This time the atmosphere was awful, despite there being more fans in the ground, both fans were quiet and if Turf Moor was vibrant and intimidating in the past it certainly wasn't today. A victory from Burnley didn't change matters, the big terrace on the side now replaced by seats was quiet and the open terrace now boasted a two tier stand, but at what cost?. Maybe it was an off day and we weren't much of an attraction? Perhaps it was the introduction of all seater stadiums? Football post Hillsborough? Whatever the reason it certainly seemed different today.

Luckily the night in Liverpool was a good one. After arriving back on the coach it was back to my Mom and Dads (a stint that lasted nearly a year) in Crewe for some food and a quick bath before getting the train up to Liverpool. It was like being a teenager again, I would see Becky every other weekend and one night in the week, but the other weekend would be a combination of football, pubs, gigs and clubs. It hadn't been what I wanted with Kate or Becky, but things had been that bad that I had to get out.

In some ways I had got the best of both worlds, a part time dad to do the nice things without the responsibility and time for the pleasures and school preparation at work. When thinking rationally I thought I should make the best of the times with Becky having as good a time as possible, she loved her trips to Crewe seeing her cousins and Nannie and Grandad.

In more irrational times I thought have we fucked up Becky as much as much as we had ourselves? No it wasn't easy for me trying to keep her on the phone when she wanted to rush off and watch her favourite programme on television, coming off the phone in tears. Having a 4 hour drive on a Sunday to take her back home after a great weekend wasn't always easy.

Yes, I did have a good night in Liverpool. Yes, I did end up in some lovely woman's bed. Yes, I probably wouldn't have visited Burnley on this date if I hadn't got divorced. Yes, I wouldn't have to juggle Becky with an afternoon's school work on a Sunday? Yes, I would have been with Becky, how guilty should I feel?

Burton Albion

This one was changed to a Friday night at short notice - which made getting there more problematic. In the end I ended up going with my ex brother in law and his lad Rob, who for the last couple of years has gone to nearly every game home and away. This was a bit problematic as Kev and my sister had recently split up. Now Kev is a lovely lad, very sociable and likeable which is probably one of the reasons he played away from home. Heidi, my sister hadn't taken the split well, but on the other hand it was important to be civil with Kev, who I liked and important that we kept things normal with Rob and going to the "Alex" was a good healing process for Rob through this transitional period. The offer of a lift was a kind offer and it made it easier to tick off a new ground - so diplomacy and split loyalties were all issues on the trip. Footy is a great talking point, so matrimonial discussions were kept to a minimum and the company and chat was enjoyable.

We parked near a roundabout and went to the ground. There is a lovely bar in the away end which is situated in an area between the turnstiles and the ground. I met ex-student Nigel Roberts at the bar who I used to teach and went to school with his Dad. He was one of those students who I really liked and will always remember.

The away end was covered with good acoustics. However, the first half was tainted by some quite offensive chanting about Dario Gradi by some of the younger lads who didn't see him in the same light as older fans. Yes Dario did probably go on too long, but the abuse was disrespectful and inspired me to write to the Crewe Chronicle that week. No-one, including me confronted the fans in the ground - it was my guilt that inspired me to write, a less brave alternative. In the second half another ex-student I taught, Bricky, was instrumental in getting the fans to get behind the team and it seemed to raise the team to a more spirited second half display.

It was an enjoyable journey back, Kev was a good lad but he had hurt Heidi and she was hurting for a long time. It was another situation that was more problematic than football.

Bury

This was an unplanned visit to Gigg Lane when I was 17. On day release from the Post Office doing Business Studies, I met Steely by chance who I knew from various Undertones concerts. I met him by the lift at about 4 o'clock and he said he was off to catch the coach to Bury. I thought he was a good lad so I took this opportunity to extend our relationship.

Luckily, there was room on the coach, plenty; in fact I was one of the 17 on the coach for this midweek localish derby. Younger fans would find this hard to believe, but it shows us what the pre-Dario days were like.

We stood in the first half behind the goal in the covered end which is the home end now; it was spacious, covered and I liked it, it had character. About 4 of us managed a chant before a handful of lads told us to "shut the fuck up" We were outnumbered in the away end by some Perry boys our casual lads weren't on this trip, we were dressed in donkey jackets, straights and Docs. We did as they said and in the second half we did our best to be anonymous in the paddock underneath the stand.

I returned to Gigg Lane in the 1990's. Kate took myself Phil and Keith in her Mini (car and skirt).We were dropped off by the park on the main road where we were to be met after the game. We went to a couple of nearby pubs which were packed with both fans; it was boisterous but trouble free.

With both of us on course for promotion frivolity was in abundance with both fans creating a great atmosphere.

I met up with Garf at the game, he had come with a mate from Manchester University and they wanted a lift back to the station, with his mate. Kate obliged but that journey wasn't half uncomfortable! Kate had been around Bury town and their market, which she said was impressive, returning with a handful of bargains. These were the days when she was happy to mix shopping, my mates and the football together and a good day was had by all.

I returned again in 2011 in the car with Kev my brother-in-law at the time, his lad and Robbie Campbell - who both went to my school. We parked by the park that has been previously mentioned. By the ground Kev and I were interviewed outside for a new website that was being launched, but I let Kev do most of the talking. We watched later that week, how technology and how we watch the game is changing. This year we were in the opposite end which is deceptively larger than it looks on the television. The toilets have the original features with lovely brickwork and would especially appeal to my wife Jackie, who loves classic architecture like that (but not enough to visit!). However, the young fans just think it's old and shit!

Cambridge United

My mate Phil, who is a bit of a nomad and whom was living in Cardiff at the time, came up to see me In Kidderminster on the train. He was late as usual, but this time he could blame British Rail.

From Kidderminster Station we went straight to Cambridge - a much shorter journey now due to the improved A14. We had some trouble finding the ground and also missed most of the tourist attractions. I do fancy a return trip for the weekend in the future, with or without football.

We took a walk across some green land next to the Abbey stadium to a pub which was friendly enough and had a mixture of both fans in.

The ground accommodated the away fans in a small open end with a small section at the side of which there is some seating and terracing.

One of the memories of the game was meeting up a friend Dave Meecock who was 'paralytic' sitting on the terraces oblivious to anything going on around him. I never found out if there was any particular reason for his state, Dave does like a drink and loves the "Alex". He did miss a lovely goal at our end by Wayne Collins, one of my favourite "Alex" players.

Phil stopped the night in Kidderminster after the game. It was fine until Phil and Kate got into a row. Kate always saw Phil as pretentious and would enjoy winding him up with all kinds of issues;

issues they would probably agree on but for the sake of a row take different perspectives. Kate stormed off to bed, not the first or last disagreement between the two of them. Torn between a friend and a partner is an unpleasant situation and one that does crop up from time to time. Life does get more complicated with age and balancing your partners and friends can be a big part of it.

Cardiff City

This is one that has often coincided with seeing Phil who has had two periods living in the Welsh capital. Phil was living in Manchester in the early 90's on our first trip to see Crewe there and he came to Kidderminster. We were nattering in the car non-stop and we missed the Cardiff M50 turn and ended up having to cross the Severn Bridge which was a costly debate with the toll.

The weather was getting increasingly worse and we were lucky to get over the bridge, because not long after that, the bridge was closed due to adverse weather conditions, mainly wind and rain.

There had been vast amounts of wet weather recently and the game commencing was beginning to be in doubt. It is funny how in such conditions that you keep convincing yourself that the game will be on. We shared stories on how we had played in much muddier conditions and we remained optimistic although we tuned into the local Welsh radio to be sure. Just as we were getting to the ground it was called off at about 2.30.The rain was really torrential in Cardiff and it wasn't surprising but you still have this sense of disbelief when a game is called off. Did the radio get it wrong? Is teletext right? Has the website been up dated?

Not knowing when I'd be back, I made up my mind to go in the ground, the gates were open and we wandered in to the Cardiff end behind the goal Not many can say that without feeling bruised!. I remember thinking that the end looked smaller than it appeared on the TV and that the pitch was unplayable.

Fortunately, we were stopping the night down there, staying at a woman's house whom Phil had lodged with when living down here, so it wasn't as bad as people who'd arrived on the official coaches and had to go straight back. We went out drinking and ended up going to two parties that were dominated by older Welsh nationalists/socialist types. We witnessed an amazing rendition of Sweet Chariot (Swing High Swing Low) in a wonderful gospel style, Irish rebel songs and some songs in Welsh. It was interesting but the people were more politically bold than I was (I supported most of their views but didn't share their commitment) or wanted on a Saturday before Christmas. However, the hospitality was amazing and it suited Phil's interests at this current time.

My second trip to Ninian Park coincided with Kate being pregnant. We decided to make a weekend of it in 1993 and we set off early Saturday morning picnicking around Monmouth/Chepstow. The journey through the Forest of Dean on the Welsh/English border is surely one of the most breathtaking views in the country.

We booked into one of the big hotels and lapped up the luxury, showering gratuitously and watching MTV. Lennie Kravitz's hit of that year seemed to be constantly played every half an hour. We checked out the town centre with the impressive castle and I treated myself to the baggiest pair of jeans I had ever bought which turned out to be good quality for the money!

We parted our ways at two o'clock and I drove to the ground. We were in the corner of the seats by the open end. Apparently this had been very intimidating last year, we had stopped them getting in the play-offs with a draw and the "Alex" fans were trapped in the corner on both sides and by hundreds on the pitch at the end, showering the "Alex" fans with coins. This year there was another big crowd, they were on a good run and a win would have made a club record. Consequently the open end was full again and a little hostile.

Bobby Moore had just died and there was a banner saying Bobby Moore RIP hanging from the side opposite us on a day where there was a minutes silence for his death. This was a remarkable sight; I couldn't imagine a respected Welshman having a banner in England although the death of Gary Speed many years later was a really positive exception. This was largely respected, apart from literally a handful of lads who made as much noise as possible (which is loud during silence) which predictably increased the amount of Eng-er-land chant from the "Alex" fans in response.

About 200 of us made lots of noise (I remember starting lots of songs off today) that afternoon to make a good atmosphere (their Ayatollah chant and hand waving chant is original and impressive) and bring Cardiff's winning record to an end with a draw. It was fairly peaceful, apart from one fan that calmly walked over to us at the end who told us he wasn't a 'sheep shagger'. Fair enough I suppose, I didn't see many sheep in Cardiff!

Getting in the car in the car park opposite the ground by the athletics stadium I could spot several fans lingering around the coaches, at this time this seemed a rare occurrence but will not come as much of a surprise to many away fans who have travelled to Ninian Park.

After going back to the hotel, we went for a drink before going to the old Odeon cinema in town. This was followed by a meal to round off a really good day. The drinking was limited due to the pregnancy, hence a rare trip to the cinema for us which makes it even more unlikely that I can't even remember what film we saw!

The third trip to Ninian Park was on my own, travelling from Kidderminster to Phil and Sarah's flat in Roath. We were situated in the open end on a sunny winter's day, a big end that must have looked pretty sparse. The "Alex" were terrible that day and trailing 1-0 until the Alex got an injury time equaliser. From the kick off the incredible happened, we went down the field and scored again. We danced, jumped and dived all over this vast end to celebrate a situation that most fans will have enjoyed, or walked away devastated, at some time in their football history. It either feels great, you are set up for the night or it could ruin your night/weekend/week! When you have been awful for 90 minutes it makes it even better. I was slightly brought down to earth when leaving, one Cardiff fan pleaded "where's your boys?" .He must have been devastated by the result or more likely he'd have said it anyway. Nobody was up for mither and everyone kept their head down and walked away.

The night out was great, good company, many beers and a sing song in a bar with a drag artist Now that was a first for me and I'd recommend it if the atmosphere on such nights is as good as this was. Some flirting with one of Sara's mates rounded up the night nicely. Cardiff, a great place, great castle and never dull. Ninian Park was a cracking stadium and I look forward to hopefully not being disappointed with their new stadium in the future.

Carlisle United

I drove to this which is not as long as you think due to the journey being all motorway, and the less busy part of it at that. It was 1991 and with no tape in the car we had to make do with various local radio stations. Many were playing dance music by Rebel MC and Shabba Ranks in between a certain record from a Robin Hood film that was still being flogged to death. Carlisle is also a decent trip on the train - something I would like to do on a return trip to Brunton Park

I went with the Johnson brothers to this one. Rick has been unwell and doesn't go to the "Alex" any more. Pete has been a good friend for many years. Pete is ten years older than me but has often hung around with people younger than himself .We became friends after getting talking to him in the Duke of Bridgwater pub in the early 1980's. He has always been an "Alex" fanatic since the sixties, following them home and away through the good and awful periods. I have always seen him as my "Alex" dictionary - he can remember scorers and the build up to goals of games 30 years and 30 days ago, which puts me to absolute shame. He has been so committed to the "Alex" that he puts somebody like me into the part-time category.

Passing through Carlisle, I couldn't help being pleasantly surprised by some impressive buildings and architecture, including the castle and the railway station which was particularly pleasant on the eye.

After parking up, we found a pub near the ground which wasn't hostile and we had a pleasant couple of pints (this hasn't always been the case for those interested read 'She wore a Scarlet Ribbon' by Jules Hornbrook which is a really good read)

We walked along a footpath passing a dilapidated covered terrace that we were located in. We were situated along the side with a decent view. A brilliant Carlisle goal stood out in a fairly un-memorable trip north.

Charlton Athletic

This trip to the other CAFC was made on the coach not long after meeting my second wife to be Jackie in the 1997/98 season. The Verve were becoming massive at the time and 'The Drugs Don't Work' was now being played on the mainstream radio stations as we travelled south to the capital in the optimistic days of a new Labour government for the first time in eighteen years.

Pete Johnson was on the coach but I nearly missed the coach after squeezing some extra time out of Jackie, so I ended up sitting next to a lad who was good company. He worked on the rigs and can't make every game but he certainly had a passion for the lads. I also found out that his girlfriend at the time knew Jak, that's living in a small town for you! He accompanied Pete and others in a friendly pub near the ground where the coach was parked. Prices were dropped for this game - such is the pull of the "Alex", five pound for kids and away fans, which led to 15,000 fans and an excellent away following. I remember spotting the block of flats you always see in the corner at the Valley that I had seen on the television. There was an excellent atmosphere despite the hostile stewards in a game that the score line suggested was closer than it was in reality, a 3-2 defeat.

One quite interesting game on the coach played with some fans is "Guess the exact time of arrival in Crewe" (when you get to around Birmingham). I'm sure other fans have similar benchmarks to what time they get back from away games, differing whether it is from the North or South. Some cheats try and change the time when we get to Keele. On arrival today it was straight to the Brunswick on Nantwich Road to meet Jackie and some mates. I'd got some polos handy before meeting her! We arrived at 8.50, I can't remember who was the nearest to that predicted time.

Chelsea

Chelsea was spray painted all over Crewe around 1980. A lad from Crewe was as mad about spray paint as Chelsea and any visitor may have been foiled to think they were in West London (well not really, but you get the point).

I remember the 1-0 league cup victory in the mid 70's (and even more success in 1961 for older fans to reminiscence about), hence the away FA 3rd round cup draw really captured the imagination of the town in 1990. The town was buzzing. I made the trip down on the coach and we were in the big visitors open end. The West and East stand stood proudly to both sides, but this end, like the opposite Shed, had the past written all over it.

My memories of this end on TV were often to see a small section of away fans surrounded by no mans land segregation (not forgetting that unique little stand in the corner). Well today the end kept filling until eventually we had the whole end. I can only remember seeing this a couple of times at Stamford Bridge, most notably when Liverpool won the title here. I don't know who was more Surprised - us, the police, stewards or their boys in the West stand. When the "Alex" came out, it was like a carnival.
Then in the second half the incredible happened, we took the lead through Steve Walters. I epitomised my emotions in the following quote from my wedding speech that summer:
   "I'll never forget that day after meeting Kate, walking alongside the windswept Mersey together

cuddling each other excitedly………….. nearly as good as taking the lead at Chelsea." (I had met her at Liverpool doing my degree in Liverpool). Well it got a laugh from everyone, including Kate.

Unfortunately, going back to the game, they equalised and we lost the replay, but it was a great day. It was marginally spoilt on the way back with a brief showing of Chubby Brown on video on the coach. Fortunately, somebody complained and it was turned off. I certainly felt uncomfortable knowing the racist jokes were likely to start soon but I didn't get up. Somebody thought the language was too blue for their child and it was turned off, I wish I'd had the courage to make a stand against racism before that. It reminded me of that poem by Martin Niemoller where no one is left because everybody had tolerated prejudice. Half Man Half Biscuit also did a song version of the poem in their ironic style. I digress again. Steve Walters was one of the great young prodigies the "Alex" produced, but one that didn't make the grade. He fell out with Dario and ended up at Northwich, partly, allegedly, due to his betting and lifestyle.

Later during my divorce years going out in Nantwich he was a regular face about town, it may have been this that Dario disliked. When I see Chelsea on the television nowadays it bares no resemblance to the place I visited in 1990, it has been transformed. However, they still play the excellent ska classic 'The Liquidator' by the Harry J Allstars, which is a nice touch with the past that has remained.

Cheltenham Town

My first trip to Whaddon Road was on Boxing Day of the 2003 season and the visit conveniently filled a vacuum as I wasn't seeing my daughter until the next day. This was the season we went straight back up to the Championship and the "Alex" were on fire that day, as they were most of the season, with Dean Ashton and Rob Hulse scoring goals for fun.

After the big grounds had become the norm in the Championship, it was a bit of a reality check to be at Cheltenham. At the time, the away end was a small open terrace. With some open terracing and an old stand to our right and a compact end behind the other goal, it was much smaller but more of a 'normal' ground for the older fans who hadn't grown up going to big grounds with the "Alex".

I have returned to Cheltenham a couple of times and have also found it a lucky ground for the "Alex". It is interesting that the ground is in the middle of a council estate when the town is often associated with wealth and prosperity. However, as a fan of Demob, the punk band who originated from Gloucester/Cheltenham, I was familiar, through the bands songs like 'Teenage Adolescence', with some of the problems in the two towns. I wasn't surprised to find like any other town that all towns are not exclusively rich or poor.

I have always found that the social club by the ground is hospitable and friendly and I hope that a play-off final hasn't spoilt that.

Chester City

Chester City are one of our biggest rivals, although it is nothing like the intense hate that they share with Wrexham. When we played them in the early 80's we hadn't played them much in my supporting time. They were often in a better league than us when I was younger, more recently they have been in the doldrums while we have blossomed.

My first two trips to Sealand Road were not with the "Alex". When I lived near Walsall I had a good friend called Ian Pearce. We kept in vague touch when I moved to Crewe and then his dad died (his mum had died earlier). He then went to live with his older sister in Rossett, six miles form both Wrexham and Chester. He took time to settle and I visited him at weekends fairly frequently at the start. One visit coincided with a Chester–Walsall game, a game of interest knowing our football mania and former locality. Ian was more football mad than me, and a Wolves fan. We used to play Subbuteo for hours, commentating and making crowd noises. He used to push rather than flick and I always remember him having a runny nose.

We went in the main stand near the Chester end, which gave us a great view of the non–football action. Walsall had brought many fans and had taken their end. However, as the game went on Chester seemed to reform and more entered the end with both fans making plenty of noise, with sporadic fights and surges taking place. I remember leaving the ground to a huge chant of 'Walsall boys will be back in town again'

At a similar time of being aged 12 we went to a local derby with Wrexham. Ian was now a bit of a Wrexham fan. Rossett was in Wales and Wrexham were pushing for the old second division and his new mates seemed to follow Wrexham. I think there was more segregation the year after and we were in the open end behind the goals on a sunny day. Two Chester fans infiltrated the away end and got a kickin' which seemed an incredibly brave/stupid thing to do.

The game was delayed at the start due to a Wrexham fan throwing an empty bottle of whisky at the crossbar, which smashed in the goalmouth. I think this was before the days of crossbar challenge! It was a strange sight seeing lots of stewards on their hands and knees clearing glass.

When we played Chester for the first time in ages there was a real buzz, also fuelled by it being the first game of the season. I was working at the Post Office at the time and all the young lads were going there. We decided to get the train, only 19 minutes from Crewe that got us into Chester for 11o'clock ish. There were plenty on the train but luckily no escort, although there was a police presence on the station. There was ST, sacrificing man City for this one and Swinny. Swinny was respected on his estate but in many ways stood out from the others by working and being ambitious, a life of crime wasn't a certainty although he was no angel. At first we went in one of the small hotels by the station. A quiet, friendly, bar it gave us chance to talk about the game and the possible adventures that inevitably lay ahead.

With a few beers down us we headed towards the town centre, about 8 of us walking down the pedestrianised area. Chester has a great city centre, but I don't think you appreciate places as much if they are on your doorstep and you visit them frequently. You enjoy it but you are sometimes oblivious to the wonders of the River Dee, the walls, the amphitheatre and the cathedral when you are shopping or drinking. Today we definitely had other things on our mind.

The exclusive Grosvenor Hotel lay ahead, so with a few beers down us we tried to blag our way in with the doorman. It wasn't really our scene and we weren't really expecting to get in but it was a laugh. Unfortunately during this humorous banter we started to realise that we had been sussed out by some Chester boys. There were about 20 visible but on a Saturday afternoon in town there could have been many others lingering around, I for one was worried. Should we try and hide in the Grosvenor? Should we try and fight our way out? Neither seemed realistic to me, fight or flight?

Just as their boys started moving forward and giving us verbal abuse we heard a big chant of "Crewey boys we are here…oohh." The cavalry had arrived just in the nick of time. ST sensed the odds had changed and moved forwards and with this new mob coming from behind. Chester retreated down the pedestrianised area. However, our now 50 strong squad still had to be wary. Chester have got some hard lads (many tourists are unaware that Chester does have some tough areas) and the old original shops all have balconies from yesteryear but are excellent for looking out for opposing fans and throwing objects.

We all piled in a pub near the Racecourse after the town centre. I consumed another 4 drinks and was feeling really drunk in a good atmosphere until a brick was thrown through a window. The atmosphere quickly changed and people were outside looking for retaliation. I don't recall too much trouble here, but the landlord with the help of the police decided to shut the pub so we walked in the August sunshine to the ground.

We had the open end and half of the terraced side. Similar to the earlier visit with Wrexham, Chester had a couple of fans in our end. The inevitable fracas led to most people ambling into the open away end. To curtail the trouble the police closed a gate in the corner of the open bit and the side leaving me and about 50 others who had not been involved in the open end trouble on the side with most others behind the goal. At half time some Chester fans climbed over the segregation fence and got into our bit on the side. They were really up for it, one took off his belt and one bearded Crewe fan took him on, most of our fighters were behind the goal and for the second time today I thought the worst. However, as before the cavalry arrived for the second time. Suddenly a couple of hundred "Alex" fans ran across the pitch to help numbers out on the side. Calm was restored before the second half started, but the game was fairly immaterial. I remember we had an escort back to the station, pockets of Chester fans kept appearing and taunting us, but it was all fairly peaceful. What a mob we had that day, on the train you spotted every 'nutter' in the area from aged13-40.

We were straight in the pub from the station, starting off in the Royal and drinking until last orders. I think I had about 13 pints that day, a record for me that still stands today. A day trip on the train is definitely more exciting, interesting and more dangerous than the coach.

The "Alex" were at Chester at the new Deva stadium on the last game of the season a decade later when they clinched promotion. It was a sell out and I couldn't get a ticket. Kate and I travelled up to Chester for shopping; I felt I had to be near even if I couldn't get in. I saw some familiar faces around and witnessed some similar running battles through the pedestrianised area. One "Alex" fan kicked a street artist's cap in the air, knocking his money everywhere, which was gratuitous as he had nothing to do with the football. This annoyed Kate and I, Kate used the incident to put down football. I didn't blame her, it wasn't nice but I've seen worse.
Now I do love shopping, but on a crucial day like this I couldn't concentrate, wishing I was at the game, wanting to know the score, trying to listen for a radio commentary or scan a TV shop. It didn't really work. I would have been happier with Radio Stoke or Teletext, I tried to please Kate, myself and the "Alex" but it didn't work. I was delighted to

find we had gone up, but it was all a bit of an anti-climax. I had missed one of our great celebratory days.

I did make the Deva Stadium for a Johnstone's Paint Trophy game just before Chester went out of the league. It was a rushed job, we drove for the night game on the first day of the new term, so fellow teacher at Shavington, Pete Rhodes and I were a bit pre-occupied.

As a result we set off late and got in late with many other latecomers. Due to the lack of appeal in the JPT's early rounds there were only 2 sides open, we were on one side and they were in the other. The new ground is lacking in character on an industrial estate and similar to many other characterless small grounds.

Like the start of any new term, there are often so many things going on in your head with all the things you have to do, which isn't helped with the big holiday (apologies to those with shorter holidays). In some pleasant weather the game petered out and into a draw. This prolonged the night further and with penalty misery at least we could get home to think more seriously about education!

I look forward to visiting again, with Chester back in the Football League and in a far more relaxed manner.

For Chester at Macclesfield see Macclesfield Town.

Chesterfield

I travelled up from Kidderminster for my first trip to Saltergate. I was supposed to meet Garf in their social club. I arrived there early; surprised by the quick trip, the A38 is certainly a good quiet road.

In the bar I got talking to an ex-miner who gave me honest answers to my questions. I was an active socialist at the time and the strike has had such an impact on future working behaviour that the chat had quite an impact. In the 80's, I had helped organise a benefit gig for the miners in Crewe One lasting memory of that was the miner we invited down to talk to the audience ended up copping off with one of my mate's sisters! We also talked about several coaches going to see Man United from Chesterfield that angered us both.

It was a good job we chatted because my mate Garf didn't show. These were the pre-mobile phone days. In the ground I found Pete Johnson, the away bit is quite large with some cover at the side, an open terrace and some seats on the other side. Now when you haven't brought many, having your fans spread out has a detrimental effect on the atmosphere. Pete and I tried to get some singing going on the side, but with pockets of people spread out it was a losing battle. The 3-0 defeat and a poor display didn't help matters.

I returned to see the "Alex" play at the new ground. I went with Pete Newton to this one, I was getting particularly disillusioned with teaching at this time and I apologise to Pete for boring him with the details.

The ground was impressive for a new one and was nearby to real houses, pubs and shops which made for a refreshing change.
We were seated behind the goal and a healthy number had made the trip, some like me to tick off the new ground. We were treated to a real treat and nightmare. There were goals galore to treat both fans but with a 5-2 lead near the end we thought we were coasting. Bizarrely we ended up capitulating and drawing 5-5. It had been a wonderful life experience but we were absolutely gutted to be leaving against promotion rivals with only one point. It had been a great atmosphere and the new ground certainly seemed to have been a positive one with a large passionate home crowd.

Colchester United

Despite being in the same league for many years, I only just made the visit to Layer Road before they moved to their new ground.
Colchester frequently played on Friday night in the past and with the added distance it had one that nearly slipped away.

My main memory of Colchester is a meaningless end of season game in 1982 at home. On a beautiful day with an even smaller crowd than usual we were sitting on the terrace basking in the sunshine, going through the motions This was the kind of game that the superb playoffs has largely eroded. Suddenly a mass brawl between several players broke out, but why? There had been few tackles and no malice, perhaps they wanted to instigate some memory to this unmemorable game. Two Colchester and one "Alex" player were sent off. I have a vague recollection that it was two brothers in the Colchester team.

My boys were quite young when I attended this old Third Division game/league one game. This is a hell of a journey and the coach didn't make the ground till 2.40, meaning no time for a walk around or a drink. This was frustrating as you don't get chance to get a feel for around the ground which I see as a big part of the day trip. The "Alex" won, Steve Jones got a cracker and I particularly enjoyed the old school end which was ideal for making a great noise and had real character - even if there wasn't that many of us and it had seen better days. There were seats in the opposite end which was unusual for old grounds like this, but it gave it some originality. The home crowd made lots of noise to our right, the toilets were really small, antiquated and full of graffiti, they reminded me of some of pictures of the toilets in the classic punk venue CBGB's in New York.

This was a game that played on my consciousness. My obsession with new grounds had meant that I had left the house at 7.15am to leave – leaving? Jak on her own with two young children. I wasn't going with a particular mate and my time to reflect on the coach was making me feel selfish and guilty. I kind of made up my mind that I wouldn't do a long away game unless it was a vital game or until the lads are old enough to do along trip with me.

This year we are away at Colchester on the 29th of December, the kids are now 9 and 12 and it our wedding anniversary, my dream would be a few days in London and taking in the game. The initial interest from Jak hasn't been that optimistic, let's hope its not grounds for divorce.

Coventry City

Coventry are the kind of club that seem to generate little interest in most fans, me included (ironically their financial mess in the 21st century has put them in the public eye as much as that glorious FA cup victory).This all changed after I met my mate Michael Keane while studying at Liverpool, a football fanatic and close friend and who has been my best man twice. I have now changed the view held in John King's 'Football Factory' that "Coventry City are fuck all" as what usually happens when you have a friend from another team, you suddenly take a major interest where before there was very little.

My first trip to Highfield Road was as a newly affluent, working 17 year old following Everton. I made the trip with my mate Tappy. After changing at New Street, two non-scousers started talking to us, asking if they had seen us at other Everton games. We were suspicious and said we were going to see a mate even though we thought it was unlikely that Coventry would have some 'boys' who lived in Birmingham. Interestingly enough we met them later in the Everton end and we had a laugh about it. The Evertonians were from Telford!

Now in those days Everton were poor, but despite this their songs were often about the players: "Ronnie Godless down our wing." It's funny how Scousers and successful teams tend to have more songs about the players. In the Midlands and other less successful clubs, I suppose predictably, fans tend to spend time singing about the opposing teams in an aggressive manner.

Incredibly Everton couldn't put a foot wrong and ended up winning 5-0. We were in the open terrace and were jubilant, such a score line being such a rarity. After the game there were buses to take fans back to the railway station, but not enough for ourselves and about 50 other scallies. We set off across the park near the ground which I was later to visit with Michael, living a 5 minute walk away in Welland Road, Lower Stoke. Now as we got nearer to the town an enormous mob was growing on the other side*. The contrast of styles was obvious - Coventry were dominated by skins and punks, Everton's boys had flickheads and casual wear (I had my casualish uniform on, hair was brushed down and not spiked, I would have felt more comfortable with the Coventry mob). I was too 'woolly' and not interested enough to look similar and sharp as the Toffeemen. "Part-time Punks", well yes I was when I followed Everton. However, my mate looked the part in his bubble coat.
Everyone was shouting "stand" and "stay" as isolated Coventry fans ran in and the ranks looked depleted against such a mob. Everton fans were standing and doing well against all odds but I was thinking "Where the fuck am I? I haven't a clue where the station is and at this rate we're more likely to find the hospital". Suddenly several police horses came from nowhere and the two mobs were eventually dispersed. The coppers made everybody get on two buses that were still stuck in traffic and it was standing room only, we were packed in like sardines. We were certainly

contravening any safety laws on how many were allowed on a bus. As we passed the Coventry lads, everybody was deriding the Harringtons and Doctor Martins worn by the Coventry lads which made me think how this was my usual attire. On the train back some Evertonians raided the buffet car and we were greeted by the transport police at Crewe. The train was delayed and when we eventually got off, after pleading innocence to the coppers, the tannoy said: "The Liverpool train has been delayed due to the behaviour of football hooligans". Working at the Post Office, I kept my head down as some working postmen collecting mailbags from the train were among the people who looked at us with disdain.

I was again left to ponder my love of Everton and felt further pull toward the "Alex" and music.

My other trips to Highfield Road, a handful, have all been with Mick against other top flight teams since 1990. One, against Chelsea for a morning kick off was a dull 0-0 draw (due to being Grand National Day) in 1990 with such a quiet atmosphere. We were in the open end in the home area. This was part from the odd Eton Boat song and 'In our Coventry homes' which are fantastic anthems and songs, but not on a game with a morning kickoff. This was the first premiership game I had seen for ages and I was surprised to see both fans being let out at the same time without trouble. Things were certainly changing during this period.

More recent visits were in the lower tier of the East Stand where the atmosphere has been one of the best I have seen in the nineties. However, it can be a little uncomfortable. Everybody stands which I prefer and you can without hassle from the stewards which is rare, but if you are right at the back and tall, which I am, your head hits the ceiling of the bottom of the upper tier. Hence, if you are on the back rows you have to stand partly upright and hope there isn't too much to jump up about. No hope of that Mick!

If a visit to Michael's doesn't coincide with a game, the conversation is often dominated by politics and women. Cov isn't the best place for a night out, but we've certainly had some fantastic nights out at Browns or the TikTok club in Hillfields. Dave Nellist, Peter Billing and Cyrille Regis are all great people from this City who have been worthy talking about. I have been to Highfield Road with the "Alex" as Cov have slipped and the "Alex" had a period in the second tier of football. The first was during the ITV digital period, bringing live games to 6.15 on a Sunday. Now what a good idea that was! That year I went with the Crewe fans but in a later season I went in the upper tier of the East stand to watch Dean Aston get a winner - it was a shame I couldn't celebrate. The same season I again met up with Mick and we had a drink with Kenty and Potty. We had just sold Dean Ashton and we were stuffed 3-0. We didn't win a game the rest of the season until the last game when we won to stay up, against Coventry City.

The next time I saw the two clubs, the club had moved to the Ricoh. I went to the game with Becky and we travelled on the bus from his new home in Chapelfields to the ground. It was a freezing night over the festive holidays and Becky and I went in the away end with Mick. The ref gave us everything that night and the locals were fuming that night, with one or two getting on the pitch to complain and it was a bit edgy outside; Cov seemed to have a fair crew that night.

I missed one of our greatest nights for the JPT Northern Final which was watched by 32,000 - the second largest crowd ever at the Ricoh. Cov had one eye on Wembley and it was a night that was supposed to bring the good times back. Unbelievably, the "Alex" won 3-0 to kill the tie and unfortunately any hopes of lifting away from the financial gloom. My delight was overshadowed by some sorrow to a club who I had grown to have some affection for.

We returned for the league game 3 days later. Pete Johnson and I got there early and we went to Mick's house for dinner. Dylan and Reuben came too and they played with Mick's kids who all know each other quite well. We went in the family corner of the Coventry end, all the kids and adults together which was nice. It's a shame when you have to separate for a game when you don't see each other all the time. Pete Johnson actually celebrated our winner which could have led us all to be thrown out. In games like that how many times does the other team win after the other has won the cup game? I bet even Mick, who has feelings for the "Alex" even had difficulty not liking Crewe that day. Things have got even worse since this, I almost blame the "Alex" for their position, and if they had got to Wembley would they have gone further in to this mess? Yes of course they would, Cov fans know who they blame for their predicament.

Coventry City, no passion? Who said that? They've obviously not met the fans who are fighting for their club in 2013.

Crawley Town

Kevin my ex brother-in-law took me to this one with his lad and two of his friends that both went to my school. As a result the conversation often included grounds, footy, students and teachers which was better than conversations about my sister who at the time was still not coping with the break up.

We started out after 9, and as a result we didn't get to Crawley until gone 2.30. We parked by some trees and walked under the subway toward the grounds where there were queues everywhere. Apparently the new stand was opening and this had an added interest to the visit of Crewe. Accordingly it was chaos everywhere and both home and away fans were going to be getting into the game late.

We were situated in a covered terrace which covered half of the end behind the goal and a small section of the side. A new ground and an excellent run under Steve Davis meant that about 600 had made the long trip and were making a lot of noise. The new stand eventually filled up and I think I am right in saying that this was Crawley's biggest league crowd at the time.

It was one of those trips and towns when you are not really much wiser on the town you have visited, having only seen ring roads and not had the time to explore.

Crewe Alexandra

Well this is a difficult one to write, I don't want to go on to much about the "Alex", this book is about life, growing up and being a footy fan although I'm sure you readers of other teams will forgive me, probably being as fanatical yourselves.

I see myself as a 'Crewey' although I didn't move from the Midlands till I was 8. Having lived and worked in the Midlands in my adult life, the area still has an big influence on me but *My Identity* is influenced by the lads in Gresty Road. It was this Midlands connection that took me to my first Gresty Road game. An FA cup game with Stafford Rangers sparked the interest in my Staffordshire mother who decided to take myself and my older sister. Mimicked by some when I first moved for being a Brummy and telling people I supported Everton and Walsall I went to this game with mixed feelings. Do I support my new hometown or the underdogs who spoke with a similar accent? I loved the trip to Gresty Road; the "Alex" won 1-0, although trouble on the terraces was a feature of this 6,000 crowd, 4,000 more than a regular crowd at the time. It wasn't long before I was a regular at the "Alex"; the assimilation process was fairly quick.

For me and probably many visitors, the old Gresty End held many memories, partly due to its uniqueness. The end was covered but wasn't straight with the pitch. The end had some wooden steps at the back, where the singing usually took place. In your secondary school days you moved from the front wall where you hung your scarves over, to the steps at the back. This was a stage of trepidation, a place where you might sing together or get threatened by somebody harder from another school. I also had to keep an eye on the popular side fairly frequently because this was where my Dad stood, smoking had to be surreptitious and if major violence occurred he would stand with me or make me reluctantly follow him to the Popular side. Either was very embarrassing but being a parent now I can't blame him. I always remember my mate Faz stamping on a bottle that made a really loud noise during a quiet period. A copper thought it was something more sinister and threw him out of the ground and he was loudly clapped out by the visiting Wigan fans.

When trouble did break out, it became like a Western. Below the wooden steps there was a flat area covered in dust, shale and gravel. This flat surface was ideal for running battles and taking our end. Any skirmish or running battle would create a cloud of dust, and there were many smogs especially when Stockport County and Northampton Town visited in the 1970's. I vividly remember a Northampton fan being knocked unconscious directly in front of me with a Kung Fu kick in an encounter with the Cobblers.

On the field, the 70's were terrible with the league cup being our only outlet of success. Chris Duffy, Dennis Nelson, Hugh Riley, Ray Lugg, Tommy Lowry, Dai Davies, Geoff Crudgrington and Hughie Reed were all heroes despite having to apply for re- election nearly every year in the

1970's. I remember walking around a housing estate with friends trying to find the house where Hughie Reed lived.

Despite being more of an Everton fan, in the early days my fondest memories were for the "Alex". At school age there is a pressure to support a big club and it was "Everton Rule OK" that I wrote all over my school desks in Ruskin Road, but it was the "Alex" where I formed friendships, acquaintances and have the fondest memories.

It was Dario that moved us from mediocrity to marvels! Supporting the "Alex" was a bit of a joke in the 1970's, it wasn't like the Championship days where it was easier to say you just supported the "Alex". Now the "Alex" has a team that is respected by every premiership team and produced some fine England players. It has been our youth policy that has won us this respect.

Everybody loves their club and is proud of them but from a personal, maybe Socialist point of view we can be proud. We play football the way it should be played with no big stars or wages. I don't have to defend some overrated, greedy bastard or a team of dirty twats who kick and boot and cheat their way to victory. Yes, for me they are the perfect team and I hope they keep the same principles post Dario. The 2013 Cornwall incident was very 'UnAlex 'and difficult to cope with. We couldn't be morally superior any more!

Well after the Bradford fire the cover in the Gresty End had to come down and we became more familiar with the Railway End, which was also not straight and also with gravel and dirt at the back. The popular side eventually emerged as the side where some noise was generated although some scallies flirted with the A stand and D stand when the hooligans headed for the seats in the early 80's. The paddock would sporadically make a noise underneath the old wooden stand. I eventually found a patch on the pop side terrace which was eventually replaced by a seat in the mid 90's. In 1999 the ground was transformed with a big main stand and the Gresty End was returned as a home end. The Popular side was now an away side and the Railway End is either a Family End, or if there is a big away following the away fans get an extra side. I have flirted with the Main Stand and the Gresty End, before eventually settling for the Gresty End again. I enjoy standing and singing in that end with Pete Johnson. We are at the older side of the end in an end that it dominated with the younger fans and as a result tends to be more optimistic than the Main Stand. I now attend with both of my lads who go to most of the games and are season ticket holders as well as myself. I love our walk to and from the game and sometimes I think the kids enjoy this ritual as much as the game. The landmarks that are important for the kids are running through the sign that's like a goal post on South Street, the raised concrete on the corner of Ruskin Road and the kids racing back to get back to a warm house.

I'll try and perceive Gresty Road from an away perspective. On the field it must have been a banker away victory but that changed in the late 1980's.

In the Championship, the big teams would have expected to win at Crewe but some often went home with their tails between their legs.

I suppose the old Gresty End must have been a relatively easy and exciting end to take in the 1970's - especially as the ground is fairly central for both Northern and Southern fans, made easier by the excellent rail network, especially for London fans. The ground is also around the corner from the station which makes it easier and safer. The railway factor also enables the "Alex" to have a reasonable away following; many enjoy free or cheap rail fares or have more appreciation of public transport than other areas.

The ground is just off Nantwich Road, the 'Golden Mile,' with numerous shops, takeaways and pubs which not every club can offer. On the whole, away fans can expect a safe, friendly scoff and pint without going far from the ground.

The first new Gresty Road included an open end of 6 steps and ledge on the wall for fans to stand on which housed about 1500 fans. It was not great if it rained or for atmosphere. I remember Birmingham fans getting absolutely drenched one game and Walsall fans were squashed like sardines there in a playoff massacre by us. This was replaced by a covered stand of 950 which although it looked like a Subbuteo stand compared to the big new stand it did generate a good atmosphere for away and now home fans being close to the pitch.

One of my darkest hours was when Sheffield United visited when we were in the old fourth division to clinch promotion. Due to the Sheffield demand for tickets, the "Alex" fans were told to go in the Gresty End while the rest of the ground was for the Blades fans.

On the day there were over 7000 fans, about 2000 of them being "Alex" fans. I had a drink at dinner time in the Bitter End and United were in there a pub that was a long way from the ground.

United took the lead early on and the pitch was invaded again and it was clear that there were many Sheffield fans in our end, designated for us. Early in the second half, being 2-1 up, some of us plucked up enough courage to sing and make ourselves known. Suddenly, a copper dragged me from the singing group and I assume to be harshly thrown out. When I get outside I find myself put into a 'meat wagon' and taken to the station to be arrested.

I pleaded innocence, but maybe the arrest taught me a lesson and did I a favour in the long run? Maybe it helped me grow up?

In a cell with a Sheffield United fan from Rotherham-laces out-photo taken-fingerprints taken-17 arrests on the day-one "Alex" fan arrested, me-my Dad at the game in the paddock-Being let out of the police station-picking my bike up from Strainy's house after the game- Strainy and Faz's disbelief and laughter-Strainy saying fighting 5000 of them did the coppers think you were mad?-Faz trying to put some humour into the event by putting 'Police Oppression' on the turn table by the Angelic Upstarts- Strainy getting threatened in the Grand Junction pub that day-telling my Mum and Dad that night-my Mum's birthday the next day and how I had ruined the day with relatives-my Dad a headmaster and the case being in 2 local papers, god he must have died with embarrassment-Dad going to the cop shop and pleading my case-pleading not guilty-prolonging the agony till September-2 court cases-saying I said "lets get the Sheffield bastards" in court-not true- daft singing twat yes- but not that!-newspaper report headline that said "Alex" fan Kicks out-torment and piss take at work-a lecture by my head teacher 11 years after getting my first teaching job after the incident comes up on my CRB check- Oh boy did that make an impression on him- getting the respect of some hard lads-Lyndon Oakley speaking on behalf of me in court-thanks mate-police statements-going through the facts-the incident becoming a blur-being sure -having doubts-solicitors and courts- a new experience- a 3-2 defeat.

Moving on and forgetting all the above, the "Alex" are always there for you, a friend and a mate who doesn't betray you. When your girls rejected you, when works a drag and stress you can try and get 'lost' at the "Alex", like any other club. Sometimes it's wet, awful and cold, but it's great, you can chat to the old and young friend or stranger. You are part of some imagined community that does exist. I love my 15 minutes walk from there one of the reasons why I have bought my last two houses. Sometimes it all gets too much, too self indulgent, obsessive and boy do you need that summer break. However, Crewe Alexandra is like a class

"A" drug, really hard to give up and you know you will be back in August.

Crystal Palace

What a lovely name, definitely on of my favourite London sides when I was seven. This opinion was extended when they had those lovely kits; the purple one with the really thin white and yellow stripes, a classic. Then there was the white one with the red and blue diagonal stripes that has been copied by some teams more recently.

My new brother-in-law Pete is a big Palace fan so I'm hoping there may be more trips to South London. I hadn't visited there until the late 1990's.

Well with 2 away games in 4 days, one at Hartlepool which was a new ground, I decided wasn't going to go to Selhurst Park. I might have been seeing my daughter, Becky, my ex Kate hadn't decided which day was best to pick her up. I'd also just paid my MOT and Green Flag and my road tax was later this month. The bills were a bit like buses.

Now I had been to Selhurst Park to see the Wombles so I could do it another year but on Friday afternoon I was getting restless. I knew Pete was going and it was an extortionate price at 20 pound to get in. Kate had confirmed I couldn't see Becky till Sunday and nothing special was planned. Jackie finished work early and knew I had something on my mind, guessing it was to do with my ex, Becky or the "Alex". She said I should go to Palace, what a woman, but it was early days! I had ten minutes to book the coach (I would only drive to London in extreme circumstances) as I couldn't afford the train. Luckily, they had places left, yes, I was on my way. Must take some butties to save some money, First away game, while on holiday, not going? Was I kidding myself? Sort of new ground, I had to go, didn't I?

Well was it worth it? The weather forecast was for hot and sunny weather, especially in the South so I decided on t shirt, combat shorts and baseball boots (despite the drizzling rain) as I closed the door to walk to the "Alex" for the coach. A minute into my ten minute walk to the ground, the heavens opened and I arrived at the coach absolutely drenched. Thankfully our coach wasn't full so I spread out a bit on the back row in the middle, with plenty of leg room for my long self. Even at our stop on the M40 it was still dull so I was feeling a bit daft dressed in summer attire. I used the blowers in the toilets to dry my shorts and shirt and treated my self to an expensive cup of tea to keep warm. Thank god I had made 8 rounds of sandwiches and other goodies.

The coach is better than normal as I am seated near Pete Johnson with lots to talk about. Pete, who having waited 45 years before getting engaged, has split up from Clare. Pete seems happy, the split seemed amicable and a love affair with an "Alex" fanatic, one that I thought would stand a chance of lasting, was over. Apparently she was very untidy around the house, for many years Pete had been meticulously looking after him self so I guess events were perhaps predictably strained. The internet and mobile phones were also explained as other irritants, a problem when going for a younger model!

Mick from Stockport was also on the back row. He has followed the "Alex" ever since Neil Lennon came to the "Alex" (both living in Stockport) and has stuck with the "Alex" ever since. He had been working in Tenerife for a few months and keeps us amused with recent activities over there.

Austin from the Post Office is somebody I have got closer to since leaving the Post Office and we also caught up with tales of a few old colleagues, recent gigs and our love lives. The decent banter made the journey a tolerable one especially as the journey turns out to be one of the worst I've been on; the M25 is a nightmare, as is the route up into London around Coulsdon, Purley and Croydon. Should we have travelled through London?

We arrive at Selhurst Park at 2.40, too late for a drink or mooch, although it is sunny and my baseball boots might get dry eventually!

When we get there we have to queue at the ticket office rather than pay at the turnstile. Football is becoming more like going to the theatre all the time. 20 pound today is more expensive than some theatres.

We were situated on the covered side, near to the new two tier stand. There is a good atmosphere from both fans with the "Alex" fans having a few jibes at the Eagles' financial plight. It is an even, entertaining game with some of the new players and "Alex" youngsters looking useful. A penalty save and a 1-1 draw leaves us feeling quite happy.

At the service station I call Jackie and arrange to meet her in the Brunswick at 9.45. I won the guess for the time of arrival with 9.24   we actually arrived at Gresty Road at 9.25. Pete joins me in the pub but we all only have a couple of drinks, leaving to have a takeaway on the way home. It's been a great football day but I haven't got the stamina to watch Match of the Day, we've already seen ours.

Dagenham and Redbridge

My memory of this ground will be dominated by the weather. This was the hottest October day on record in 2011. As a result shorts were worn for the early walk to Gresty Road to get the official coach. It was a long day, and as a result I didn't take my lads Reuben and Dylan - which meant a long day on her own for Jackie such situations mean trying to be especially nice before and after the game!

I met up with Pete Newton and his lad for this one. The coach was sparsely populated, which meant plenty of room to spread out. We arrived very early in East London and quickly realised that it was even hotter down here. We walked across a park near the ground which was busy with people enjoying the late summer weather. It was a good mix of people which was good to see, the area had been famous for BNP activity in recent years and I wasn't to sure what to expect. I had recently watched a documentary with my sixth formers about the acrimonious election campaign where the once successful BNP had been beaten by Labour. A group of black lads playing football tried to give us directions to the nearest pub, but were not very sure; clearly going to the pub wasn't a major part of their life. Eventually we did find a pub which had a good mixture of home and away fans, some of whom were students, ex students and parents of students that I had taught which was nice and bizarre. It's strange that at an away game you can go into pub miles away and meet other people who have made a similar commitment to your club.

After a couple of pints, we ventured out into the scorching heat and I did something I have never done before a football match - buy an ice cream! It was a very enjoyable experience too, but one that is unlikely to be repeated very often unless the "Alex" gets a run in the Europa league in the future!

We walked down the street that leads to the ground, past the open home end - where the home fans would surely need hats today. We were seated in the shade in the new stand behind the goals. It seemed a bit odd to see the away fans in the most modern part of the ground, but this seemed to reflect the friendly nature of the club. The friendly East End! The atmosphere was pretty poor, you certainly didn't need to jump and sing to keep warm. It's these kind of conditions that surely promote the passing, possession game although on the day the "Alex" didn't do this very well.

Perhaps I need to return to Victoria Road in January!

Darlington

This was a coach trip in 1992. Phil and Pete were on the coach but none of us are sat together. Pete turns up early and is a well known figure and his back row is full. I turn up about ten minutes before departure while Phil grabs the last seat, lucky they've not gone without him.

I'm sat next to this gross looking fella about 30, my age, but the guy looks nearer 45.He also has a distinctive stench of spunk. Now I know you can sometimes surprisingly get lucky and make have to rush for a game but you make some sort of effort, wash or even splash on some of her perfume on! No evidence of that here, I'd be surprised if his spunky night was shared with anybody, a porno night if he was lucky! He doesn't seem keen to speak after some polite questions are met with monosyllabic responses. "Anyone injured?" "Been here before?" or are ignored which comes as a relief.

I am an enthusiastic teacher and I have brought a book 'A long Way to Go' which is not about a trip to Feethams but about a black conscientious objector in London in World War One. We have 30 copies of the book at school so I'm sussing out whether it is likely to engage a year 9 class. I actually enjoy the book, and think the students will as well. However, when I actually read the book with them they didn't really take to the book. God they should have seen the traditional books we had to read at school, if they had done did then they may have enjoyed this better.

The North East, unless the traffic is bad, is now a relatively short trip so we arrived early enough for a drink not too far from the ground.

The area seemed quite affluent around the ground which puts some of the stereotypes about this area to test. The approach to the away end is unusual and oozed with character, walking down a cobbled alley with some turnstiles at the end. You almost expect horses to be tied up at the turnstiles. Once in we are in a standing open corner fairly reminiscent of the corner you used to get at Gillingham. We were bloody awful and lost 3-0, still only another 3 hours with spunky man to go!

I always remember playing 'Darlo' at Gresty road in the mid 70's they were on top and brought about 10 coaches. Not long before the kick off this fog descended on Gresty Road and the game was called off just before the kick off. I do believe the Darlington fans were not very happy, I shared their frustration and I only had to walk home!

I visited the new ground just before 'Darlo' slipped out of the league.

It was a warm August day for this league cup game. I went with my nephew to this one, he was starting to enjoy the buzz of away games and I wanted to tick this new ground off so we both travelled enthusiastically.

We arrived in 'Darlo' early for this night game and the driver, for a change was imaginative and stopped the coach in the town centre for a quick bite to eat/drink/ wander. It was evident to me this still was a prosperous town the town wasn't filled with empty properties and had some original and exclusive shops. He then took us to see the old ground for a short trip. The ground was still partly there although run down with weeds .The cricket ground next to it was thriving and again we saw some wealthy properties around this part of Darlington. It wasn't like the 'Darlo' I had recently seen in a Panorama programme on the division of gender roles in the job market which I had shown for a Sociology lesson. It goes to show how there is often two sides to every town, the rich and poor often living very different lives.

When we arrived at the new ground I was struck by the enormity of it for a club the size of Darlington. We were located behind the goal and the 200 made a tremendous noise that night as did the home crowd. You'd have never guessed there were only 2000 in there and only 3 sides of the ground open.

It was a lovely warm night with victory for us, this, with the added bonus of the magical mystery tour before the game led to a really enjoyable trip. I hope Darlington can move up the league pyramid and look forward to a trip up there again soon.

Derby County

I have visited both the Baseball Ground and Pride Park. Now the Baseball Ground was a ground ahead of its time if ever there was one. It sounds so like one of the new grounds that pops up like the New York stadium at Rotherham United. I didn't go to Derby in the mid 80's when the "Alex" played them in the first round of the cup. It was the year I was getting into education at night school and thinking of the leaving the Post Office. It was mainly home games only that year for me. Saturdays would often be taken by homework, in retrospect I wish I had gone despite the 5-1 defeat.

My first visit to the Baseball Ground when I was about 7. As a Toffeeman in the Midlands I was taken to this one as a treat. One of my main memories was of young kids walking around with little wooden stools. When I got in the ground I realised that some of the terracing was below ground level and kids stood on these to get some kind of view. Wish I'd known? Health and safety officials would have been in their element. The most memorable moment was when the ball went into the crowd and my Mum caught it! Howard Kendall came to retrieve it and my Mum threw it to him. "The day I threw the ball to Howard Kendall" is still a story she still repeats today.

My other visit was in 1979 when I was in the fifth year at school .I went with my mate Kucky (Mark Kuspisz a lad from Poland. Crewe has always had a small community a long time before the larger influx in the noughties). He was one of those lads who vanished after school, that nobody has seen or heard of. Maybe I should go on Facebook?

These were the days when there were frequent crowd troubles at Derby. Away fans were in the corner next to the segregation fence with half of the terrace in the paddock as well.

We took the train from Crewe and walked to the ground through many rows of terraced houses. It was a game that I noticed and increasing amount of different casual clothing and quiet Evertonians. I wasn't sure if it was due to the mediocre Everton performances or if less singing was part of the new casual fashion. We were escorted back to the station, but it wasn't as intimidating as I had expected.

I visited Pride Park for a Tuesday night game on a school night I drove there with Pete Johnson and as is often the case for these night games you are in the dark and don't get a real feel for the ground, you rush and get to the ground and come straight back often with other things on your mind.

I remember seeing Chris Lines and Craig Parker, good lads from school. I recently found I out that one of the dads from my lad's football team is a good mate of his. Small town England! (Brilliant song by New Model Army)

There was a great crowd as ever at Derby with great vocal backing, they are a bigger club in my opinion than many give them credit for.

This is a new ground that I would like to return to in the future; maybe I'll find Kucky again and make the trip together for a re-union.

Doncaster Rovers

Well another new ground in the League Cup first round, easy if you are a teacher and still on holiday. The "Alex" had won the first leg 4-1 so the trip always looked a non-entity with no atmosphere but you never know?

Kate comes along to this one with Pete, his brother and Phil joining us. We arrive early in my Talbot Horizon and see the impressive Racecourse and the less impressive football ground. We go for a drink in the Rovers Social Club after paying a nominal fee and drink in a friendly atmosphere, Pete starts up a nostalgic chat with some Rovers fans. I could have been one of those fans. I have a vague recollection of visiting Doncaster when I was 7. My Dad had an interview in Doncaster and we went for a gander around the town not long before he got his deputy head job at Ludford Street in Crewe.

The ground is not helped by two open ends and on this occasion a one sided 2 legged game. Why 2 legs in this competition in the early rounds and semi-final? (Changed now I know). Pete reckons it was to help the big clubs, after an all 2nd division final between Villa and Norwich in the 1970's, the decision was taken. The odd new ground out of term time is the only advantage I can think of. We are situated in an open end which looks better than the one at the other end. The covered terrace at the side is where most of their fans congregate and has some character, although some may make resemblances to a cowshed. Opposite to this is a tall stand but only covers half of the side with some open terrace either side of it.

The "Alex" win handsomely at Belle View in a 4-2 second leg but it's not got the excitement of a usual victory with this score line. We stop off at a pub North of Manchester, just off a junction near Worsley to celebrate on the way back.

It was in the Northern final of the football league trophy that I made it to the new ground. The new ground certainly offered more shelter from the elements but was similar to many other grounds that are part of a retail outlet. With the chance of a first final in this competition and a trip to a new ground, the Millennium stadium for many, the game attracted a vast amount of interest. When the coaches arrived I noticed that there was a larger than usual amount of youths on the trip. The cheaper prices for this competition often seem to attract the youth and it was these youths who were stomping around the ground and singing in a very aggressive manner. I'm not too sure if it is me or the Rovers fans who are most surprised. At half time we are 2-0 up on the night and appear to be Millennium stadium bound. By the bar at half time the Fratellis play and everybody is jumping around in a jubilant manner, the atmosphere is electric. Unfortunately a 3-2 collapse in the second half takes the stuffing out of the fans and at the end there is an abundance of vitriolic abuse by upset and angry fans. Even the 2 legs were no help this time and our dreams of a day out in the Welsh capital were over.

Everton

Living in between Cannock and Walsall in 1970 did I want to support the Wolves, the Albion, the Villa or even Walsall? Not me, I've always been an awkward sod and wanted to be different.
My favourite letter was E and I chose the Toffeemen instead of that other club in Devon that I still haven't been to. Alan Ball became my favourite player; he had the number 8 on which was also my favourite number. I remember waking up early as I still do today and reading the paper and finding out Alan Ball was going to Arsenal for around £125,000, I ran into my Mum and Dad's bedroom crying.

Before I moved to Crewe, Walsall were drawn away to Everton in the FA cup 3rd round. This was my favourite big team playing my favourite small team which created one of my first major dilemmas! Everton got the edge on the day and it was their scarf I wore on the Walsall coach I travelled to the game on. I bet I got some strange looks and my Dad had a lot of explaining to do that day.

Once in Crewe I still followed Everton although Crewe were beginning to compete with my emotions much more. Everton were the team I was associated with, sung about and wrote on the desks at school. Most people at the time supported a big team, but were more likely to attend more Crewe matches. Up to the age of 15 my Dad would take me to the odd game - but a paper round and working at the Post Office at 16, made trips to see Everton, Crewe and gigs far easier.

One family trip which included my Uncle John, who was a mad Wolves fan, saw Wolves come out on top and me with vertigo at the top of the Main stand (I think). I was amazed that you could go in a lift to a part of a football ground. Goodison Park was and still is a fantastic ground with great character and originality.

One other memory as a younger teenager was when I went to see Crewe reserves play Everton reserves. At this time reserve games were actually played at the home ground which is fairly rare nowadays. I went to the game with my denim jacket on with my 'Up Everton' and Everton wing badge proudly worn. During the game, a lad left a group of teenagers and approached me, I was with one quiet lad called Tim. He said to me "You called me a sky blue bastard" and punched me in the face. This Man City fan was older than me and I was flabbergasted I didn't even know the lad and would certainly not have called him that. I was really upset when two other older lads Kenny Everall and Dave Meecock came over and told him to 'do one.' It was all a bit bizarre there were only about 30 people in the ground at the time. I don't think I ever went to another reserve game again.

Gordon Lee was one of my favourite managers as he originated from Cannock and his accent sounded like most of my relatives, although he wasn't the most successful. I also have fond memories of Billy Bingham and his soft Irish accent and red face during interviews. Recently, I moved house and found a silk scarf with 'Bingham's blue army' on it. His period was fairly mediocre on the pitch as well. I also cherished my 'George Wood is safer than the pill' badge which I though was really funny and clever at the time! "We all agree Duncan McKenzie is magic" we sang and he was a real player with flare and style and one of the few players who stood out in a fairly grim period while I supported them.

At 18 I had lost interest in following them, my trips to Goodison Park or away games were often solitary or in pairs and I enjoyed going to see Crewe in groups far more. I remember sparking up a ciggie on a bus downstairs on my own and being asked to put it out kindly on a trip from Lime Street to Goodison. I felt like a right dick/woollyback, I didn't even know smoking wasn't allowed on the bus down stairs. Crewe is small enough not to get the bus! As a kid I walked and biked everywhere.

The walk from Lime Street was too far and I would often worry if I was getting the right bus. I often didn't ask because I didn't want to give the impression I was an away fan. Even when we had colours on we occasionally got hassle. In punky attire and scarves after a 2-0 defeat by Middlesbrough, Tappy and I got ran by some Perry boys by Lime Street Station. Even if I tried to dress the part, I still didn't feel I belonged enough, so I thought I'd stick with the "Alex" and dress how I liked. I think it depends on the kind of person you are, At the "Alex" I have sometimes spoken to this guy who sits on his own and travels up from Solihull. He is polite enough, but I concluded that he actually enjoys being on his own. At the time especially I wanted more than solitary trips. I'm sure I could have persevered more and I'm sure I could have made some mates. Maybe I was a small town boy? Maybe I just liked getting home to watch final score for home games? Maybe it was a case of wrong decade and fashion or the age of tribal warfare? Even my Love of Wah, the Bunnymen and the Teardrop Explodes didn't help my assimilation? Community is important for me, meeting people you know is as important as the game, chatting to somebody you know from the hospital or Post Office, somebody you used to live near or used to teach. This was a pushing factor away from Goodison and a pulling factor towards Gresty Road.

If my love affair with Everton was over, it was dead and buried during the late 1980's during the John Barnes era with the "Nigerpool" and the "Everton are white" chants. In a different but similar way, perhaps this is how Kevin Sampson felt at the end of 'Away Days', turning his allegiance from Tranmere Rovers to Liverpool FC. The other difference in being, he opted for the bigger team while I opted for the smaller team.

During my time at what now is Hope University in Childwall, I attended an FA cup replay against West Bromwich Albion on the Gwladys Street with my mate Phil. I wondered if some of the old emotions would come back on the visit but with songs like "shoot that nigger" it wasn't very endearing. We were also near one of the loudest obnoxious bigots I have ever been near to. I felt like I did at a Crewe/ Bournemouth game when some "Alex" fan was giving Luther Blissett so much racist shit that I nearly got in a fight. Here at Goodison I felt less confident and quietly listened to his hatred aimed at Albion's black players. Oh he was so funny!

This led to me not really wanting Everton to win the Merseyside cup final that year. I watched it in the Belgrave in St Michaels. This would have been unbelievable 10 years earlier. As a student I quickly grew to love the city, and feel really comfortable on Merseyside. I frequently now visit for shopping, gigs, and cultural days out, but the passion for Everton hasn't come back although I love it that they compete with the big 5 so called 'super clubs' on a smaller budget.

I have met many pleasant non racist Evertonians in my time and I don't want it to seem that my falling out of love isn't just a political rant. Our separation was more to do with community.

I did return to Goodison in the away end for an enjoyable visit after the WBA debacle. During some awful snow in the Midlands that didn't reach Merseyside I was one of about 50 Coventry fans (with my mate Mick) in the upper tier of the Stanley Park End. Due to the snow, very few fans made the trip, but being at uni, it was just a train ride away to Kirkdale for us. I was part of a noisy 50 who tried to spur them on to victory, but it was to no avail. It was a great view up in the upper tier of that end at Goodison.

I returned as an away fan when the "Alex" were drawn at Goodison for an FA cup 5th round game in 2002, deemed to be attractive enough to be televised. This was the cup run that was the highlight of a relegation year, maybe the cup run even led to us being relegated. I got there on a Post Office coach which took me back down memory lane and I attended it with Faz's lad Elliot after someone let me down. He was a teenager but was quite happy to talk and was just as affable as his dad is. He is in his late twenties and still lovely and going steady with Eve a girl I used to teach Sociology to. Small world! There were around 8,000 who made the trip that day and I was right behind the "Alex", there were no mixed emotions on the day with regards to my old team. We were situated in a large proportion of the Bullens Road stand. The "Alex" made lots of noise that day and I sung my heart out, I'm not too sure what Eliot made of this friend of his dad making more noise than himself, but what the hell. To be fair the game was pretty dull with few chances so at least the atmosphere would have been good for the TV watching public who stuck with the game. I didn't get to the replay that Everton won. I have watched the game from every side at Goodison, something reserved for very few clubs which gives you many good and different perspectives.

Ironically, as my trial separation with Everton began, the mid eighties saw the club being more successful than they had ever been during the time that I loved them. I suppose this analogy might be explained by an ex girl/boy friend blossoming with beauty or weight loss after leaving you. I guess that's something than most of us can relate to.

Exeter City

This is one that I keep missing and it's getting ridiculous. I missed my chance when I was younger and we seem to miss each other even when we get promoted or relegated. If it goes on much longer St James' Park may have to be visited during a holiday to Devon.

It's you Middlesbrough and Arsenal that I want when the cup balls are in the bag!

Fleetwood Town

In 2013 the Johnstone Paint Trophy gave me an opportunity to visit a new ground. On a Tuesday night in October it is a busy time for teachers and even though I only do 3 and half days a week, it typically didn't fall with an early finish. I spend my day off on a Monday as a Health Care Assistant bank worker. I enjoy the complete change of scenery, which is made even more attractive because you never have to look at a computer.

The work can be physical, it can be smelly and dirty but it is nice to be able to help people who want to talk and be helped although sometimes I don't think I'm as competent as the other staff. It is more honest than what teaching has become. Teaching is complicated in that not only do the kids have to learn but they have to really enjoy it as well; you have to be like a magician nowadays, every lesson, everyday. It is easy to burn yourself out. Even 6th form lessons have to be all singing and dancing. The kids are going to get a real shock at university where it's not all pair work and fun.

The official coach was going at 4.00 o'clock and school in Nantwich finishes at 3.30. This took a traumatic turn when the detention rota was changed and I had been put on, yes you guessed it, for 3.30 on the day of the game. Luckily a kind member of the Maths department came to my rescue and swopped his Thursday for me. It was still going to be a tricky getaway; if I got away at 3.29 ish you leave the chaos of the car park and an extra 15 minutes off your journey. Leave it till 3.32 ish and getting to Crewe was going to be tricky. The problem would be helped if I could find a trusted colleague to cover my last 2 minutes who was also free. I would then just have to have everything e.g. jacket/ticket/ refreshments ready in the car. Alternatively I could pretend that I was on bus duty and pack away a couple of minutes earlier.

There are other non-school complications; I am assistant coach for Dylan's team Ruskin Park Rangers who train on a Tuesday night. When I am there I also take his brother Reuben. So I am putting Damian the head coach under a bit of pressure and it is a bit of extra running around for Jackie which isn't going down too well. In my defence, it is my first away game of the season and its going to knacker me for the week! Anyway I got away and made the coach in time with time to spare in the end. I sat next to Mark on the coach. As part of my work as a HCA I had to deliver a package to the pathology laboratory and Mark works there and our eyes met at a distance but we couldn't speak. He knew I was teacher and was clearly shocked to see me in a different context. We discussed my changing career and his marital problems on the way, such as life is in your forties.

The journey was relatively traffic free for a Tuesday rush hour and we arrived at six o'clock. Some glass trees stood out on the outskirts of Fleetwood, part of the grounds of a glass company, the impressive statues surely had one or two health and security issues. A couple of miles later we passed the Fisherman's Friend's factory not long before arriving at the ground - for many years I have associated the cough sweet with Fleetwood and they have been life savers in times of illness.

After being dropped off by a park, I walked around the ground and treated myself to some chips and mushy peas at the Highbury chippy, eating them outside on a lovely mild evening. From there, I went to Jim's Bar which is at the back of the home end. There were a lot of Crewe fans in there and I found my mate Pete Newton. I hadn't seen him for a while and was good to catch up with him and make arrangements for the next Half Man Half Biscuit gig in Birmingham. His lad Tom was there who was with Scott an ex -Sociology student of mine who is a lovely lad. It was moments like this that made me stick with teaching.

I also caught up with Brian Johnson, an old friend from school and again we swopped nostalgic stories although his memory puts mine to shame! It was nice to catch up and talk about other issues but the "Alex", a subject that he can be a little negative on!

We walked around the ground and entered the entrance by the bar and club that is at the side of the ground by the away end. This is exclusively for home fans, it seemed a strange policy but it wasn't a problem on the day.

We were in terracing with a cover; it was a decent end with a good view behind the goal. To our left by the Highbury Bar was a very good screen for this tier of football and a small stand. To our right there was a stand with boxes and an arc shaped roof which was impressive. The opposite end was of similar size to ours with some unused boxes behind it.

On the pitch our dreadful form continued but despite the 4-0 deficit, we bombarded the goal in the second half and we could have scored six! However, the awful run continues but the support today from young and old fans alike was positive. Surprisingly the support was vocal and still not critical of Steve Davis, yet. Crewe seems to give managers more time than most.

As it was my first away game I had enjoyed the trip. If it had been colder or I had been to every away game I probably wouldn't be feeling as content but a return for a weekend fixture was on my mind as we said goodbye to Fleetwood.

Fulham

This one was the only new league ground I could do in the 1999/00 season, bar some good cup draws, so it was meticulously planned for a long time, making sure that it was a weekend that I hadn't got my daughter Becky.

As it happened Becky had been ill that week with suspected impetigo (an illness that is due to not cleaning properly and deprivation!) Accordingly, she has been aware of her contagious spots and had missed some school at a time when she had been struggling at reading. At this age I saw her once in the week, phoned everyday and saw her every other weekend but at a time like this situations seem beyond you, especially if don't live in the same town anymore. Confiding in nicotine and alcohol isn't the best solution.

I had planned on making this a train trip with Pete Johnson, being a tourist, drinking and browsing; but Pete's new life is now more complicated and led him to saving money for a Millennium holiday so it's the cheaper and less exciting official coach trip.

I have much to ponder on the journey. On our 2nd anniversary Italian meal out, Jackie and I talked about trying for children which is a pleasant surprise. She doesn't want me to be an old dad and I'm keen to be a house husband. I have been particularly disillusioned with teaching recently and the opportunity for a career break and possible career change add to the appeal Are the above the real reasons or am I keen to have another child? Yes I would like to have more children, but I don't fancy juggling quality time with a new child with a set of books, seating plans and OFSTED? But if I do make the break, what can I do after my kids go to school? I'm not good on the computer, not scientific enough for nursing, and social work would be just as stressful? Why is it such a long away trip this week?

A library job might suit but could I afford to re-train? Working with the elderly does appeal, I do tend to have a good rapport with them, but would it be different every day, could I afford to do this work and would the hours be very antisocial? Why am I so impractical? If I was a footballer I wouldn't have such worries at the age of 35.

Austin was on the coach we were on, it wasn't that full. I sat in front of him and Connie and enjoyed spreading out on a seat of my own. Incredibly we had a 15 minute stop at Hilton Park services where I rang Becky whose impetigo was eventually clearing up. This was pleasing, as my parents and Nan were blaming the situation on her/mine/Kate's vegetarianism!
I also managed to get a quick call with Jak before having a fag and being last back on the coach - rare for me being a very good time keeper.

At the start of the school year I tend to get really stressed, and this year was no different; in fact it seemed to be getting worse rather than better. When you're starting to think of careers rather than football then things must be getting bad. At another break on the M40 at Welcome Break, we are greeted with spurting fountains rather than hostile rival fans.

When we arrive on the outskirts of London, it's always interesting listening to conversations about housing, about multicultural Britain, graffiti, traffic and the tube. The consensus is usually that being from Crewe we are lucky to live out of the hustle and bustle. The above subjects are generally not seen with envy.

A group of tourists are huddled around the gates of the iconic BBC building, desperately attempting to see some stars. We deride them categorically, but I'm sure they'd do the same if they knew we had set off at 7.30 to see Crewe who? Play!

When we arrived at Craven Cottage, we were surrounded by well trimmed hedges and well maintained Victorian houses - unlike many of those seen on our trudge through London. This part of Fulham looked well and truly gentrified.

The coaches parked by a park and we had a quick stroll and gazed at the Thames. This park was just behind the away end and the Thames flows behind the stand where both home and away fans sit. Heaven help them if the Clash's prediction "cuz London is drowning" is proved correct.

I loved the cottage and the bricked side on the opposite side to the Thames, it oozed character at a time when so many grounds look like warehouses. We asked two stewards for directions to the nearest pub and we weren't very satisfied with the answer. Both sent us in opposite directions and one said we could get a drink in the ground. We set off on one direction tentatively and when it looked like a wild goose chase, we asked for further directions, again and again until we ended up in the road where we started off. We sadly came to the conclusion that if it that if it is that difficult to find a pub, if we do find one it will be absolutely heaving so we decided to try the ground for a drink - although I had this bad feeling that ended up being correct. The away end was 'dry.'

The ground appealed to me and standing up is a bit of a novelty in 1999. Through the gates from the outside, the Fulham end looked impressive, and a vast terrace with a cover for those at the back. The away end was a vast terrace accentuated by giving us the whole end which is uncovered leading to a lacklustre atmosphere at our end. A good turn-out, but being so spread out (with Austin and 250 others in the seats at the side) meant we had little vocal support, especially as we had little to sing about. We were 3-0 down in half an hour and outplayed for most of the game which brought more gloom to a deteriorating day. Pete my mate from Sutton didn't make it either, so I wallowed in several cigarettes thinking this could have been a much better day and vowed to return in the future.

Thankfully, the trip back wasn't too painful and we made the Brunswick by nine. The first pint with Keith was drunk swiftly. During the second I met up with Simon and Tricia who had just solved some babysitting problems, so we all knocked the beer down our necks and let ourselves go. The topic of work and stress was a major talking point, we were turning into a load of '30 something's' but at least I wasn't walking around in a circle for a pint!   A drunken bath beyond midnight, after a take away and my troubles seem far away. An equally intoxicated Jackie arrived later after seeing a Jam tribute band. The night was young and work troubles were far away for now.

Gillingham

This one was when I was with Kate, pre- Becky in 1992. The game was on Easter Monday. We had arranged to go to Torquay on the Good Friday with some friends from Kidderminster. I say this fairly loosely, the couple were our friends but I didn't feel particularly close to them. He was mainly a friend of Kate's, somebody who had grown up with her and knew plenty of her history! He had also been part of her history! I did like him and his girlfriend, but even a weekend with your closest friends isn't always a bed of roses, so I did have reservations (especially as his brother and friend were also stopping at the hotel). They were all more into cars than football and that always alienates me.

Accordingly, I felt I had compromised a little for the trip (although it turned out pretty well). Torquay was lively and the weather and company was half decent. Anyway to cut a long story short, I thought it wasn't unreasonable to go to Gillingham on the Monday as we were leaving that day anyway. Another new ground, great! I knew Gillingham was on the coast and thought a Bank Holiday there might not be too bad. Well the journey was quite interesting at the start; we travelled through Dorset and had a quick stop. However, time was moving quickly and the vast distance of travel ahead of us was dawning on Kate and me. I started to put my foot down a little which was annoying Kate. The whole West to East coast was an alarming journey; thank god I didn't support Gillingham or Swansea!

Eventually we arrived in Gillingham at about 3.00. After 5 hours travel, I don't think the nicest place on earth would have cheered Kate up and certainly Gillingham wouldn't! No disrespect to Gillingham (Crewe isn't the prettiest place either) but it was a dock town (not a seaside town) which is grim and closed on a Bank Holiday. We struggled to park and Kate was fuming. She declined the offer to go to the game, maybe she anticipated a more enticing couple of hours! I left for the game feeling guilty and shit but excited by the prospect of a new ground. We were in an open corner in a similar position to Feethans, Darlington. The sun was shining and we won 1-0. Pete Johnson was there and Sutton Pete and his wife Monica - who I hadn't seen for a while. Pete and Monica offered us a bed for the night which we put to Kate on returning to the car, but she was almost hysterical and turned down the offer in an embarrassingly rude manner.

I got in the car and we headed North. I dared not put on any football scores and left Radio One on. I remember she didn't speak to me until we were way beyond the Dartford Tunnel. When she did speak she explained how she'd been abused by some drunks outside a pub while looking for a shop that was open and bought some magazines to read in the car. On returning to the car her reading was interrupted by somebody who didn't like the fact that we were parked outside their house So when she asked me if we could pop in at her friends in Welwyn Garden City, I could hardly decline.

The story of the day was re-told, but this time a few red wines with her old mate and the events seemed a little funnier (although I was still not forgiven). I was a bit fed up at not seeing Pete and Monica, more my friends - although I did really like Brian and Diane. A good drunken night was had in Welwyn, a strange place, lots of houses and greenery but hardly any pubs or shops (a theme for the day for Kate). I don't think Kate will ever return to Gillingham. I certainly won't forget it. This was certainly a ground for divorce.

Grimsby Town

This was a long time coming and one I shouldn't have done, but for being a new ground obsessive. This took place on a Tuesday night during the busiest school term in October of the 1998/9 season. Luckily, there were no meetings or school clubs although this was the night I often see Becky so I would see her the next night making it a busier and more tiring week than it should have been.

I quickly got changed after school and set off for the East Coast from Bilston where I taught. I stopped, rang Becky and Jak and got some food before continuing East. East Coast journeys can be a real drag. I approached Scunthorpe thinking I was nearly there only to be told by the sign that there were still 35 miles to go. I took my "Alex" car sticker out of the car before entering Grimsby, (Europe's Food Town apparently). I had read and heard off from one or two people who had had trouble with the Mariners and advised discretion in the town.

I parked up after finding the ground unusually easy. I got some chips but gave the pubs a miss. My mate Austin and 200 others had made the long midweek journey. It was a ground I liked, compact, covered with character. The "Alex" made some noise which helped make the trip seem more worthy. It didn't seem that intimidating today although some "Alex" fans complained about being attacked by a laser pen from their impressive tall stand to our left. Hi-tech hooligans!

We managed a 1-1 draw with a tasty goal from Rivo (Mark Rivers). When the gates opened, I stood near them for a quick getaway on the final whistle when 4 lads entered on BMX bikes maybe doing a scouting job for some of their boys. They didn't seem too interested in us, perhaps just a bit of bravado to show they were here if anybody wanted a 'pop' at them.

It was only another 155 miles to my Nan's house in Cannock. During the transitional period of my divorce I would stop at my Nan's abode 3 nights a week. I was always very fond of her and it benefited everyone - it saved me petrol and time, stopped my Mum and Dad worrying that she was lonely or vulnerable every day or night.

My Nan enjoyed my company and I enjoyed hers - even if she was a bit of a right wing bigot. She was still intelligent enough to enjoy some political banter in her eighties. I couldn't believe the fixture list in June. When you are scouring the fixtures for the new grounds it is a devastating blow to find that your new ground is a night game. I got some chocolate for my energy and really put my foot down. The A19 from Grimsby was deserted and I got home just after 12 (which was too quick and too fast but I had to get some beauty sleep to educate the kids of Bilston in the morning!). Driving to Crewe would have been out of the question, the short journey from Nan's house would help me be relatively alert for my year 10 lunatics. Mind you, was I the lunatic driving 310 miles on a Tuesday night to see the "Alex"?

I needn't have bothered killing myself on that Tuesday night as in the early 21st century we were drawn at Grimsby for the first game and the first one is an easy one to go to being a teacher.

Austin drove and this time we went to a pub about 10 minutes from the ground. There were a few Crewe fans in there and it was friendly enough again. At least I didn't have to drive to the east coast; I wonder how many other teachers went to Cleethorpes over the holidays?!

Halifax Town

This was a game that I was allowed to go to; my dad wouldn't let me go to Stockport County due to their fan's reputation, so The Shay was the next best thing! I first went in the 1978/9 season travelling on a sparsely populated coach. Despite the two clubs only vying each other for bottom place, in the days before automatic relegation, as a 14 year old I was just excited to be going to an away game.

On the day, not that many were! The crowd was 980 with less than 50 making the trip from Crewe. The Shay had a speedway track surrounding the pitch and it was strange to be so far from the pitch. There were two open ends and at the two sides there was a cover half of each side was terracing and the other half was seats. We stood under the terracing on the one side with seats to our right. We could wander round to the open end, but we decided on standing at the side, thinking that we could generate more noise.
The small crowd was treated to a 0-0 thriller.

I ended up visiting The Shay for the next two seasons. The results or the ground didn't change much over that period, we lost the next two trips to The Shay, but at least the crowds were more than a 1,000.

On the last year we took a few more than the previous seasons, and there was nearly a skirmish after the game with both fans running and shouting a bit at each other by the coach. I was with Tony Ralphs and he had a friend with him who picked up a half brick and threw it, it missed the Halifax fans and hit a car windscreen. The police clearly saw him do it and he was arrested as we trundled back to the coach. I don't recall ever seeing that lad again, maybe he settled in Yorkshire or ended up inside?

Hartlepool United

When I found out this first round Worthington Cup on teletext in the summer of 1999 I was delighted. A new ground for next season when I was only expecting to go to one was a real bonus. Phil hadn't been either and also treated the draw with much enthusiasm.

I hadn't seen Phil for ages which added spice to the tie. That morning I was taking Becky back to Kidderminster after a lovely couple of days, but I was starting to get travel fatigue. Now I ought to be used to it, living in Crewe, working in Wolverhampton, daughter in Kidderminster but it had been hectic.
Saturday -Palace and back.
Sunday -Kidderminster and back.
Monday- Gulliver's World, Warrington and back.
Tuesday -Kidderminster and back, Hartlepool and back.

I must admit I was relieved to arrive in Crewe. I had been imagining, during my journey back about the possibility of breaking down and missing the 3 o'clock coach from Gresty Road. Still it took my mind off leaving Becky, especially as she was a bit upset today as I left her. My emotions were a combination of excitement, sadness and guilt. Keeping busy is one way of coping with the harsh realities of life.

Well I had to time to make a mountain of butties and a short romantic and lustful note for Jak before jumping on one of the two coaches, especially as Phil was inevitably late calling for me.

Phil's daughter Willow is now about 9 months and Phil is moving again, this time to Birmingham to buy a house for the first time. Ironically Phil used to talk disdainfully about the city but has recently changed his view partly due to his partner's sister living there, so I can understand his change of opinion.

Steiner Schools are already a possibility for his daughter for whom he has great expectations. I spoke about them being good in principle, but a bit removed from the real world and wasn't Phil vehemently against private education?

We went through his realistic and pipe dreams, he has one planned called 'Northern Soul' a geographical and musical play about his different musical interests. His realistic plan is to leave teaching (don't we all) and do a psychology degree and become an educational psychologist (he did and still is).

This is one of his famous five year plans that have been prominent ever since he left Crewe Railway Works. To be fair he often puts them into place (unlike many others). More children, an eventual return to Cardiff and a bigger house were other plans, most of which have been achieved.

On arrival in Hartlepool, I was surprised at how nice Hartlepool was, especially around the ground. I had a preconceived notion that Hartlepool would be rundown, but in 1999 this part of the town looked more pleasant than Crewe. A museum, an Art Gallery, a Marina in Liverpool Albert Dock style and Multiplex Cinemas gave it a rosier image than James Bolam described in the classic 1970's "Likely Lads" series. Even the sun was shining, although it was a bit nippy for August drinking Al Fresco outside at Jackson's Wharf. It was a tranquil and pleasant scene.

The ground had been modernised and was compact with some character. The outside of the Cyril Knowles stand looked impressive and tasteful to the tourists who would pass this stand on the way to the marina.

We were equally impressed by two beautiful blondes with knee length boots and short skirts outside the ground. Surely going out with some of the players but stunning enough for us to try and successfully spot their lovely legs in the ground during a dull period of the game.

Today it wasn't very intimidating, although reports on the Radio 5 phone in and my Macclesfield mate suggest it can be. About 7 of their boys were in the corner where you go to the toilet try some banter at half time but today we can relax.

Six goals, four of which could make 'goal of the month' make for an entertaining 3-3 draw. Hartlepool seem good up front, but their inability to take a point or score in their first 2 league games suggests the defence may be suspect.

It's strange coming to Hartlepool. For years we played and visited places like this, and now we are in the Championship I hear superior comments made by Crewe fans, which for many years have been maligned ourselves. Swings and roundabouts I suppose, we should enjoy it while it lasts, but pride often comes before the fall!

The journey back is also quick as we arrive at 12.20 after discussing smoking, drugs, porn, women, the film 'Human Traffic' and Radio 2. I'm not going anywhere in the car for days, I'm feeling jetlagged!

Hereford United

This was one that I looked forward to as a 15 year old teenager. I went with Rick Johnson and Tony Ralphs, all in the same year at school and all equally excited for the trip. We went on the lovely train route to Hereford which only takes 90 minutes, which partly explains some of the friction between the two clubs. You should add on another hour to the journey by road.

We had a look around the town wasting our money on sweets and cigarettes and the usual rubbish that appeals at that age. I can even remember dossing on a bench by the cathedral. The ground is memorable and unusual with lots of cover. The away end was divided in half, each half going in as you get towards the middle, so it almost looks like an acute angle from the sky. There were terraces at the back with a wide open flat bit in front of it with big fences, ideal for hanging banners.

After the game, we decided to try and get back on the coach but the stewards wouldn't let us despite some empty seats, so we left the coach and started to leave the now fairly empty car park. Suddenly a gang of Hereford fans started singing at us and then ran towards us. It must have looked quite amusing to the fans on the coach, but we were in a panic, panting and running rapidly. Once on a main road we dived into a lingerie shop and hid behind the stands of stockings and tights, too worried to be turned on! The staff in the shop were sympathetic and let us stay in until the coast was clear.

While waiting on the platform, sitting on a bench, 5 of the now smaller gang appeared and started talking to us. Two were skinheads and clearly recognisable from a group who were near the away end. We spoke about different fans and music. One spotted my 'Stiff Little Fingers' badge and talked about how he had seen them in Cardiff. They also talked about carrying weapons in an effort to frighten us (that worked). It was only when we got up to get on our train that they decided to aim a few harmless kicks at our backsides, to show they could mean business if they wanted to - but I don't think they thought we were worth it. They knew we'd spread the Hereford reputation back at school on Monday.

The year after we returned, this year there was an unofficial coach of unsavoury characters going. We tried to get on it, but it was full and we were too young and 'soft', so we ended up going on the official coach. We didn't fancy the train after last year.
This year we had found pub culture, and predictably at that age and in Hereford, we sampled the Scrumpy cider. I remember it kicking off outside the pub and near the ground. Similarly at home, many past Hereford games seemed to see mither with skinhead culture seeming popular amongst the Hereford fans in the early 80's. One year my mate Garf got chased right up to the other end of Bedford Street - which is a long way! It must be all that SAS training and country air!

While living in Kidderminster I returned to Edgar Street. I was driven by my brother-in-law Ian who is the most 'unfootball' person you will ever meet, he hasn't a clue, and he is far more interested in computers and films. However, he was bored and loved cars too, so he jumped at the opportunity to show off his driving skills and took me to Hereford. It was like being with a 6 year old going to his first match. He was looking at the stands and floodlights (old school and prominent at Edgar Street) humoured and fascinated by the chanting, and genuinely excited when the goals went in. He was continually going to the bar for food and drinks (which was useful). It was a nice gesture to take me and a good bonding day. He has been more interested in footy as he has got older and I hope this game was a spring board for this.

I returned to Edgar Street with Dylan - one of his first away games. It was a game that you could easily visit on the train; this was good as he could worry about going to the toilet, being on the train was ideal. When we arrived he did want the toilet immediately and we went in the old classic cinema 5 minutes from the station. I had planned a route that took us towards the park by the river and we headed there for a picnic. While eating it, we were entertained by various youths jumping off the bridge in to the river. After we headed in to the town for a brew and wandered by the cathedral before heading to the ground. The flat bit at the front of the away end was ideal for a soft ball that we had in our bag and we had a kick around, which was probably better than one we saw on the pitch that day. There were quite a few "Alex" fans on the train that day. When we got off the train at

Crewe many started singing 'bring on the scousers', the league cup draw had become common knowledge. Dylan was shocked at the noise, this was the noisiest the "Alex" fans had been all day!

My last bit on this section returns back to a home game in 2011/12. Hereford brought a lot of 'boys' to this game and had an EDL flag removed from their end. Racist scum! During the game there was a small group who were clearly up for trouble. They had been taunted by the "Alex" fans for being Welsh during the game which hurt them, probably as many of them were English Nationalists. I'm not too sure if the "Alex" fans were rubbish at geography or it was just a wind up chant!

I was at the game with Dylan and Reuben who were 9 and 7 at the time. Pete stood near us as usual, he seemed a bit more fired up recently, may be it was the indignity of working at Tesco's on the minimum wage after being made redundant as a printer after 40 years.

As we walked up Gresty Road after the game on the left hand side pavement, the Hereford 'boys' were opposite on the right. As we approached the tuning on the left by the church and tile place which is our usual short cut, some of the young "Alex" fans were just behind us. About 5 of them started singing "Wales" at them and they were shouting things like "we're English you thick twats" etc. As we reached the turning, the Hereford fans ran across and chased the 5 young lads right down this side street and the young "Alex" fans scarpered. The Hereford fans were walking back to Gresty Road shouting "You're nothing Crewe.... Runners" This was too much for Pete who started shouting at them "you're going to the Conference ...Who are you?" I hadn't seen Pete so fired up and I wasn't going to stay around and told Pete I wasn't. So I took my lads around the corner as Pete took a couple of swings at one of the Hereford fans. I took the kids out of sight until I heard one of them shout coppers and they legged it. I came back around to see Pete on the floor, apparently a Hereford fan pushed Pete from behind and he hit his head on the pavement. You're not that balanced at 60 and should know better!

Luckily, he had his "Alex" woolly hat on and it protected him well, but he was still bleeding badly. I told him to put his hat on and we made a rapid exit before the police came asking questions. As we walked down Nantwich Road my youngest kept asking if Pete was ok. I felt really worked up, I had left Pete on his own, even if he should have kept his mouth shut and ignored the provocation of his beloved club, but it wasn't something I had wanted the kids to witness.

I walked the kids back home, they seemed fine with the incident, and it was me that was more worked up. Jak was level headed and didn't go off on one saying you can't take them to a game again. This was something I really respected her for. She recommended I take Pete to A&E, and this was where we spent most of the evening. A calmer and level headed Pete spoke about history and the merits of vinegar as polish as we waited to be seen. I think the incident shook Pete up and maybe football doesn't bring out the best in him, although his passion is usually directed in the right way. I can honestly say I had never seen Pete try and strike anyone in his life, at football or elsewhere. I think as you get older you think you can say something and get away with it. This volatile situation clearly wasn't one of them.

Pete had a family meal the next day; I wonder what they might talk about? What is it about lovely cathedral county towns and trouble?

Huddersfield Town

I never made it to Leeds Road, my Dad was not keen on me visiting there and I was also a little apprehensive after some of their visits to Gresty Road. While at school I was threatened outside the ground on a night game as four enormous donkey jacketed men barked at me! The same game also saw a fight on the corner of the pitch at the Railway End in which a corner flag was thrown as a weapon. A dull 0-0 end of season game in 1977 saw Huddersfield take over the whole ground with several pitch invasions. I remember trying to be anonymous with my mates in the middle of groups of older men. Huddersfield fans were trying to pick fights with you all the way through the game. I was even threatened by an Asian Town fan which came as a surprise although he was from Huddersfield!

Of course the bad old days were largely over when I visited the McAlpine Stadium. I think this is one of the better new stadiums, partly because of the unique design of the arc shapes and partly because it is in 'real Huddersfield' rather than miles away on the outskirts. They sell beer there and this helped the excellent atmosphere in the "Alex" end which saw the "Alex" win 2-1 and looking like they were really competing to get into the 2nd tier of football. It was a great result and atmosphere.

I returned with my Dad on the last day of the season in the second tier, just having guaranteed safety at the previous home game in the 1998/99 season when relegation had seemed a certainty for so long. It was such a surprise that 3,500 travelled to Huddersfield for a carnival and a rest after months of checking possible slip ups, victories and draws. I personally felt the trip by car was a disappointment and anti-climax. I felt uncomfortable in the first half because my Dad and I were sitting behind some pissed and racist fans. I understood their drinking (unlike my Dad) and relief if not the odd racist comment.

I felt like I'd focussed on staying up for so long and intently that the game seemed irrelevant. At least I saw the last game of Seth Johnson, a quality player, I looked forward to seeing him on the left side of England's team in the future, and unfortunately I was disappointed with that as well.

Hull City

This was during the Emlyn Hughes glory years at Boothferry Park in 1983 when we were pretty awful.

In my eyes this was quite a big game - even if Boothferry Park was starting to be dilapidated. Personally, I thought it was great, the side and their end were vast terraces with a good cover. We were in the corner, with cover if you wanted to be near the City fans or on an open terrace that twists behind the goal and supermarket, similar to Burnden Park Bolton.

Despite the pull of a sleeping giant on top of the league, the coach was half empty, travelling with Steve Brereton who used to be a super speed driver so at least we were safe on the coach! We found a large pub on the corner of a housing estate (which was heaving) for a couple of drinks.

We got hammered on the pitch but did have a penalty save to cheer about. Near the end when the gates opened, our end suddenly got fuller with many Hull City fans entering ; many not more than primary school age. As we watched the game, one ran and pushed me from behind, causing me to topple down a couple of steps to the amusement of the watching others. We were left to grin and bare it, there were only about 8 fans under 30. Being an away Crewe fan in those days made you an easy target if people wanted mither, because there were so few of you (apart from the

FA Cup and some local derbies). How things have changed?

I did return to visit the new ground; I again went on the coach although this time I had a drink in the ground instead. I think this is one of the better new grounds, compact and still within distance of real communities. We took a decent following and made a lot of noise despite the vast noise coming out of the home sections to our left and right. They were derided with chants about being the worst town in Britain, something I'm sure the Hull fans have heard before. I wonder if Crewe is in the same 'worst' league!?

Ipswich Town

I was looking forward to this one. Portman Road was frequently on the television in the 1970's when they were a great club with Muhren, Whymark and Wark. It always looked a compact ground with a great atmosphere. It didn't disappoint, although those who prefer the newer stadiums would probably disagree.

It was 1997/8, our first year in the second tier. This was the last game and we were safe from the drop. A carnival spirit it was and much more enjoyable personally than Huddersfield away in similar circumstances. It was a 3-2 defeat with plenty of action and singing, away fans now being housed at the side, we were in the upper tier. Much of it referred to the two cities, Stoke and Manchester who were now incredibly going to be in a lower league than us. We were staying up, that's what really mattered to me but the radio reports coming through of the game between the big two added some spice to the day.

It was an early kick off and all the coaches were there for 11.30 with the pubs on Sunday not opening till 12 o'clock. We were allowed in one near to the ground but they couldn't serve until 12, it really showed how ludicrous the licensing hours were in those days. The bar was knee deep with people waiting to be served, getting irate, resulting in everybody getting more than one pint when they did get served and accordingly I got a quick one in at 12.30 with the kick off at 1. Absolutely absurd but a great day in the town, home of one of the greatest punk bands ever, The Adicts.

Kidderminster Harriers

I lived in Kidderminster on and off from 1989 and properly from 1991 to 1996, living with Kate's brother and Dad for much of this period.

I visited Aggborough about once a season while I lived there. It is situated on a hill not far from the railway stations (steam and modern). It was an area with several pubs and takeaways and is an excellent away trip on the train. The Market Tavern, one of the pubs used to be an excellent music venue where I saw the UK Subs, The Selector, Space, Catatonia, The Subhumans and Leatherface. There is a magnificent viaduct if you approach the ground from behind the away end, again with a couple of pubs and food outlets.

The ground had been modernised, unfortunately too late to get into the league which was a travesty. At the time it had a bigger capacity and was probably a better ground than Gresty Road pre-1999. At Aggborough they knocked down the quaint old stand on the roadside, but left the club bit at the back to keep its character. Both ends now have modernised terraces, both under cover and the cow shed side (by the cattle market) is functional and under cover.

My first visit was against Man United in a friendly, one of those games where there were supposed to be stars playing - but there wasn't!

I visited Aggborough for an entertaining 2-2 against Macclesfield. The supporters changed ends at half time which reminded me of pre-segregation days at the "Alex". They were fond memories and gave you a chance to focus on the strikers all the time rather than the defenders.

A trip to see them play Torquay United in the FA cup in 1995 brought a large crowd which attracted less desirable elements with racist singing and monkey noises, this was the last time I have heard racist abuse on a large scale at a football match and hopefully the last time. I was that outraged that I wrote to the Kidderminster Shuttle newspaper and got my letter printed.

It was ironic after splitting up with Kate in June 1996 that the "Alex" should arrange a friendly a month after at Aggborough. I was temporarily staying at my parents' house in Crewe and visited Becky at dinner time in Kidderminster. I was playing with Becky while Kate nipped to the shop when the phone rang. Becky said you better answer it, and it was Kate's new boyfriend. It was a horrible experience at a time when I was still cut up about the split. He was friendly and apologetic and we now get on quite well. He is a fellow northerner who follows Stockport County and also a big fan of Half Man Half Biscuit - my favourite band. To be honest I probably get on better with him now than Kate, and that also follows for him. It was funny how she went for somebody again who was mad on music and footy.

It was strange afterwards, leaving my old house feeling confused and walking past St Ambrose Catholic Church where we got married to see the "Alex". The smell of the sugar beet in the

Kidderminster air bizarrely reminded me of more pleasant times I had in the town. The visits will now be sporadic and uncomfortable pick-ups. I had a drink in the Harriers social club and met Pete in there. This was a club where I used to attend Labour Party branch meetings. It was a good way of meeting new people in Kidderminster and I was pretty political at the time. However, getting involved in local politics actively can be dull and monotonous with plenty of back biting. I strangely enjoy politics more if I'm less involved - although I don't mind posting leaflets for the party. The meetings were often on Monday evenings when the Harriers sometimes played, if they did I longed to be at the game instead.

The "Alex" hammered Kiddy that day which was enjoyable. I felt in some way it was repairing the pain and misery of the split. We even had a bit of a sing song, very rare for a friendly. There was a further Kidderminster connection when I was a bit more stable and playing the field again. Incredibly we got the Harriers in the FA cup that year, why was I again being reminded with memories of the town? I can't remember ever playing them and now we were playing Kidderminster twice in a year, a year of my separation.

Football certainly wasn't helping the separation. It was not until Dylan was born in 2001 that I stopped staying over at my father in laws every Tuesday. Tom didn't have to put me up but he knew it would help my relationship with Becky and we loved each others company, enjoying lots of political banter. I still ring him up every couple of months for a chat, to the annoyance of my ex.

Tom informed me that there were many early drinking coaches making the trip to Gresty Road. I was really excited going to the game and took pleasure in the 4-1 stuffing, where a young Lee Hughes stood out. We tried to sign him not long after this game, it's a shame because he has been a nemesis over the years, taking pleasure in scoring goals here for a number of clubs. Dario didn't get Hughes, but did sign Marcus Bignot from the Harriers who did a decent job for the "Alex". It was no surprise to see a mob of Harriers fans leave the game early. We later found out that they had trashed the Barrel pub near the ground. It is funny how these big games (Crewe?) in the FA cup always bring out the 'nutters' who usually aren't regular fans.

Kidderminster, through my daughter Becky, will always hold memories for me. It's a nice underrated town, similar to Crewe but a bit wealthier. I often thought it was bit like Crewe in that both towns are derided because they both live in the shadow of old historic towns, namely Bewdley and Nantwich. I loved living in Imperial Avenue where we lived with Tom and Ian. The Victorian terrace has many memories for me and most of them were good.

I will always look out for the Harriers results because relationships and football are often closely connected, even when there are grounds for divorce.

Leeds United

A damn good third round FA Cup tie for the "Alex" in 1994, and a new ground for me. This was a car trip; my brother-in- law drove to this one. One of the few games my sister Heidi let him go to! My Dad and Phil made up the rest of the passengers on the trek over the Pennines. There are certainly some breathtaking views in between Rochdale and Huddersfield, there is tendency to romanticise the towns even though they have probably never have one day free of rain!

We parked up on one of the trading estates near to the ground and went into the South Stand without having a good look around the ground - which I regret, and am surprised at not doing, especially as Phil usually insists on this. However, Phil is a Leeds and "Alex" fan, so the ground was not new to him although the circumstances were strange for him. His split loyalties were only evident when an "Alex" fan taunted the Leeds fans with "You'll never win the league." He was a Man U and an "Alex" fan; some may say a glory hunter for the day.

We had the whole end with a huge following of about 3,000 and we made a huge racket that day in a crowd of only 18,000. Some pull we were! On the day Elland Road didn't seem very intimidating which wasn't really surprising against us, although there was a small mob in the corner of the East Stand who looked like they could be up for it.

We scored one of the most memorable goals of my "Alex" watching history. Tony Naylor scored a great individual goal and I was really disappointed that it didn't make Match of the Day headlines that day. It gave us hope at 2-1, although we eventually lost 3-1. It was a great performance and atmosphere even though my long legs were a little cramped to say the least. It was definitely a case of slapping seats on terraces!

I returned to Elland Road in 2008 with my son Dylan. It was the best opportunity of the season to show him a big ground that wasn't too far away. We set off on the coach early and unbelievably we decided to stop at the service station 10 miles away from Leeds. Still my lad, nearly 7, was not good lasting on a road journey without going to the toilet so on this occasion I won't moan too much. We still arrived early - on the other side of the ground this time. We sat by the Billy Bremner statue in the sunshine before wandering around the ground. It was still early and I swallowed my principles and treated my lad to a meal In McDonalds which he ate outside on a lovely September's day. If you are not a regular the questions 'aren't half complicated'. My lad just wanted a burger but it's never as simple as that!

We made our way to the ground; we were in the other side of the South Stand in the corner in the upper tier. There was a big mob to our left in the lower tier of the South Stand who taunted us despite being Crewe and few. Kev was there with his lad, Rob was now older and Kev was going to far more games now as Rob was getting the taste for away games.

On the pitch it wasn't ideal with Leeds scoring five, although we got two back near the end. Many had left, although a hard core were doing a conga when we were 5-0 down.

We got back to the coach safely, although there was one bloke with his young lad who was game for a fight with somebody by the coach. He painted quite a sad picture really, but it was just an isolated case.

I'm not too sure how much Dylan remembers of the day but if he gets obsessed with trying to attend all the grounds it's another he can tick off.

Leicester City

This coincided with a Christmas 1996 piss up with my mate in Coventry. We had both finished school on the Friday. I hadn't seen Mick for a bit, and I still hadn't been to Filbert Street, so we went out celebrating on the Friday night. We had a great night chatting about school, footy and girls. I was having a good time post-divorce and we ended up stumbling into the Irish Centre in Coventry. The place seemed full to the brim with older divorcees. We were too busy chatting to get involved in 'cattle market antics' but we ended up having a good laugh with a few women in some drunken dances later on in the evening. I bumped into one attractive 45 year old who I had chatted to earlier while waiting for a taxi and enjoyed being pinned against the wall for a lovely snog and fondle. It was one of those chance moments that are brief and memorable and in that small amount of time absolutely perfect. The moment becomes even more enticing when the moment is fleeting, hazy and anonymous due to the amount of beverages. We didn't go all the way, but a brief fumble and embrace can really perk you up and can be a great talking point for the next day.

Well we certainly needed it, it was absolutely freezing on the Saturday, add to this a terrible hangover and end of term fatigue. We approached Filbert Street, leaving the car about 15 minutes walk away. Well the lustful memories of the night before were soon blown away as we entered the away section down a narrow terraced street.

As we entered through the turnstile, we seemed to have entered a war zone. Leicester fans were banging on the corrugated iron as you walked past towards the seated area at the side, making you feel extremely intimidated. It had been a while since I'd witnessed scenes like this.

Once in the ground, both fans goaded each other in the corner - this was going to be a full bloodied Midlands Derby. All the Coventry fans stood on the seats and several were being smashed and the stewards did nothing. At the time at the "Alex" you could get confronted by a steward for just standing up!

I don't suppose you could blame people for standing up as the away side is at ground level and below for people at the front. Somebody was passing burgers around the end; obviously somebody had placed a large order and left without paying. I quietly refused not giving the vegetarian argument at this particular time; I don't think the context was quite right! There were big sauce bottles being passed around the fans generously.
Coventry were deriding Filbert Street "You've only got one side" referring to the side opposite and "what the fucking hell is this?" (Pointing to the away side).

All these goads were exacerbating the already pugnacious Leicester fans. Being a traditionalist I liked the compact ground and although the away end wasn't perfect, it was all close to the pitch invoking passion and atmosphere.

I did witness an absolutely fantastic extended version of 'Twist and Shout' by the Coventry fans, which would have made the Beatles proud to be from Coventry, which they are not! I was particularly interested in the ex "Alex" player, Neil Lennon, and it wasn't hard to keep an eye on him because he was booed every time he touched the ball, having rejected the sky blues for the darker ones. He had a disappointing game by his excellent standards, a highly underrated player in my opinion.

It was that cold that I dared to put my black Bronx Alex hat on inside out, only for it to be knocked off in the scramble that took place after the Coventry goal. I didn't half retrieve it quickly; I wouldn't have liked it to get in the wrong hands in the volatile atmosphere.

Leaving the ground was frightening and not a prospect I was relishing. In the dark unlit terraced street in December it was not very enticing. Pockets of youths lingered along the streets and skirmishes broke out. We put our heads down and walked quickly. Away from the street by the side of the ground, the walk to the car seemed friendlier and relaxed but boy had I seen some passion and aggression today, even in the 1970's or 1980's I think that corner would have stood out. This wasn't even a derby that I had heard about or perhaps it was like this in the corner every week?

I returned to the ground for a league cup encounter at the new ground with the "Alex". I went with my next door neighbour to the game.

The family are "Alex" fans and we often chat about the game on the front of the house, but this is the only game we have been to together. We set off for the midweek game too late for my liking and as a result my neighbour certainly put his foot down. We arrived late and saw some hefty parking prices. While lingering on whether to pay, an Asian guy guided us to his house tempting us with half of the price to park in his yard. The guy was friendly and offered us the use of the loo (which was really nice and needed). It was one up on kids asking for money to park on the street which used/still does happen at Merseyside and Manchester games.
I like the fact that the new ground was in the same area as the old ground and was still near real communities.

We were in the corner of the ground in a really thin but long strip of the ground. There was a decent atmosphere, although it was far more civilised than my last trip.

We got back to the house with the guy opening his gate for us and helping us to reverse out of his yard. It was a lot more surreal and friendly on this return trip.

Leyton Orient

Becky, Kate and I travelled down to London early Saturday morning from Kidderminster in the 1994/5 season. We were stopping at Kate's friend Maria's house who was a nurse in Wood Green, North London. I had vowed, after going to a Madness concert in Finsbury Park that I would never drive again. After missing the turn it took 10 miles with one ways and no left turns to get back to Finsbury Park, returning in such a state of anxiety that we didn't go to the gig in the end. Anyway Maria's directions were good and we ended up in North London relatively stress free.

The girls headed for tourist places, while I headed for East London, changing at Tottenham Court Road. Getting off at Leyton I found a pub near the ground and read the newspaper. Near the ground I met my mate Pete who had just been interviewed for the excellent 4-4-2 magazine. We then made our way to the open end behind the goal which was larger and more impressive than similar ends in the lower league at the time. Thankfully it was a glorious sunny, April day and we won 4-1. It was an enjoyable game helped by meeting Phil at the game and Southern Gareth who I hadn't seen for ages either before or since.

Gareth had moved south and worked for the railway at Gatwick Airport. Phil, Gareth and I made our way back to Leyton Tube station only to find that it had been closed due to someone throwing himself in front of a train. I hope it wasn't a depressed Orient fan, football is serious stuff - but not that serious.

So we set off in the direction of Stratford by foot with many other people and fans. We walked past many tower blocks and the parts of London that the tourists do not see. On the walk, I remember being fascinated by a big ball cage with a huge amount of Bangladeshi youths playing football. This was a time when there was much talk of Asians not making the break through into professional football and it looked like there was a lot of talent on show here that wasn't being tapped by local scouts.

On reaching Stratford, we got a train to Liverpool Street where we drank at a new massive pub that was part of the station. We had two or three relaxing pints and I really enjoyed the 'early doors' freedom and chat. I hadn't been to as many games since the birth of the lovely Becky and it was good to combine family, football and friends with a visit to the capital.

Eventually, we went our different ways; I changed at King's Cross and headed back to Wood Green. I babysat for Becky while Kate and Maria headed off for the West End.

The next morning we headed for Camden Market which was bohemian and interesting, but life was different now and walking around with a baby in a push chair is not ideal when looking for bargains. This can be hard to adjust to but you know that children aren't young for ever and you should try and make the most of these times.

In fact I returned to a very different Brisbane Road with Becky in 2007/8. Becky was now 14 and came to visit me in Crewe for a few days over February half term. Kev and his lad Rob had planned to go and I was keen as we were on holiday, but Becky was less so. I managed to convince Becky that it was a trip to London and she would be going to bed at about 3 in the morning although I knew she would only be able to gaze at London through a coach window. We went on the official coach, it was lovely to be with her and an away game and the four of us had some fun on the coach and service station. Unfortunately, the coach driver got lost and we were going to arrive at Leyton not long before kick off. Even when we got to the ground the coach driver didn't know where to park, he stopped on the High Street and didn't know whether to park down the crowded side streets. We managed to talk ourselves off the bus before he parked up which was a minor result and went for a drink in a large friendly pub on the High Street near the ground. Fortunately they let Becky and Robert in despite being 14 and12 respectively. We had a swift two before going to the game.

This time we were in the side in the corner. The seats were wooden benches, but we had been sitting down enough on the journey so the side was ideal for standing up in. There were now two tidy little covered ends and the side opposite was also modernised. We seemed to be in the largest and oldest part of the ground.

It was one of those games where not many make the trip, but the fans make more noise as result of a long journey and a compact bit of space. The "Alex" performed really well, and we sang our hearts out, although Becky was one of the exceptions in our bit. She had her eyes averted from the pitch. It was a bit weird intruding into the lives of the people who lived in the apartments in the corner of the ground. Becky was more interested in this bloke who was cooking his dinner in an open plan apartment and watching TV at the same time. This was the highlight of city life for her on the day.

At half time, I bumped into Swinny who I have known from the PO days. He is now a manager and had done really well from humble beginnings. He was on a course in London and came to a rare "Alex" game to see if there was anybody he knew there as much as to see how the "Alex" got on. It was a real bonus to bump into him for the first time in a while.

It had been a great atmosphere and game which made the trip on a Tuesday night even more worthwhile. We were a lot quieter after we had done some people watching in London and we all seemed to drift in and out of consciousness. Becky got her promised late night and glimpse of London life through a corner of Brisbane Road.

Lincoln City

In my first year at college in Liverpool in 1987, the "Alex" hadn't been at the forefront of my mind, but the pull of the FA Cup first round and a new ground whetted my appetite. Garf was living in Nottingham at the time and said that quite a few people were going to the game and stopping over for a night out in Nottingham, this third offer made up my mind to go.

Anyway I sacrificed a Friday night at the Haigh building (the old Liverpool Poly) and stayed in. I got the train from Lime Street to Sheffield on Saturday morning. There are some breath taking views when you get to the other side of Manchester, so I enjoyed the scenery and pondered on my new life and glimpses of my old life that were going to clash today. The trip was a bit expensive but my only alternative, I'm sure taxpayers wouldn't mind contributing towards my student grant to see the "Alex" play away!

The trip was going well until Sheffield, where a guard told me that the Lincoln train was the one after the train in the platform had gone. I watched the train disappear realising ten minutes later that this was my train. An hour wait and arrival in Lincoln at 3.12pm was making me think I should have gone to the Poly Disco.

I arrived at Lincoln station and panicked, I got a taxi, and people who know me would be shocked at that, being both thrifty and walking a lot. This was exacerbated when I found out that the taxi was an embarrassingly short distance to Sincil Bank. There was a large drunken following as per usual for the FA cup, and I found myself at the side of a large open terrace which was segregated down the middle. Lincoln has just been relegated to the Conference and ended up beating us, in a year that they went straight back into the football league. I had thought the days of FA Cup embarrassment were over.

I missed many of the tourist parts of Lincoln in the police escort back to the station. I had visited Lincoln before in the 1980's when I was seeing Debbie and we visited her grandparents for a few days on the way to Skegness. I remember the break fondly as it was the first time that I had had sex in a house and a bed rather than outside or in my Maxi. Lincoln has some good shops and attractions similar to other county towns like Stafford or Chester. Her grandparents lived in a terraced house that had such a big slope you that you felt like you could fall down it. My Maxi just about made the steep hill. The streets were as steep as some of those near Hillsborough.

The train was full of "Alex" fans, some of whom had been a bit mischievous in Lincoln. Garf and I got off in Nottingham with a variety of music buffs and beer monsters who were also sleeping at Garf's poky bedsit in Lenton. The night was a good one although I don't recall that much about it. It was a good job because that many people sharing one room wouldn't have been a very pleasant experience sober.

I do remember enjoying the company, some of whom I hadn't seen for a while. Many students often used to moan that they had grown apart from their mates back home, but I still felt happy in both camps, although it was more complicated, yes I did make some new friends but I wasn't disowning my friends from Crewe.

On the Sunday I made my way back to Merseyside and caught up on the gossip from the weekend. This was a game where I remember that I had moved on and embraced new experiences, but hopefully not forgotten other people from the past. Maybe I was feeling a little less sure and I was convincing myself I did belong in two camps as Julie Walters did in Educating Rita?

Liverpool

My first visit will be a shock for younger fans. I travelled to Anfield to see the "Alex" play Preston in a 1976 FA cup second replay which was always played at a neutral ground. What a wonderful choice to whet the appetite of the fans. I went to the first tie at Gresty Road when their fans broke the turnstile and generally ran amok.

Well the second replay captured the interest of the town and about 20 coaches made the trip, unheard of in those days of half a full coach if you were lucky. The "Alex" fans were still outnumbered in a crowd of just over 7,000.

I went with my Mum at the age of 11 and stood at the Anfield Road end, to the right of the entrance that used to be in the middle of the old end. I think the Centenary stand was closed. The ground was mixed, but it was the "Alex" that sung from the Anfield Road end with Preston fans more likely to be in the Kop. I vividly remember a PNE banner being set alight in the Kop but this was done by the locals rather than "Alex" fans. Neutral grounds give you an added dimension with another set of fans to look out for. However, on this day it is fair to say that the Liverpool fans seem to be less hostile to the underdogs and more hostile to the bigger PNE.

However, while waiting for the coach by Stanley Park all fans were asked to put their heads down because the mid 1970's was a thriving time for the fashion of bricking coaches.

The "Alex" actually visited Anfield for a League Cup 2nd round game in 1990. We filled the majority of the Anfield Road end and sung our hearts out in the new seats. That middle exit, such a feature on the TV in the 1970's and 80's had now disappeared. Being in Liverpool at the time was strange, was this like a home game for me? Was it more or less exciting because I lived here? Whatever my emotion, the impossible actually happened, we actually took the lead against the greatest British side of the period. We ended up losing 5-1, and 9-2 on aggregate, but we gave a valiant display.

During my college years I visited Anfield to see Coventry twice. The first year I stood with my Coventry mate, Mick, on the Kop for a 0-0 draw. The second year we went to the Kop's only paying turnstile which was full, so quickly we went in with the Coventry fans (My friend Phil was keen to go on the Kop before it was seated, but ironically it was his late arrival that meant we didn't get on the Kop) My friend Mick and I were happier and the Coventry fans sung their hearts out, especially after a Cyrille Regis winner. It was refreshing to see several Asian faces in the Coventry end at a time when this was extremely rare. Incidentally, I have never seen Coventry lose at Anfield.

During that time, we also stood on the Kop for the visit of Millwall. On this occasion like most of the others we would get the train from Central Station to Kirkdale and walk the rest of the journey.
One of the most memorable visits was when we walked to Anfield. In the 1987/8 season Liverpool

had already won the league but were parading the trophy at the Southampton game on May Day Bank Holiday. We planned our route from our Halls of Residence in St Michaels Road in Aigburth through Toxteth, Edge Hill and Shell Road. We thought the walk would save us some money, keep us fit and improve a geographical knowledge of a City we had both grown to love. It was a Bank Holiday at the end of the season, a good day for football and bonding. We got in with surprise ease and we were amazed at the near silent Kop. They had just won the championship and it was just polite clapping, like a Sunday stroll, no fervour. As Coventry and Crewe fans, we had been short changed with success and were happy to go along and be part of a joyous Mardi Gras. The Southampton fans made more noise. As we walked back we couldn't believe it, going over the events with disbelief. The only conclusion we could come up with was that they had so much success that they had become fastidious. I bet the next time Liverpool win the league it will be different.

We arrived at the Halls of Residence when the staff were clearing away the evening meal. After hearing our adventure the staff took pity and took the trouble to give us an over ample meal. The staff at the halls were always more pleasant and generous to the lads. I should never have moved out after the first year!

After living in Wavertree and Garston, I left to work in the Midlands but Mick worked in Merseyside for a few years working at Plessington School in Bebington. He met his wife to be Gabby at the same school. On numerous visits to Liverpool we always had a great night at the McMillans, the Mardi Gras or the Blue Angel (The Raz). On the night I went to tell Mick that Kate and I were splitting up, England played Scotland in Euro 96. There were a lot us that watched the game and we ended up at The Raz at the end of the evening. Gabby's friend Rachel took pity on me that night, dancing and comforting me on an evening I was drunk and confused.

When I visited afterwards she never came out, I thought she might have been a little embarrassed although nothing really went on. The following Easter she did come out and we got it together although in our entire month relationship we never went all the way. According to some of Mick's friends they have had similar 'unexperiences.'

The fact that we got it together was a shock as I thought she had avoided me the last time I came up. As a result I had been encouraging Andy from Portmadog to try and cop off with the lovely Rachel from Swansea when it was me she actually wanted. I honestly didn't see it coming. It was during our month relationship that I made my next trip to Anfield in very different circumstances. This time a music benefit gig for the Hillsborough disaster was the reason for going to Anfield. We had a drink in Hanover Street before making our way to see the excellent Space, Dodgy, Manic Street Preachers, Beautiful South and The Lightning Seeds. This time Rachel and I were in the main stand where you couldn't get on the pitch to watch (unlike Mick and Gaby where you could from the Kop). It was a nightmare to get beer at the kiosks, they kept running out and they were hopelessly undermanned. I was glad that we'd had a few at the Hanover before the gig.

The next day we spent a wet afternoon at Speke Hall before she wrote to tell me that "I deserve someone who could give me more love". So I went looking.

Luton Town

I ended up going to Luton twice in the 1996 season. In the league I went on the coach, when we approached the predominantly Asian area where the ground is, I didn't hear any disdainful comments which suggested that attitudes were changing for the better.

Kenilworth Road is an amazing unique ground, despite being derided for being antiquated. First, there are the turnstiles that almost go through the terraced houses. Then when you get in you are practically in several people's gardens - I bet the Asian community was petrified on that infamous visit by Millwall. By the proximity of the gardens it is fascinating but very intrusive. I hope the club sends all the residents a present at Christmas.

To the left of the away end there are the executive boxes that look like flattened sheds. These are all part of the individuality of the ground; I would definitely recognise these if they came up in a pub quiz photo. However, in the away end you are very close to the pitch and it has a good roof, both helping to create a good atmosphere. This was pleasing because I didn't want to ask myself why I had decided to wear my jeans with a hole in the knee today, it was freezing.

It was one of those days on the pitch, a sending off and a 6-0 defeat. Despite this, we kept on singing and moving about trying to keep warm. To try and cheer us up, we decided on the coach to make a night of it in Nantwich. After a quick bath we were out and ended up in 'Gregs'. Pete had a successful night copping off with Clare, half his age and an "Alex" fanatic. Surely this was everyone's perfect dream? Maybe not in the post Jimmy Saville period!

We returned to Kenilworth Road for the semi-final of the play offs. We had bounced back after the hiccup earlier in the season at Luton. My mate Mick from Coventry fancied this midweek game so I left school in Bilston and met Mick at a McDonalds just off the motorway near his Catholic School in East Coventry. We shared the phone box to speak to Gabby and Rachel who shared a house in Allerton in Liverpool (little did I know this would be the last time I would speak to her, before getting my Dear John letter on the Friday). Thank fuck I had a Wembley trip to take my mind of the rejection.

We parked up, and Mick was as eager and excited as I was. Going 2-0 down didn't silence us, but I for one thought we'd lost it until Colin Little put us back in it. 2-2 was enough to take us to Wembley again. I must praise the Luton fans at the end who invaded the pitch, at first it seemed menacingly, only to come to the half way line and applaud us and wish us all the best. I don't think I'd have been so generous in the circumstances.

Macclesfield Town

My sister used to live in Macclesfield for a while. A picturesque town with the Peak District leaning on it adds to its character, but also decreases the temperature to freezing. Even in summer you could set off from Crewe in relative warmth only to be shocked by the adverse weather conditions that greeted you.

My main interest in Macclesfield came from a lad called Phil who lived with Mick in Liverpool. A stalwart fan who travelled to Yeovil on a midweek night spoke passionately one night about the Silkmen on various nights in Liverpool. On one night in the Blue Angel his lovely sister (who also follows Mac) was nearly pushed over a wall with a 30 foot drop down while getting fresh air as Phil told me the perils of travelling to Meryth Tydfil with the Silkmen. It was the same night of the England Scotland game in Euro 2000 and the night I poured my heart out about my separation from Kate and got comforted by Rachael in the group. Hopefully it's the only semi-cop off I've had when somebody felt sorry for me!

Well my only visit to Moss Rose was to see the "Alex" play Chester before the new Deva was ready. In the 1990-91 season, relegation was a possibility but a fantastic win at St Andrews and a home win had given us some optimism. A Bank Holiday weekend made the trip up from Kidderminster easier and Kate decided to try the shops out. The local derby and the importance of the game meant an increased troublesome element in town before the game and at one point

Kate was advised to stay in the shops before kick-off time rather than the streets.

Unbelievably, we were 3-0 down at half time, capitulating to the fourth tier of football. We had half the ground - I stood under cover at the side of the pitch, while others stood behind an open end to my right. At half-time, 20 "Alex" fans invaded the pitch in a half hearted attempt to get the game stopped which looked a bit pathetic, 20 fans was not going to cause the local constabulary much stress and just added to the misery of the day. We pulled one back but we were down. Knowing we had outnumbered our rivals at their ground wasn't much consolation (Even though they were homeless). After the match there were some predictable skirmishes but fairly tame compared to previous clashes. We even won our last game 4-0 too good to go down eh?

Moss Rose was a ground I was keen to return to as it had changed and I felt I needed to see Macclesfield next time. The opportunity arose for a Christmas fixture in 2010/11.

Jak had a friend in Mac, and we arranged to meet up at her house before the game. She lives near a school and Sainsbury's. After a bite to eat her husband, their eldest daughter and my two lads decided to walk off all the Christmas indulgence and walk to the ground. This meant a fifteen minute walk to the town centre and then a walk along the London Road to the ground - a fair walk for three children under nine (and when you do the same walk home afterwards on a cold December evening). It was decided that we would go in the Macclesfield seats as children were let in for free and we couldn't please everybody, so I went along with it. We were on the same side as I was on my previous visit, but it was now a smart small stand that housed both home and away fans. The game was disastrous from our point of view as we were 3-0 down early on, and the Mac fans sang amusingly "you're just a small town in Sandbach". The afternoon for the "Alex" fans on the open terrace to our left didn't improve as we eventually lost 4-1. The kids all seemed to get on together and happily walked back - although they were happy to get back to the house for a hot chocolate. It was different combining and adjusting to footy and family, but today had been a lovely and a successful experience.

I returned in 2012 when we were on a great run and attempting to get in the play offs. Jak's mate was on holiday, so I went without the family. I had recently decided to go teaching part-time and Jak was concerned for me to make savings wherever possible so I decided to get to Mac in a cheap way without inconveniencing Jak as we were now a one car family. Accordingly, I decided to get the long journey on a special bus ticket. There were about 30 others on the bus that was due to get to Mac town centre about 2 o'clock. Unfortunately, there were major road works going on in Congleton that day and we were way behind schedule. I was starting to get a little worried as we didn't enter the outskirts of Mac till 2.30. The plan had been to maybe meet up with mates for a quick one but the town centre was ten minutes away so I used a bit of local knowledge and got off on the main road and turned right through a variety of houses and made my way to the ground from the other side of the ground away from London Road. The open end was heaving as promotion fever was alive.

I stood with Faz's lad who was with his girlfriend who I used to teach Sociology. It worked out with them on a day when you were bumping in to loads of people that you knew.

At half time, people were smoking all over the place, hard nuts in our end seemed to outnumber the stewards and letting the smoking rebellion seemed the best solution. We came away with a draw, which wasn't ideal for either club, both of whom were fighting for points for very different reasons. After the game I met up with Craw and Garf and we walked down London Road before taking a right turn and finding a decent boozer just off the Main Street, I think it was The Railway. It was nice to catch up with them and have a drink after the stress of the bus journey; Craw was brilliant supporting me with my teaching in a period where I was lacking in confidence, and it was great to see Garf happy again. He was with Jane, his childhood sweetheart, 20 years on which was nice and not just because she is an "Alex" fanatic. We then ventured into the town which also had a nice mixture of home and away fans without any trouble - which was refreshing for a local derby. I returned to the bus and said goodbye to the rest who were getting the train home via Kidsgrove. The journey back was a lot more relaxing and quicker, the only problem being my weak bladder! I was gutted that Mac slipped out the league and not just because you can get there on the bus!

Manchester City

City were always a cool team to support and a popular team In Crewe and amongst the kids when I was at school.

My first trip was with my Dad while at school with Everton in the late 1970's. We sat on the benches in the old Platt Lane stand in an unsegregated stand where there were very few Evertonians. The Kippax looked a great vast terrace to the right. We walked back to Oxford Road station where I saw Geoff Davies and some of the other cool City fans.

My second trip was with a City fan who was a roofer from Handforth who I met on day release at South Cheshire College whilst at the Post Office. We met up at his house after the easy and short trip on the train from college. Although Handforth is close in proximity to prosperous Wilmslow - the bit where my mate lived could have been a million miles from it. We again went for the Everton game and sat in the corner of the Main Stand and North Stand. I didn't have to curtail my excitement when the Toffeeman scored; they rarely did in those days.

Incredibly, promotion to the second flight in 1997 meant a trip to Maine Road with the "Alex". This was one of the most talked about games of the season. The midweek game saw us gobble our ticket allocation, including the temporary scaffolding in the North Stand. Bizarrely, City only officially got 950 tickets at Gresty Road that season meaning that we took more fans away than they did, incredible!

The visit seemed to bring every 'Tom Dick and Harry' that you hadn't seen for years. The "Alex" played superbly, apart from some missed chances. A 1-0 defeat was unfair but didn't take the edge off a trip that showed how far the "Alex" had come.

We went to the game with my Dad and Kev. We met a City fan, who Kev worked with in Stockport, in a bustling back street pub. We met some Crewe Blues in there, my old school mate Geoff Davies and Paul Reade from the Post Office.

The 'Blue Moon' song was sung by both fans who claim it to be their own. We sang it first at Stockport when a bright moon appeared above us in the open end; we think some City fans at that game may have adapted it. However, on the night the city fans probably sang it better with a more up tempo beat with clapping compared to the slower version adopted by us. And yes we do play in red!

I returned to Maine Road in the 1999/00, it was a memorable one. Not really for the 4-0 thrashing, but for the day out with my mate Garf.

The day started off badly. Garf lived in Stoke at the time and was going to meet me on the train at Stockport. Garf was going to join me on the train, but couldn't see me so he didn't get on. As the train was speeding off, I saw him, so I had to wait at Piccadilly till he got the next train; luckily there are lots of trains from Stockport. When he got there we got a couple of CD's from the excellent Vinyl Exchange on Oldham Street before going to the Wetherspoons on Piccadilly Gardens. After a couple of pints we got a bus that dropped us off somewhere on Wilmslow Road. I remember us both buying an apple from a corner shop and asking the guy who worked there if he recommended a good curry house. He gave us directions to a place called Shazans which was cheap and tasty. It was a dry curry house so we got some beer from a place over the road.

After the game, we slowly walked our way back to Oxford Road stopping a couple of times for a pint on the way. We spent a while at a white and green pub that used to be an old cinema, which was busy with a great atmosphere. Garf and I left each other at Piccadilly about 9 o'clock - it was the most I had drunk for a long time.

When I got back, I met up with Jak and her mate Mandy. We had a couple more in the Brunswick and ended up having a second curry in the Taqadir further along the Nantwich Road. Now that was a first for me, god knows how many calories I had that day! I remember being very drunk and feeling a bit jealous of her friend Mandy, such is the lethal combination of insecurity and too much to drink. There was also a disagreement over the merits of the Grand National which was linked to the jealousy.

The next trip to Maine Road was more cultural and family orientated. Jackie, Becky and I went on the train again and this time after a quick look in a few shops we walked along Oxford Road stopping for the odd snack before going into an Art Gallery along Oxford Road. It was more to break up the walk than the culture, but it made a change than the usual pre-football entertainment! I once remember reading that this is quite common amongst some Italian football fans to do that, Manchester is as good as Milan! It was a lovely day and the walk was pleasant and interesting, I love getting out and seeing different places, walking makes this much better than being stuck in the car.

It was a cracking atmosphere in the North Stand again despite the 5-2 defeat. We even walked all the way back to Oxford Road station, although Becky was struggling a bit towards the end, having to be bribed a bit with some bought food and drinks for a change. It was here that the Italian theme changed to Pizza!

Overall, I have had some great memories at Maine Road; I hope to get to the new ground in the future, although the likelihood of it being with Crewe in the league is increasingly unlikely. Incredibly, in 1998 we were in a higher league than City, how football can quickly change.

Manchester United

My first trip to Old Trafford was when I was 17. I went on the train with Tappy, getting off on the short journey to Warwick Road station (sadly there is no direct train anymore). We left the station and walked passed a group of Everton boys who were hemmed in by a load of police by the cricket ground. After a brief walk around their awesome stadium we joined rest of the Evertonians in the Warwick Road end. It was Gary Birtles' first game for United after an expensive buy from Forest, and he made an inauspicious start to his career, to the pleasure of us all.

During the game we spotted ST from Crewe (a City fan) and his Man United mates walk along the touchline in front of us. This was amazing, at Crewe you might spot somebody you know but not at Old Trafford! The Evertonians at the front taunted the four of them as they walked by. Apparently his mate had cut his hand and they were going to First Aid. It didn't half make us chuckle, ST on show walking past the scousers.

We were kept in for ages after the game before we were escorted to Warwick Road station. When we got there we tried to explain that we didn't want to go to Liverpool but we were bundled onto the platform. As the train pulled in (and many Evertonians had boarded the train) United fans started to ambush us from behind the wall at this tiny station. It was pandemonium, Scousers wanted to get off the train to fight, the police were trying to get everybody onto the train and debris was being thrown over the wall. It was during this that we were pushed towards the train and in the confusion and chaos we reluctantly decided that getting on the train was the only option (staying behind on the platform would have clearly identifled us as Evertonians to the number of rcds waiting on the other platform).

Of course at Lime Street we were trying to board a train to Crewe with a ticket from Manchester. The ticket collector was obstinate and wouldn't sympathise with our plight and we ended up having to buy another single ticket. Apparently we had travelled from Manchester to Liverpool for free and we were lucky not to be prosecuted. We arrived back in Crewe at 8.30 from Manchester! No wonder following the "Alex" was becoming increasingly attractive.

In the mid 80's I went to spend a weekend with Phil and Damon who were living on the Palatine Road in Didsbury (Tim from the band James lived next door). Phil had got a year's grant on a unit in Affleck's Palace and with Faz they had a clothes shop called Bugle clothing. They sold new and second hand clothing. I helped them out with a purchase of a beige jacket with a hood even though the arm had a twist and didn't fit correctly. The expensive things you do for mates!

Anyway at dinner time, Damon and I fancied a spontaneous trip to the footy on the first day of the season. United were playing QPR and we turned up at 2.30 and got in, paying at the gate. Imagine that happening now! We were in the corner of the Stretford End and the South Stand which was 'chocker'; I kept losing Damon in the constant swaying up and down the terraces. This was the worst I had ever experienced; it was so distracting that you couldn't concentrate on the game. I loved standing up, but this situation did make you think of terrace disasters like the one at Ibrox that I read about in the 1970's and had always stuck in my mind. We tried to forget the 0-0 draw with a drunken night at the pretentious PSV Club in Hulme.

Now I didn't see the next two visits coming, but it's strange what life throws at you. Jackie's Dad is a Man United fan and took every opportunity to manipulate the kids in a similar vein with shirts and merchandise at every opportunity, especially birthday and Christmas. Accordingly, both Dylan and Reuben are both Man United and "Alex" fans; although I would like to think it is the other way around in terms of allegiance.

It was for this reason that I found myself and my eldest Dylan attending the United and Wolves League Cup game in 2010. The game was in October half term and a late night was allowed. This competition gave me a chance to get a ticket quite easily and Wolves are the team that I look out for more than any other club after Crewe (family, work, friends) so I was keen to attend this game more than most.

We went to the game on the Manchester United Crewe branch coach. I know the bloke Andy Ridgway who runs it and he is a good guy. I also know a couple of other people who go on it ,one used to teach Geography at my school and John

Hulse I have known since I was kid playing down the park.

The coach is cheap and during the journey it has a sweep on who is going to score as well as other quizzes and entertainment. Dylan and I caught the coach from the Earl on Nantwich Road and we parked by the War Museum in Salford after a nightmare journey with traffic. As we were late, we avoided the club shop and made do with a cheap scarf off one of the unofficial lads around the ground. We were in the South Stand near the front, to the right of the manager's seats and to the left of the away end. I made sure I smuggled lots of food in to make sure we didn't add further to the profits of Man United. Of course there were very few Man United stars on view being the league cup (Bebe!) but at least I had bought him on his first visit Old Trafford.

It wasn't a bad game with United shading a 3-2 victory. The crowd were extremely civilised around where we were, staying seated for the majority of the game. The Wolves fans made plenty of noise in a fairly quiet atmosphere on a crowd of fewer than 40,000. I thought it was sad that there were some United fans next to me who sounded like they were from Wolverhampton, and even sadder that there were other from further a field (who were also not following their local team). Did Dylan enjoy it? Did he enjoy it more than the "Alex"? Did I? Well it was good to go a ground that had changed a lot and I'm sure we spent lots of time taking in the surroundings. We also saw a few bigger names than normal! As for me, I did feel a bit of community on the coach but at the game it all seemed a bit too big and soulless.

Anyway, the next season I had promised to take my youngest Reuben as well and I thought I ought to take them to a game with some stars in (Rooney was actually rested). We ended up, through Andy's connection, getting to use 3 people's season tickets priced 35and 40 pounds. It was part of their Christmas present, but not the only present, and as a result it wasn't a cheap affair. We went on the same Crewe Reds coach for the morning kick off on New Years Eve. It was friendly on the coach again and Dylan won the sweep with the name of one of the Blackburn scorers.

We went to the pub to meet some guys who were loaning us season tickets for the day. We were going to meet up with them in big pub that overlooked Salford Quays. We waited upstairs in a big room and the lads were excited and enjoying having a coke with Andy and some others off the coach. Unfortunately we were waiting and waiting and my eldest who is super organised was getting frustrated and Reuben was getting super restless. It was the day that there was going to be a tribute to Fergie before the game as it was his 70th birthday. We got the season tickets 20 minutes before the kick-off, and by the time we got in the ground the game was about to start. Not only had we missed the tribute, but getting in the ground had been a hassle and a rush.

Andy was apologetic it wasn't his fault and he had helped out any way. Dylan was going to sit with him in the North Stand, while I was taking Reuben in the upper tier of the Stretford End. We couldn't get 3 seats all together.

To be honest I was really impressed with the top of the Stretford. The songs were original and everybody stood up and showed passion. This was the Man United that I thought had gone missing and I was pleasantly surprised it was still alive at home games. If I was a red, I would like to be up here. Unfortunately, it is not the best place with a 7 year old. Reuben is used to standing up in the Gresty End at Crewe, but in our bit there are plenty of empty seats so he can always see. Here he had to stand on the seat to have any chance of seeing and even then his view was limited.

Dylan was watching in a more civilised area, but the 3-2 defeat did test the civility of the prawn sandwich brigade.

I think Dylan had enjoyed it more this time, Andy had treated him and the view was good. I don't think Reuben enjoyed the experience that much. Since then they haven't begged to go to United and seem to enjoy the "Alex" more and are keen to attend away games. I will have to see how it pans out in the future. I don't mind taking them once a season; it will be when they get older that they will have to make bigger decisions. Will they adopt for the bigger or the smaller club? Will it be the big city club or the local club? I chose local and I hope they do, but there are plenty that enjoy following a club away from their own town.

Controversially, I do walk with them even with their United shirts on. How many United fans would do the same if their sons went Sky Blue or Scouse? I have taken them to United but I would be happiest if they were armchair Man United fans and go to the "Alex". I could live with that.

Mansfield Town

I was living in Kidderminster for this one. While doing our weekly shop on a wintry Saturday morning my car wouldn't start. Accordingly we did our shopping in Kate's Mini. My car still wouldn't work after we got back from shopping, so I was still a bit worried that she might not let me use the Mini in the afternoon. I was thinking we've done the big shop, she could walk into town and treat herself in the afternoon with my cash card (she did anyway). Yes I can have the car... I hope you see some clothes you like…. of course… I'll drive carefully.

I set off about 1 o'clock - maybe cutting it a bit fine. The radio in Kate's car was awful, I thought of trying for local radio to keep an eye on any traffic problems, but the sound wasn't much better so I decided to try a new tape we had just bought. Nirvana had just released their follow up to the classic 'Nevermind', it was the first listen of 'In Utero', it sounded pretty good but it was always going to be a difficult album to follow. The catchiest song was 'Rape me', I remember thinking I'm sure its not as bad as the title suggested, but I made a mental note to listen to the lyrics carefully at a later date.

The car didn't clear air well and the windows were steam ridden for most of the journey. It was getting too cold to open the window, and the further North we got, the worse the fog became. As a result, I slowed down and arrived near the ground around 2.45pm. I hate arriving late for away games although for a home game this would be early. I prefer to look around the ground and town and have a drink, something I rarely do for home games, and if I did it would probably be in the Brunswick.

Parking was particularly difficult around Field Mill, probably because the DIY shop near the ground was more popular than this fixture. In desperation I mounted a grass verge which didn't look that bad in a Mini and hoped I wouldn't be penalised. On the open terrace I met a few familiar faces including Beckett, a lad who I had known from school. I don't remember him looking this cool. He had gone to Nottingham Uni and had been a big part of the Alternative /Goth scene in the city and was now a club DJ, but he hadn't forgotten the "Alex" on this musical journey.

The fog prevented us seeing a view of all the ground clearly, but it did have some character. The paddock and main stand looked quite impressive which couldn't be said for the game or atmosphere. It wasn't a memorable away game but I had 'done the ground' thanks to Kate's Mini.

I did return to a transformed Field Mill in the early part of the 21st century. I travelled on the coach from Crewe and this time I managed to find a decent boozer not too far from the ground. The "Alex" fans were now seated behind a covered end, and the end opposite and to our left had both been modernised. The "Alex" had a field day scoring five on the pitch and we were able to celebrate in style - much to the dismay of the

Stags fans to our left. This second journey was a much happier and warmer affair.

Middlesbrough

As we got promoted to the second tier in 1997, this was a new ground that I was looking forward to visiting, especially as I never made it to Ayresome Park. As a child watching on TV, the away end, with a large amount of seats was strange, especially before the Taylor report. In the corner of this was an away terrace, hemmed in between the large seating area and the side. I could imagine it might have been quite intimidating. The home end looked a great old style end.

Unfortunately, the fixture was a midweek one in a busy week at school and reluctantly I decided that the trip would kill me off. I would have had to sacrifice my usual midweek visit to my daughter because school commitments meant I could only see her on the night we were at 'Boro'.

A hectic week would mean pressure and stress and a trip to the North East could have been the nail in the coffin at school. It's funny how kids can sense, tiredness, illness, hangovers and lack of preparation. I decided to go for the alert option at school.

However, I did manage to go to the home game in October with Dele Adebola scoring one of this greatest ever "Alex" goals against class opposition. I was a bit pre-occupied at the game with my washing. Graham and Nic and Patricia any Yestin were coming up from Wolverhampton to visit for a night out and they were staying over. I had only been in my Crewe house in Smallman

Road a couple of months and four people was the most I had entertained. I concentrated on the food preparation but left washing the bedclothes until late. (It's funny how having visitors seem to turn even the most meticulously domestic person to stress out). With no tumble dryer I was praying that the bed linen would stay dry and the weather didn't break. Luckily, it was only the 'Boro net that nearly did!

It was also a first showing off of my newly acquired next door neighbour, Jackie, to my teacher mates. She was also conveniently near if the October sunshine changed. I needn't have worried, the night went well, I am still with Jackie but I still haven't visited the Riverside stadium yet.

My only other connection with anybody who supported 'Boro was a lad called Jamie who was a student with my mate Phil at Derby. He was a photography student and took the photograph for the cover of John King's Football Factory.

Millwall

In the 1996/7 season I made my first trip to the New Den. On the official coach I didn't have the same trepidation that some fans might have making their own way there. Mind you the song "No one likes us" could be compared with no one hates us as barr the odd mild exception we are not treated with much malice compared with a Milllwall away fan who must attract the wrong sort where ever they go.

We met a police escort at the Dungeon tourist attraction near the Thames before entering South East London. The New Den is a modern, compact stadium that like most modern grounds sells alcohol, which if the football guides are true is safer than drinking in Deptford. Mind you a drink in the tourist areas and the train makes for a more exciting day than a coach trip.

The upper tier gave a good view, and as expected the atmosphere was quiet, we weren't worthy of intimidation! Darren Huckerby shone on his loan spell and helped seal the points for the Lions. Half-time was good, as at many London games you bump into Crewe exiles. I hadn't seen Jo for ages, an ex-punk, mod, casual who was the girl fiend of an old mate. She was a solicitor now and I still found her attractive although she wasn't obviously so. I always wondered if she knew it, unfortunately I don't think I was her sort. She offered to put me up in London, boy do I wish I had gone on the train as I was single and over Kate. The offer was an offer of friendship, but a boy can always dream can't he?! I also had a wedding do to go to as soon as the coach got back to Crewe, so I declined the offer thinking there may be better potential there (There wasn't as it happens and I'd even left some tooth paste and deodorant in my car by the coach, Saturday footy trips are not conducive with good breath and smells)

As the coach drove away from the ground, I have never had so many friendly waves leaving a football ground. Was it genuine spontaneous amiability or a policy devised by the club? One thing's for sure I came away from this game with no animosity to the club, can many other fans say the same?

I did return to the Den with Phil. Phil was living in Birmingham at the time and I drove to him from Crewe and we drove from his home in Selly Oak. The plan was to leave the car in North London and make our way south of the river. When we got to the Brent area, we planned to park up on the road somewhere and get the tube in. We naively thought this would be simple but hadn't thought about permit parking which seemed to be the rage in this part of London. As a result we eventually gave up and decided to park in the Sainsbury's car park. We made sure we bought some items on arrival and leaving and hoped that the car wouldn't get a ticket. We got a tube ticket to London Bridge and got off and had a quick mooch around by the river taking in the Gherkin and other well known attractions on the skyline. We resisted any temptation to be tourists and joined the tube to Bermondsey thinking that we not far from the ground.

The journey clearly showed the contrasting two cities from the new wealth that surrounded Canary Wharf to the forgotten areas surrounding the Millwall ground. On arrival we quickly realised that Bermondsey and South Bermondsey were no where near each other. When we got out of the station we walked out with trepidation, but attempted to be casual like locals. We scanned the street hoping to find some clues of where the ground was. On either side of the road there were maisonettes or tower blocks and none of us fancied drawing attention to ourselves by asking the way. We did spot a lad with a blue top on and we followed him for ages before he entered a park to play with his mates. He was probably relieved to find his mates; he might have feared he was being followed by two paedophiles! We then bravely decided to only ask the elderly and women for directions to the ground. The last person was a young woman who joked about how she ought to send us the wrong way but she must have thought that two Crewe fans were not worth losing! She joked with us and practically escorted us to the ground, she was our own private bodyguard on the day and made sure we got to the ground safely on time.

We joined a couple of hundred others in the upper tier and met our mate Pete from Sutton who had made his way from New Cross Station.

After the game, we were a little wary walking back to the station, this time we got on at South Bermondsey to save our tired little feet. We decided that we wouldn't open our mouths till we got to London Bridge, but in all honesty I don't think there was any threat that day, it is just that a team's reputation can make you extra cautious. It is at safer grounds that sometimes the unexpected can happen.

We got some food at the supermarket before returning to our car which, thankfully, hadn't been clamped. As we headed towards the motorway we relaxed and joked about our magical mystery tour around Bermondsey.

MK Dons

I went here in the 2012 with Pete Johnson; we went on the official coach which set off early giving us plenty of time pre-match. We wandered around the ground which was lively due to it being a family day, and to be fair the club had set up plenty of activities. After passing ASDA, he was reminded of work, so Pete decided we should find a pub. He was a printer for 40 years before being laid off and has since cleaned at Tesco on the minimum wage, including New Year's Day - an absolute disgrace.

We wandered through some trees and a lake before finding a friendly pub, more geared up to decent food than football fans after a decent pint, but it was pleasant enough and away from the retail nightmare that surrounds the ground (although I'm sure the kids love it)

For a new ground at this level the ground was impressive with a good vantage point for the 700 fans that had made the trip. The atmosphere was enhanced by the family day cut price tickets, but still a little lacking due to the enormity of the stadium - although the club have lofty ambitions for bigger stages. The new ground had brought some old faces down to the game and it was nice to catch up with likes of Pogs, Steve B and Ian Crawford, as well as a lot of my students from school.

The game was soured for me at the end by an old guy who had criticised the team, being threatened physically by another middle aged man. I mediated and calmed it down a bit but the Neanderthal bloke was a total arsehole!

Morecambe

The trip was a family event coinciding with the Easter holidays. My wife Jackie, and my two lads Dylan and Reuben made the trip on the train. We changed at Lancaster and got off at a small station that dropped us off away from the centre of Morecambe. No it wasn't because of a pre-arranged scrap, Jackie had sussed out an excellent park that was decent and not too expensive with somewhere to eat our picnic. From there we made out way to the front and walked our way from the quieter end to the centre of Morecambe where we treated ourselves to a brew and cake in a café. We had covered a long way walking and deserved the rest. From the town we took the long Main Road to the ground passing a few pubs with Crewe fans in on the way.

When we got to the ground, we were recommended a cheap family ticket by somebody, so we proceeded to a portakabin at the ground and got a good deal which meant we were still in the away end. I loved the away end, a good cover with a flat bit at the back. We always keep a small ball in our bag so this was ideal for the lads to play when they were not watching the game ,they were both still young so this kept them occupied and also it amused a few drunk fans who appreciated that this children's game might be just as entertaining as what was on the pitch. As it turned out the game was pretty eventful, the "Alex" were 3-1 up until the last 5 minutes when we capitulated and lost 4-3. Little did we know that the last Morecambe goal was scored by David Artell who did become a bit of a legend at the club not long after this humiliating end to the game. It was fair to say that there was some anger at the end given to players and management.

After the game we walked back into town and had a brew in a café near to the station. We joined some other disgruntled fans on the train where we alighted at Lancaster. Some other "Alex" fans got off and went into some boozers near the station while we got a taxi to a Travelodge on the outskirts of the town, chosen for its price rather than its proximity or character.

After a hearty breakfast we tried the pool and sauna before leaving, the guy on the reception had actually been to the game and picked out a couple of our youngsters out for praise, despite the defeat. After that, we spent the rest of the day in Lancaster. We got the bus into town where we scoured a few charity shops (excellent for keeping the kids and us entertained and with some cheap treats) before taking the long walk up the hill to Williamson Park with its lovely views and statues. Later on, we did a bit more sight seeing near the prison before heading back to the station. It had been a wonderful weekend despite the result and boy had we done some walking. Jackie and I are not averse to walking everywhere with kids, but even we thought we had over done it this weekend!

I intended to go to the new stadium two years later where we had a last minute winner, but didn't due to having three car accidents in a month - partly through having a rough time at school. I was starting to get more stressed, more disillusioned with new initiatives and seeing an increase in 6th formers who were less equipped for A level. At the same time I was now teaching more lower school as well which can create different demands! Accordingly, the cost of the accidents meant Jackie banned me from Morecambe! I look forward to visiting the new ground soon.

Mossley

Another non-league defeat! In 1980 we were drawn against this very small non-league club, this wasn't a Yeovil, Telford or Hereford and as a result we felt very superior on the coach while entering the small town squashed between Oldham and the Pennines. I remember talking to Graham Fox about "Bank Robber" by The Clash on the coach. He wasn't even a football fan, he was just out for the day out, such was the pull of the FA cup in those days.

Unfortunately, this optimism was ill-judged and we got beat 1-0. The game also attracted lots of 'nutters' from the area and at one point the "Alex" fans got legged along the open terrace. It was not a day for holding your head up high.

Nantwich Town

I only went to the old Nantwich Town ground once when I took my daughter Becky to see a charity game between some Brookside and Hollyoaks stars. They used to play at Jackson Avenue.

Interestingly Clive Jackson was one of the investors and was on the board at Nantwich. Clive attended Edleston Primary School with me and lived in Gresty Road with his Mum. I'm not too sure exactly how he got his money, but he had certainly shown ambition and graft to get into that deserved position. He is a nice lad that deserved it.

I rarely go to friendlies and as a result my only trip to the new Nantwich ground was to play on it against a Malbank Year 11 team. These games are eagerly anticipated by students, but defeat is something that teachers fear, even if it's very near them leaving and there is little chance to be teased by the students. It is a huge issue of pride, especially for the macho PE teachers!

The new ground is a tidy new ground with two open terraces behind the goals. There is a covered terrace on one of the sides which is opposite the seating.   Behind the seats you can have a drink in the bar at half time. The ground is quite exposed being surrounded by fields so I would recommend a hat and lots of layers for most of the season

The ground is very near our school and the opportunity to play in a real ground before the pitch was re-surfaced for the new season gave the game some added spice. On a personal level, I remember it very well because I saved a penalty from Chris Hill to ensure the game was a score draw. It wasn't unknown for him and his mate Smithy to give me a bit of stick so I saw the save as a bit of a 'result'. I taught his brother Andy for Politics afterwards and he joined the army after school. He was a lovely lad, and I believe he is doing really well. This was the year group Ashley Westwood, ex-Crewe and now of the Villa, was part of but he was too good and thankfully he watched from the stand.

I am more familiar with the 3G pitch behind the ground where the staff have done battle with our local school town rivals Brine Leas on numerous occasions. The buggers are usually far too good for us!

Newcastle United

I missed Crewe's only meeting in my lifetime due to an away midweek fixture during my busy first years teaching in Birmingham. The prospect of going to St James' Park came from an unlikely source, a stag do.

My mate Ben was a rock fan and had visited the city several times due to the legendary Mayfair rock club (sadly now demolished). An electrician for the council, he often did fairly simple jobs for the impractical me. On one of these simple jobs for the inept me, he alerted me to this trip in 1998. He was driving a minibus early Saturday morning and we were to stay at a decent hotel near the railway station.

An assorted collection of people boarded the bus early on this Saturday morning: rockers with long hair, rockers with shaven heads, rockers who had lost their hair (this must be really depressing for rockers, it's bad enough for me) and punk/indie/ fans like my friend Keith and I.

An old friend Dano was on the coach (who was also a very good friend of my current girlfriend Jackie). I found this a bit strange, sometimes they go out occasionally as friends, I trust Jackie and I have always liked Dano, but you can't help feeling like Othello sometimes - natural I suppose if you love someone? Or bloody stupid! Jealousy can be so destructive, my green eyes were probably not helped as my ex-wife was an expert at flirtation.

The traffic was awful; we were stuck in a jam outside the impressive Angel of the North and at Catterick. When we arrived, it was a quick freshen up and out early afternoon in Newcastle. People spit up for the afternoon and we were due to meet up in the hotel bar at 7.

I stuck with Keith, we wandered through the town, taking in the odd shop and walking passed a big statue at a bit of a crossroads in town. We headed to the student area where we got a cheap and filling meal to set us up for the day. At 3pm the Newcastle/Nottingham Forest fixture was on the radio which I thought was a pleasant surprise for a student café. The football was also on the radio in the nearby record shop, again highly unusual - boy this town was football crazy!

I didn't know when we were going to arrive in the city, so I didn't try and get tickets for the game, although I believe that it was very difficult at the time. I didn't want footy to dominate the weekend but the chance of a new ground was very much on my mind.
Neither Keith nor I had been to the ground before and it was our intention to get into the last few minutes of the game and we would claim we had been, although I'm sure dedicated 92 ground clubbers would dispute the authenticity of the claim. We sauntered to ground which is adjacent to the town centre - something that really appeals to me and my admiration for grounds. Being part of a community or proper town centre is a huge part of my subjective criteria.

We walked around the ground before trying to get in, something that wasn't as simple as I first thought. We got into the outer area of the ground easily enough, watching some of the game on the TV monitors but getting up the steps to see the game proved difficult. None of the stewards would let us, claiming that seating grounds can't allow people to sneak in like they could do in the past when there was terracing. It was probably a fair point.

However, I was more worried that I couldn't really claim a new ground if I hadn't seen the match, so I zoomed up one of the steps passed a steward, had a quick glimpse of the match before being escorted down to the outer area with a telling off. When most of the crowd had left we ventured into the ground to have a nose.

There was a great view with no posts impeding your view but somehow I wasn't as impressed as I thought I might be. I thought it looked too grey and I prefer grounds that have four sides rather than perfectly curved all the way around.

We had a quick look at the goals on one of the TV monitors in the outer area before venturing back to the hotel for a shower to freshen up.

In the hotel bar we looked a right Motley Crew, well not literally but some of us may have done 10 years previously. We were mainly dressed casually with some long hair and PVC, but unusual enough to be advised by a Geordie guy in the bar to keep away from the Riverside area and stay near the Bigg Market student area near to the Bus Station (which was where we were intending anyway). We went in an array of rock, studenty, non- dance music bars before arriving at the infamous Mayfair.

It had a lovely large foyer, reminiscent of an old dance hall. Further inside the club there was a large dance floor and seating area surrounded by a balcony. It was furnished lavishly and kept in a pristine condition. The clientele was a collection of old style rockers, 1990 metallers, casuals and crusties. It was a very friendly atmosphere with plenty of room to wander around. The main room was soft and traditional rock mixed with the odd punk and indie track. A small room off the main hall played commercial and some obscure dance music, while the other smaller room concentrated more on thrash/rap/metal. I danced on all 3 dance floors during the night, bonding with some people on the minibus I didn't really know. The 'Rockafella Skank' by Fat Boy Slim stood out as the song of the night for me for a good shuffle on the dance floor. Dano embraced the song and we jigged to the song (which was played several times on the night!).

On the way home a takeaway is a prerequisite on a night like this. Incredibly we had difficulty finding one; surely they are plentiful in any City, and especially one like Newcastle that is renowned for its night life. We did find one eventually, but when you "Find yourself in a Strange Town." We didn't get this classic Jam song on a night like this.

The next morning, everybody seemed to make it for a hearty breakfast, where beer and the night out were the obvious subjects although the night seemed to pass without any major incidents in all the important areas!

Getting our deposits back at the hotel (only for large groups of potential male delinquents) was a time consuming process and as we hadn't swung from the chandeliers and trashed the place, like some of our former heroes, we got our money back.

The minibus journey was inevitably marred by some horrendous smells and some teasing surrounded some of the more salacious stories from the tabloids. Sadly the Mayfair has now been demolished; I hope St James' Park will be there for a while longer for me to make a proper visit to the ground.

Newport County

Back in the league I still need to do this one soon. My mate Pete Johnson has been and I know all about the Black Country history of the town which intrigues me, so let's hope the wait isn't too long.

I do remember as a kid some Newport County graffiti at the back of the wooden steps in the Gresty End, so I know they have visited Gresty Road.

Northampton Town

The name Northampton immediately makes my memory turn towards childhood and some of my most vivid memories of soccer violence.

The sound of Cobblers meant trouble in the mid 70's; these were the days when there weren't always away fans and no segregation. Northampton always brought a mob and would usually take the Gresty End by running amok in the dust at the back of our very empty end. I can clearly remember a long haired youth in side pocket flares being knocked out with a Kung- Fu kick right in front of my Dad and I. To this day I am still surprised how quickly he went down` thud` on the concrete terrace. Was he dead? This was going to be the most memorable part of the day and still a very vivid one. Excitement and fright rolled into one. Certainly a reminder that the fun of running battles can have a devastating end but a great story to re-tell with your friends; especially when Kung-Fu was massive at the time.

Later visits also meant apprehension but did not involve the violence of the mid 1970's visits. A 5-0 home defeat on a Friday night to table–topping Northampton meant our ground was swamped by hundreds of Town fans.

Running off behind the Royal also rings a bell in a later fixture. The memory of their various maroon kits over the years also stands out, the colour of kits being so important to the adolescent football anorak.

After reading the above most people would probably expect hostile memories of the County ground, but I have none to tell. It may be due to my first visit being in the early 80's when segregation was better or as some harder clubs invariably do, cause more trouble away from home.

It was on a Sunday when I made my first trip on the coach. The trip was memorable for being on the back row with Chelsea Joe. A few years older and harder, we were mesmerised by his tales of mither, we could also now put a face to the Chelsea + Joe graffiti which was all over Crewe at the time. His Dad's pub was famous for having Flux of Pink Indians on the jukebox! (Well amongst the punk fraternity)

The coach dropped us on the road by the open away end where we watched a heavy defeat, 4-0 I think. The atmosphere from the other end was good, but the cricket pitch along the one side didn't help matters. It was strange seeing a cricket pitch and stand to our left, it kept me more entertained than the poor "Alex" team at the time. Maybe we would have won at cricket!

On the way back Chelsea Joe made an audacious attempt to steal some fags from behind the counter at the service station, unfortunately for him the coach didn't leave immediately and the member of staff came on to the coach with help. Luckily the staff were satisfied to have the merchandise back, rather than involve the cops.

We were impressed by this spontaneous madness, but not surprised by the outcome.

I returned to the County ground in the 1991-92 season, fitting in a night out in Coventry on the Friday night with my friend Mick. Would he bring us luck? The next day we met Garf in Northampton town centre. His Mum and girlfriend had decided to go shopping while the 3 of us went to the pub. I remember being a bit shocked at the large size of Northampton, a sleeping giant maybe? It was a glorious Easter time day and the 3 of us had a great natter in a pub near the ground with a great beer garden where I also met Dano, which was a pleasant surprise; you are far more likely to see him at rock gigs. A 1-0 victory in lovely sunshine rounded off a good day.

I made my first trip to Sixfields for our first 3rd tier game after several years in the lofty second tier of football. I made the trip on the official coach with Becky. She was living in Crewe at the time after choosing to live with us and she lived with us in Crewe for two and a half years in Crewe before returning and staying in Kidderminster afterwards. It was great to have her up and a big shock to the system for Jackie, but she took the role of step mum seriously despite the odd knockback "you're not my mum". When Becky decided to go back, I insisted that that would be a final decision as she couldn't keep playing one parent off another and she couldn't keep swapping schools. The day she decided to live with me and not live with me, were some of the most joyous and saddest days in my life.

We arrived at the retail park area and I was inevitably less impressed than the character of the old County ground, despite its imperfections. We were seated behind the goal with a big following; the fans had stuck with us and turned out for the first game of the 2002/3 season? despite relegation. Our fans were very cocky that day, playing the role of the big club against the smaller minnows. It wasn't something I was very comfortable with and I also know how matters can quickly change on the football field. We ended up drawing the game and the "Who are you chants?" were haunting us at the end. Were we a bigger club than Northampton now? It's all cobblers to me!

Northwich Victoria

I was still flirting with Sociology and A levels at night school when we got this local derby in the cup and declined to make the trip due to being more fascinated by the Red of Karl Marx at the time.

Vic's fans should buy the excellent "She Wore a Scarlet Ribbon" by Jules Hornbrook for a write up of the Drill Field game against the "Alex" in the mid 1980's.

Norwich City

It's a bit of a journey and as a result the official coach leaves Gresty Road at 7.30. I've been getting up early for so long that I can't sleep in any more (although it is a bit early for the summer holidays!) I've packed my usual half a loaf of butties the night before and picked shorts and t shirt as the beautiful weather girl confidently told me it was going to be a scorcher!

The Johnson brothers were my main buddies on this glorious sunny day in August 1997. Pete was a regular and it was almost mandatory that Pete would be there, but it was nice to see Rick there - he had suffered some health issues and it was a rare and pleasant surprise that he had made the long trip to East Anglia.

We arrived in Norwich at 1 o'clock, where the temperature was soaring, giving us plenty of time to saunter in the sun. We walked along the river bank until we ventured into the Compleat Angler. The beer garden overlooked the river and we basked in the sunshine sharing optimism with some other "Alex" fans, something very easy in August - although not so easy when you are the newly weds in the second tier of English football.

After a couple of beers, we walked towards the ground in temperatures alien to most British football fans. Pete went to the ground, but Rick and I went for a wander, admiring the attractive station (with its old fashioned clock), quaint alleys and quiet court yards. We looked at the castle from a distance before walking down King Street on the other side of the river and crossing the bridge back to the ground. It was a lovely day, too hot for football and a walk around the town was a great temptation.

We were situated in the older, but nonetheless impressive large stand at the side of the ground with 400 others. It was a good atmosphere and I was surprised at the intensity of the home vocal support, especially as the "Alex" were gaining their first away victory in the league with two superb goals. I remember looking at one banner 'Crewe Alex not a care in the world' and thinking that was an apt summary of the day.

It had been a memorable day. Beforehand I would have been tempted to say "you can only go here once, it's too far" I am certainly considering a return visit - and that was before Alan Partridge put the town on the map even further!

Nottingham Forest

I first visited the City Ground in the 1980/81 season. It was a year I had been looking forward to, relatively affluent in my first job as a postman. I could buy obscure albums after listening to one track on the John Peel show, go to gigs, buy clothes, go out and follow the "Alex" and the Toffeemen.

Nottingham is very accessible from Crewe and the train was full of Evertonians who'd made there way to Crewe. I was dressed as casual as my punk ideals would let me and Tap was in all the latest casual regalia, bubble coat, Louis jeans and Adidas trainers.

This was the time of police escorts and we naively walked into it on arrival at the station where as the more astute or streetwise waited on the train till the last minute and jumped off at the end of the platform and waited till the escort had gone. The police were eventually beginning to be wise to the fact that hooligans didn't look like the stereotypical yob (although dressing casual certainly made it easier to blend in with family shoppers).

Nottingham has always had a reputation for good night life and interesting shops. The night life may have been sparked by the 'there's two women for every man' which seemed to be a common statement that you used to hear in the 1970's and 80's. As a result it was quickly swamped with men looking for nubile young women who were supposedly 'gagging' for it!

Secondly, in the early 1980's Nottingham Rock City was infamous for its alternative nights, anybody of Punk, Goth, Alternative or Psychobilly persuasion would try and get up or down to there occasionally. Personally I always felt it was too big and plush for such an audience, despite having a great night there. I preferred a smaller club where there was more of an atmosphere like the Planet in Liverpool, the Venue or Cloud 9 in Manchester, Chicos in Stoke or the Warehouse in Preston.

Anyway we saw little of any interest on the escort to the ground, being forced away from houses and being forced to walk by derelict factories and the Trent before urban renewal.

In the ground we were situated in the open corner on terracing by the new modern stand at the side, one of the newest stands at a time of little stadium renewal, although it didn't help the view for the away fans in that corner of the ground.

Our section was a small section and accordingly it was packed and there was an unusual amount of swaying occurring. The police stepped in at one point to quell the crushing problem and I was one of many that were randomly picked out to alleviate this. I was dragged by a policeman who took me towards the turnstiles. My insides started churning as I feared the consequences of being arrested. What would my Mum say? Would I lose my job? I wasn't even thrown out of the ground in the end, the copper pushed me and threatened me, "calm down or I'll have you in the meat wagon". There was no fear of violence in the crowd, just too many of us in one section, police surveillance should have been better and the cops were panicking. I spent the rest of the game trying to find my mate Tappy. He had been looking for me by the gates, me for him in the crowd. We eventually found each other near the end of the game. I think we lost 2-0; the game was insignificant due to the confusion around finding each other.

I returned to the City ground with the "Alex" in 1997. My friend Phil was still town hopping, this time for a brief stay in Sherwood, Nottingham. I drove over on the Friday night to see him. We went out and caught the bus up to a studenty back street pub where Sarah, his girlfriend, was out drinking with her friends from the university bookshop. I was looking for something that involved a bit more life with some dancing, but they were friendly enough and we had some games of pool and a belly full of beer. As ever it was good to catch up with Phil and it was a good start to the weekend.

The next day, after Phil was up and ready, which is an extremely long and painstaking process, we cleared our heads with a saunter around Wollaton Hall, somewhere I had visited before with Garf and I was equally impressed again. There are some lovely grounds and informative art and history, although today the nearest we got to it was drinking coffee in an historic courtyard!

Later we went out to meet a Forest fan he knew. We passed the park where the legendary Goose Fair takes place on the way, such a prominent feature in the early Alan Sillitoe novels like

'Saturday Night Sunday Morning'. I was a big fan of the Nottingham author who was partly responsible for getting my interest in reading and education. I did my degree extended essay on Sillitoe and the working class novel, something that also influenced my interest in sociology.

We had a drink near the County ground and parked on the corner near the County away end behind the goal in those days. This time the away end had been transformed, it was seated and much larger than before, I liked it but not the 20 pound price. It was an issue amongst both sets of fans, chants were sung in unison about being ripped off. The "Alex" got a bit of a hammering but it was a pleasant trip, the renovated Trent was an interesting feature to the ground and certainly adds to the uniqueness of the ground.

I made my last trip to the City ground two days before my second wedding in 2000 on Boxing Day. I made up my mind to go with Jak to the game as a break from all the preparations and fall out that seems to naturally surround all the shenanigans. I'm not too sure how keen Jak was, she certainly is not that keen anymore but we made the trip sitting together on the coach, something that isn't always guaranteed. We made Nottingham early, so we decided to walk to the town centre and have a quiet drink there than go to one of the nearer busier pubs. The walk was a long and cold one and I'm fairly sure we made the wrong call on the day. The game ended up in defeat, and the away end was almost silent the whole game, making it a very poor trip with no atmosphere. If this was test for love and married life I'd started it in a very inauspicious way. Two days later we had a white wedding with heavy snow falling making the pictures magical and the bride and guests very cold.

Notts County

My first trip to Meadow Lane was during the Easter of 1990 in the 3rd year of my degree at Uni. This meant that I could get my Dad's car making the trip a little cheaper and easier.

Kate was staying in Crewe at the time of the trip which had the potential to be interesting. Garf was living in Radford in Nottingham at the time and I had visited him there and in Hyson Green. I was fond of the City. Slab Square was always impressive and the Urban Windmill is highly unusual and impressive - the only one of its kind that I know. It is a worthy visit for both adults and families.

I have visited the castle which gives you an excellent view of the City and surrounding areas. Inside there is quite a varied museum, while on the outside I imagined myself being Albert Finney, after being just told that he had got his married mistress pregnant. I tried to emulate his cool stance with a cigarette.

Garf had been making a few trips to Meadow Lane, preferring the friendliness compared to the more belligerent City ground. He had made some friends (one through Selectadisc record shop) involved with the County fanzine 'The Pie' and arranged a football game with some County fans in the morning.

Now I would have jumped at the chance normally, the older I have got the more I have enjoyed playing football. When I was younger I was labelled a goalie, which was probably my best position, but recently I had enjoyed playing more out pitch. I think I had gained with the game putting more emphasis on passing and space than brawn. Still I do live in the town of Dario Gradi!

Anyway, during a game in Liverpool in a student league for 'Show us your Zonies', named after the bus/train passes in the city (later we were aptly re-named Shite FC) I ran my heart out with my new boots on a hard pitch. Such a harmless activity had led me to do something to my feet and lower back and as a result I had to rule myself out of this game. Phil, Garf, Rick and Pete Johnson, Sim, Pete Newton and his brother, Brass, Jud, and Melv Cotton were amongst the team that faced the County lads. Bob Newton was in goals and I think I remember Pete Newton being a reluctant but successful penalty taker. I think we won the game 4-2. Kate stayed in the car with a 'tenner' full of magazines.

An entertaining and good natured game led to a pre/post match drink with the Notts fans. A good time was had with plenty of good natured banter before we went our separate ways going into our allocated areas of the ground.

Kate left to sample some of the City's delights, apparently having some banter with some drunken "Alex" fans who were heading in the opposite direction to the ground.

Our end was a large tall open terrace with some seating allocated to us in the adjacent stand. The opposite end had a building behind it and accordingly was quite small. After a 2-0 defeat, we ventured into the town centre and met up with Kate.

We tried the oldest pub in Britain 'Ye Olde Trip to Jerusalem', built into the bottom of the castle with an array of different sections inside. We passed the Castle pub this time, a pub I had frequented on previous visits to Rock City before drinking on the sumptuous Slab Square. This was an area also brought alive by Sillitoe in his books, a square that is surely on par with Trafalgar Square as one of the best squares in the country. With its magnificent council building, pubs and shops it also attracted the alternative youth of the town who often congregated there on a Saturday afternoon.

We carried on drinking, although I was driving and unable to keep up with the same pace as the rest. We tried The Bell on the Square and Yates' Wine Lodge, on my first trip to Nottingham this was an amazing, bustling, huge spit and sawdust pub with a guy playing on the piano downstairs. The place was as heaving as it was on my first visit but it had been transformed to a modern and plush establishment, a shame it had lost a lot of its character. I don't think we would have got in if we hadn't arrived so early.

It was no surprise that Kate and Phil got into a row towards the end of the evening. Kate wasn't that keen on Phil and saw him as pretentious and when he seemed surprised on finding out Kate's age and he said "I thought you were older than that" (5 years younger than me) she went into a hump and frenzy - leaving a very uncomfortable atmosphere with the group. Kate was specifically sensitive to this; she had had responsibility from 13 due to her Mother dying and her Dad not coping. Yes she was older looking for her age and attractive, a result of having to grow old quickly in many ways. Phil knew this because his Dad had died at an early age, and he had experienced similar emotional upset. Phil had picked the wrong time certainly, although the comment would have hurt many people, including me who are vain, but especially women and in particularly a sensitive and drunk, argumentative Kate.

We left before last orders and I couldn't wait to get back. It was an icy atmosphere in the car, Phil was trying to apologise unsuccessfully and then had to ask for a toilet stop. Who says football and women don't mix?

My return trip to Meadow Lane was the last game I attended before Kate and I split up. For many years we had lived as an extended family with Kate's Dad and Brother Ian. It gave us time to clear a few college debts. We had been having a bad patch and we decided that it was time to get our own place together. We found a house fairly near to our old one and we were positive about moving forward in the relationship. Unfortunately being on our own seemed to highlight our differences and the fact that I wasn't sure I liked Kate anymore, her constant falling out with people and myself was taking its toll and I wanted out. I wanted to be happier and respected.

This was on my mind as I drove from my school in Bilston to County for the second leg of the play offs in 1996. We had drawn 2-2 in the first leg and although we should have done better at home we were confident that we could get a better result away from home. I had a drink in their club before the game before finding our way to the same end which was now covered. The 9,000 plus crowd saw a tight game, but we eventually lost the game 1-0 and the sombre mood was going to continue for me. I made the difficult decision to split and Kate didn't beg me to stay which confirmed it was the right thing to do. However, it would mean seeing less of Becky especially as all my Kidderminster connections were through Kate and I had decided to live at my Mum's in Crewe and my Nan's at Cannock until my head was more sorted and I had more idea about where I permanently was going to live.

I remember watching the England/Germany (in Euro96) game at my parent's house in Crewe and finding it really strange to not have to tidy and clear up for Becky all the time. I was restless and lost. It was time to adjust my life while seeing Becky as much as possible. Kate's Dad's house was to become another house I would stay at when seeing her. I was a nomad up to 2002 when I eventually settled back in Crewe permanently. Becky even came to live with me for two and a half years when she was 10.

Nuneaton Borough

The first round of the FA Cup was an exciting time and a non- league club didn't extinguish this excitement, in fact an away tie at a non-league side was an added buzz. At 13 in 1977 it was exciting, no Dad and off the leash with your mates.

The journey on the coach turned off at junction 12 on the M6 and took the A5 route around the outskirts of Cheslyn Hay and Cannock, half a mile where I used to live 5 years ago and where my Nan and other relations still lived. I pointed this out to my mates who were aware of my Midlands connections and often teased me for it. It was strange to be so near to a past life, both in proximity and age but I now saw myself as Crewe despite having strong affectations for the West Midlands. Little did I know at this young age that in the future that I would return to this area many years later through a job, marriage, a daughter, divorce and caring for an elderly relative.

My main memories of the ground were that the main mob of Nuneaton fans were in a large covered end behind the goal to our right. It was bigger than most ends in the bottom two divisions at the time, although I recently saw the ground in a FA Cup round up and the end seemed smaller - although it may have been altered in the last few decades. Was I deceived at such a small age on a FA Cup rollercoaster? The end was full on the day with a large number of youths, a number of which were skins. We were bombarded with stones and debris during the game, whilst occupying the covered terrace to their left. My mate Tony Ralphs took a half brick on the leg as we stood side by side. The Nuneaton fans were fighting the police continually and the 1970's song "If it wasn't for the coppers you'd be dead" seemed apt.

Still there was a sizeable following of "Alex" fans as the FA Cup attracted people in those days! On the London rail line, the away crowd was swelled by free rail passes and quarter fairs by the railway workers of the town. Many have lost those privileges with the new privatised railway companies, but the railway heritage is a reason why the "Alex" often had a good following by train.

One memory of the game was of Crewe fans spray painting the part of the ground we were in, something I have never witnessed so openly to this day. People were throwing the can to each other so each fan could add their own individual mark on the ground. I suspect the police were too pre-occupied with the hostile Nuneaton fans.

The most unusual event was that the "Alex" actually won, one of our few victories against non-league opposition in that woeful decade in the 1970's and early 80's.

Oldham Athletic

I was absolutely delighted to get the Latics in the first round of the League Cup; we always seem to miss each when moving leagues, so this was an excellent opportunity to do a new ground. Tuesday night games are not ideal but this coincided with the school holidays, it's so good when life works out like that.

It was a lovely evening as I walked down to catch the coach in my shirt and shorts. We talked about the ups and downs of the game, how we were now supposed to be a bigger club than Oldham when less than 10 years ago they were a premier outfit who were not overshadowed by their big neighbours.

We walked around the ground before the match, there generally seemed to be a good atmosphere, the weather probably helped, still sunny in an area that is notoriously cold. I liked the ground, quite compact with some good cover that seemed to maximise the noise.

I enjoyed an entertaining game, more relaxed than usual, with no school tomorrow, I was now going steady with Jackie and after having spent a week with my daughter Becky I was content and happy. There was no emotive or angry passion today, I was just chilling out in the Oldham sunshine without a care in the world.

Oxford United

Becky was one in the 1994-5 season, and this relatively near trip to Oxford from Kidderminster was something to look forward to; things were not that good with Kate and we were moving out of our extended family house to solve all our problems. So, a new ground and a sing-song was just what I needed.

In my excitement to get there, I tried to squeeze past a parked car in nearby Blakedown and cracked my wing mirror. Matters got worse, it started to pour down and it is an open end at the Manor Ground. I parked in the street and walked past a Shell Garage where some protestors were promoting the evils of capitalism. Good luck to them - they are an exploitative company, but I decided to join the terraces rather than the protest.

The route to the away end was interesting, a labyrinth of cobbled pathways leading towards a homely gate where you enter the ground. The ground has many interesting stands for you to gander at, giving it an individuality sadly lacking at many stadiums. Unfortunately, the open end was very wet that day, and my friend Pete went in the stand in the corner, thinking I would do the same. Now Pete takes an umbrella all over the place so I thought he would stand up , so we remained separated till half time. We shared a brolly for the 2nd half. We lost 2-1 but it was a good breather from home tensions, who'd have thought singing in the pouring rain for 90 minutes would be therapeutic?

I went to the new ground in the 2011/12 season.
Pete Newton decided to drive to this one; his lad
and his mate joined us in the car. It's a small
world because I recently went with my nephew to
Manchester, I was watching New Model Army and
they were seeing Beady Eye and my nephew was
with this lad. Anyway, it was a crisp, sunny,
January day and we sat outside having a brew at
the service station on the journey which is not as
long as you as you may think from the North. We
arrived at the ground fairly early and had a drink at
the pub behind the car park end of the ground.
The locals were friendly under the canopy outside
the ground which was there to increase the
amount of people who could have a drink as there
didn't seem to be too many other pubs in the
vicinity. One local claimed there was very little
trouble unless they were playing Port Vale.

We made our way into the ground after a couple of
beverages and joined the seats in a large stand
that gave us the end third near the car park. It
gave a good view especially from the back, and
we decided to stand. Pete met up with his mate
from Swansea who follows the "Alex" everywhere
despite having no connections with the town, now
that is loyal support. My other mate Pete had
made his way on the train and had seen a bit of
the town, something I was jealous of, I vow to
make a weekend in the town sometime soon.

Peterborough United

This was a visit to London Road in the early 1980's. The coach arrived early and we took the opportunity to frequent the posh pubs. Gradually moving to the town centre, we were surprised at the size of the town, it was clearly far bigger than Crewe. Nevertheless we were not daunted by the town and decided to sing our way to the ground - which was rather naïve; we were less than ten and not exactly the meanest group you were going to meet. We did get some hassle off 2 aggressive blokes, but luckily our numbers meant they were happy to just mouth off and we, luckily, arrived safely at the ground.

Boy did we make some noise that day! We may have only numbered 50 in total, but helped by an echoic end, lots of beer and a spirited 2-1 defeat, you'd have thought we were on our way to Wembley. Even the players applauded us at the end. In the 80's this kind of noise was usually limited to FA cup matches.

The ground was compact with two good ends, but an open end on the one side was unusual and for some reason seems worse than behind the goal. Despite this I have good memories of the ground and would like to return again to see how posh the new stand is.

Plymouth Argyle

January 2nd 1995, another new year and another new ground. I set off early from Kidderminster to meet my mate Phil at Bristol Temple Meads, a small journey for him from Cardiff where he was currently residing.

I stretched my feet at the Bristol station; it is lovely building and well worth a look at, a legacy of its historic links as with many other buildings in the city.

Our journey was an enjoyable and uncomplicated one, a chance to swap stories on our loved ones, ambitions, frustrations and fears. One fear was the Plymouth lunatic fringe that according to Phil's Cardiff sources can be a little tasty.

We arrived about 1 o'clock; it's surprising how your furthest fixtures can sometimes be deceptively near when nearer Bournemouth and Grimsby drag. We sauntered around the park area before getting in a working man's club about 10 minutes from the ground. These kind of away trips are one of the few ways to keep in touch, as you get older, when the meeting times become less frequent you begin to realise who you are still in touch with. This visit confirmed our friendship and we quietly saw the New Year in. It reminded me a bit like the classic 'Likely Lads'.

The route to the away end is memorable due to a pathway in part of the park. If there is hooligan danger, you almost expect it to arrive Robin Hood style from the top of the trees. We were standing in the open away end overlooking another interesting ground where cover and open bits continually surprise each other, especially to our left. Luckily it was one of those dry, bright until 4 o'clock kind of days, which was a relief. We were taunted in an amusing rather than a hostile way by a sizeable mob in the popular stand to our right. This became even more cheerful when we threw away a 2-1 lead in the last 5 minutes. Happy New Year! It probably serves me right for doing a run/dance in the vast, fairly empty away terrace when we scored. These vast ends are ideal for such energetic celebrations; Cardiff's Ninian Park was equally good.

We avoided any Tarzan style attacks by being escorted through their Popular Stand after everybody had left. Slightly deflated, we left to travel back North, but this had been an enjoyable visit. Passing several coaches from other parts of Devon and Cornwall showed the potential of the club for vast support.

Well my Dad might have bettered me by actually playing at the ground during National Service in the RAF, but he hadn't had the pleasure of seeing the "Alex's" inauspicious start to 1995. Nothing worse than last minute capitulation but we were there, Crewe and proud in Devon.

Port Vale

The Vale are generally not liked by "Alex" fans, although the feeling is largely not as reciprocal, they have other enemies, however as we have progressed I think the feeling is increasingly with rancour.

Personally, I've never been a great fan (although I would say that most Crewe fans feel a lot stronger than this); I never witnessed a victory against them till the year 2000. Their fans have always been hostile and aggressive. However, I sympathise with them, it must be hard following Vale in the Potteries with bigger fish like Stoke and Man Utd being more appealing especially during periods of gloom.

My first visit to Vale Park came on a Tuesday night when The Clash concert at Victoria Hall Hanley was cancelled. Two out of fifty punks from Crewe decided to cross the city and watch The "Alex", if they'd have all come we would have doubled the amount of "Alex" fans in the vast open away end.

After a long walk and bus journey, we arrived just before half time. We were dressed for a gig rather than an evening football match so we ended up freezing our bollocks off watching The "Alex" rather than sweating and jumping around watching Joe Strummer. We didn't risk the train back and got a lift back on the half empty coach.

My next trip to Vale Park was a bit of a disaster. With Steve Shone and co, we thought it would be a good idea to go in the Railway Paddock as juniors and save a bit of money, as there was no concessions in the away end (most of us were too old anyway). The plan was to tell the cops that we had gone in the wrong end and they would let us in the away end. Simple. Unfortunately, the police would not let us move and the corner of that end was where all their boys stood. So we spent 70 minutes standing by the cops and their boys, very relaxing! Some Crewe fans kept pointing at us and laughing - we must have looked heroic and brave, little did they know, they should have checked our y-fronts. When the gates opened we scarpered back to the away end.

In 1983, we took a decent mob to Vale for a change. After being humiliated home and away by their boys in the 80's, it was a good feeling. We were given an escort from Longport station there and back and it was nice not feeling as intimidated as usual as we sang through the streets of Burslem.

When I returned in1996 for the League Cup game, Vale had a smart cover on the away end, even if it it was bought off Chester! What a transformation off the pitch, we took well over a thousand, although we still didn't beat the Vale on the pitch. Still it was August and not too cold, so it wasn't too bad.

I returned with my daughter Becky for another visit. We went on the coach which arrived early and with a few others we headed in the direction away from the Burslem town centre and found a friendly pub that was child friendly.

A few years later I returned to Vale Park with my two lads; Vale had a great policy of letting under 11's in for nothing and I took the opportunity to make the small journey. I thought travelling by coach would be the safest bet as the coach parko right outside the away end. We arrived early, so we crossed the road and went to play in the park. The park has some lovely original features as well as a modern well equipped play area. We played with a little ball and made use of the excellent child friendly facilities. Vale were pushing for the playoffs and had a good home turn out, where as we were fairly mediocre and had taken less than a thousand that day.

We won the game with a controversial goal which had ended Vale promotion hopes and the locals were restless. Outside the ground there was a baying mob of Vale fans that were baying for blood. The police were having trouble holding back hundreds of Vale fans holding back anybody who was in the car or train while the rest of us waited on the coaches. It was getting that bad that the waiting "Alex" fans were put back in the ground for protection. The "Alex" fans were humiliated on the day, which I believe was a turning point for the "Alex". I think since this day, the hatred has increased for Crewe fans and it led to an increase in hooliganism for a new young generation at Crewe. As the coaches eventually left we were bricked from the same park which we had played happily in just hours earlier. The kids thought it was dramatic rather than frightening although it may have been different if glass would have shattered inside the coach. As we travelled down the A500 home, the glass of several shattered window panels slid out on to the road.

The next year I used my family rail card to make the trip even cheaper with Dylan and Reuben. We were met at Longport station by the police but were able to walk freely to the ground as it was mainly law abiding fans that were on our train. This following year was another sunny dry day as we walked through Middleport and Burslem. Despite some houses and complete streets being left to rot, Burslem town centre is impressive with a lovely centre with historic buildings. We took a leisurely walk sitting in the town centre for a break and some sweets, before going to the same park as last year which was a very good experience again. In the ground the "Alex" fans were in bigger numbers and a large number were in the mood for trouble. A steward was hit by a drink and several people were ejected for just being near the incident. This increased the anger in the Crewe end. After the game, Dylan Reuben and I made a sharp exit while a large group of "Alex" fans were hell bent on causing trouble.

We had a peaceful long walk to Longport Station, while other Crewe fans got out of their cars to take on Vale fans, and a large mob on the train were herded onto an old double decker which arrived with very few windows on as we arrived at Longport Station. I believe the windows were smashed by the Crewe fans on board. The youths were up for trouble at Longport Station until we all boarded the train. On arrival at Crewe, the lads ran amok at the station with some Hereford boys on their way back from Stockport being chased but it was all heavily policed.

The game has since attracted more people who don't normally go to the "Alex" and the home fixture led to 20 arrests with a pitched battle on an open area of grass in Mill Street. A new generation of young lads have increasingly turned up for this fixture in recent years.

For me my Head of Department is a Vale fan which adds added spice and interest. As a result I feel less antagonism, although it might depend on how well my teaching observations have gone!

Portsmouth

This was our first season in the First Division in 1997, an exciting prospect with many new grounds to relish and devour. If I hadn't already been divorced, I would have been after this season! However, unknown to me at the time, movements closer to home were taking place that were to influence my future.

While I was making my way to Fratton Park on the coach, my next-door neighbour was saying goodbye to her live-in boyfriend. This was the year I was going to pursue my interest in my neighbour who I found extremely attractive and as I write this section in 2000 I am busy planning wedding arrangements. I'm in love with the girl next door!

We arrived in Portsmouth early enough to have a couple of leisurely beers in a nearby pub, and Pete, Austin and myself had some friendly conversation with some amicable Pompey fans.

At the time of the game, the Fratton End was closed due to re-construction, so the ground seemed full. Accordingly, we were squeezed into the corner of the Milton End by the South Stand. Once in the ground, the friendliness that had oozed beforehand disappeared. We were continually taunted by nearby fans in the Milton End and later in the game by fans in the South Stand. This was the most intimidating ground I had visited in years, not helped by Anthrobus and

Dele scoring in the last 10 minutes to give us a 3-2 victory.

Walking along the pathways hemmed in by houses after the game, the crowd was quiet and we made our way to the coach with trepidation. While waiting for our escort out of the town, we were teased by several young teenagers who hung around until we disappeared. This really was like a blast from the past. Jubilation and relief was felt on the long, coach journey back. There is something about late wins along way from home that makes you feel great.

On arrival back in Crewe, we went straight to the pub along Nantwich Road - our own Golden Mile, and despite the long journey back we felt fantastic.

People who didn't travel were curious about the day and performance and you can talk about it with pride and see their envy. If it was only like this every week!

Preston North End

Preston's name will always remind me of the F.A Cup neutral ground meeting at Anfield in the 1976/7 season (see Liverpool) and of college mate from Preston, Alison. She was one of my best friends while studying and we had lots of hilarious moments while in halls, sharing a house and nights out.

This trip in the 1989/90 season arrived before Alison became a North End fanatic and in my 3rd year of my English and Sociology degree at Liverpool. I had met Kate in February 1989, our whirlwind romance had ended up in an August engagement with a wedding to follow in the following August. It is this background knowledge that explains why non-football fan Kate joined me on a visit to Deepdale on a cold Tuesday evening. Two years later on this prospect would have been extremely unlikely.

We met up on the Childwall campus after lectures and got the 79 bus to town to join the train from Liverpool to Preston. We were still at the stage where we couldn't leave each other alone before we were interrupted by this Scottish guy on the train who was too familiar, which on a train journey can be a nightmare. I guess if I had been on my own I might have been quite pleased but the circumstances were not right. Low and behold he was off to the game to and he was a devoted Partick Thistle fan. Some of the statistics were quite interesting, but I could feel Kate's newly found interest in football dwindling.

When we got off at Preston there was a bus to take us to the ground, and our new friend got on it. It was about 6.30 and Kate surprisingly decided we would have a relaxing walk to the ground leaving our new friend waiting for the arrival of further fans from Crewe.

We passed a large town centre, which I had visited before. I had seen Siouxsie and the Banshees at Preston Guildhall before and had a disastrous trip to Preston Warehouse. Having been to see One Way System with my mates Andy and Jonah, we were waiting for a 3o'clock morning train back to Crewe. Half asleep and tired, we were waiting in the waiting room. Meanwhile some Carlisle punks had vandalised the station and the railway police came checking tickets. We had bought half fare tickets and were 17, they booked us and took our tickets off us leaving us penniless waifs to walk 4 miles to the motorway junction to try and hitch a lift back to Crewe. Sneakily (Andy had been awake and cleverly hid on the station while we go nicked, however not so cleverly he had written Andy Crewe Punks in the waiting room and when he got off the 3 o'clock train he was pulled up by the Crewe railway police), after an hour or so of failure to hitch a lift, surprisingly (punks hitch hike in middle of the night shock horror) we decided to come clean. We walked all the way back to the station and phoned our parents who had to buy tickets in Crewe. Crewe station then rang Preston and they let you on the train. I arrived in Crewe at 8 o'clock when I was due at work at the post office at 7! I had to surreptitiously make my way off the station as this was when most mail went by the trains and many colleagues worked on the station. I had an impeccable attendance there; this was one of my few days off in my 6 years of working there. I now also had a rail offence with the police. I also had irate parents to contend with.

On our walk to the ground, I remember passing the prison and a picturesque park opposite the ground. The street lighting seemed to be really poor on route; it really did resemble very dark night time!

I think we were situated in the Town End; it had a good cover like most of the ground with a fair bit of wood rather than concrete - although my memories are little hazy, young lovers eh!! It was the kind of ground I loved and I looked forward to a return journey perhaps without a partner! I met up with Strainy and Pete Johnson; they had met Kate before and got on well. Strainy did tease her about leftism and feminism but she enjoyed the banter and he was pleased because she didn't dress like a stereotypical student as she never wore trousers.

The game was good for a 0-0 and watched by a sizeable away following for a night game. The days when you recognised all our away following were gone. Still this is progress, you can't be an indie band forevever, and quality gets noticed and supported!

We took the bus back to the station this time, but I couldn't see our friend from Patrick this time. A journey of fumbling and fondling was on!

I returned in 2003 on my wedding anniversary to my second wife Jak on December the 28th. There were quite a few exiles back in Crewe who were up the trip, and as Jak and I were going out for a meal in the evening she didn't seem to mind. I drove up with Garf, Pete and Phil and we arranged to meet up with Alison and her boyfriend Craig. We met at a large pub on a Main Road not far from the motorway junction, and I had to take a bit of stick over my anniversary celebrations. It was good to see Alison and Craig who were good company and had visited Gresty Road several times where we usually met up for a drink. She still had her long curly orange locks and Craig still had a passing resemblance to the comedian Bob Mortimer.

In the ground, away fans were now situated in the Kop End which was segregated down the middle, with PNE fans in the other half. Three sides of the ground had been modernised, it was still an excellent ground and the architects had done an excellent job. The side to our left wasn't modernised yet but still looked impressive. We made lots of noise on the day despite a rather dour 0-0, which meant that nobody had bragging rites when we met after the game.

In 2006/7 I took Dylan to his first away game at the age of five. My brother-in- law Kev had offered to take us and his lad Rob to the game. We drove up and decided to make a day of it by visiting the football museum which is situated in the corner between the Kop and the Tom Finney Stand. We parked near the park by the ground before entering the museum. The first thing that we saw was Motto's famous Sheepskin jacket which meant more to our generation than our offspring. I spent a lot of time explaining to Dylan how far we had come by showing him the league tables in the 1970's and 80's where we were generally in the bottom four only being saved in re-election by our central position to many clubs. It was a decent museum, although at aged 5 he didn't really appreciate it. I have taken him since although it is now in the Urbis building in Manchester - something I have mixed feelings on at best. There are some spectacular photographs of fans and grounds which I would recommend for the ground anorak.

In the ground we remained in the FA Cup for a further 90 minutes before going out 2-1. I have mentioned the whole day to Dylan recently and he has very little recollection of the day, but it still counts as a new ground if he becomes as obsessed as his Dad in the future.

Alison and Craig have recently emigrated to Canada, but they remain in touch with both me and PNE. I keep them informed of how our games go and maybe one day sometime I'll cross the Atlantic to see them.

Queens Park Rangers

I returned to Loftus Road 17 years after my first visit. I guess I have changed a little, 19 on my first visit while I am now nearing 37. Certainly I can't fit in size 32 trousers anymore! The ground hadn't changed that much in the two decades, although it has been modernised with some pristine toilets and seats have been added to the terraces. It is a compact ground that is close to the pitch and has kept its character. The ground has plenty of blue and badges, something our present ground lacks (of course our ground should have more red) and generally it is a ground I like.

When we drew Q.P.R. in the League Cup in 1983, they were a good First Division side and the game generated a lot of interest. The midweek fixture attracted close on a thousand to West London, at a time when 100 would be a good following to most away matches. As a postman, I finished early afternoon and had a couple of beers in the Royal with 10 others who were making the trip by train. Further beer on the train meant 10 Crewe fans were happy to be in the capital.

On arrival at White City, we went to the Springbok pub near the ground. I remember complaining that there was no mild on sale. They must have thought I was a right backward Northerner. Mind you try getting a pint of Mild in the North in the year 2000!

We stood at the back of the School End and were dismayed to see us go behind in less than a minute. Incredibly Peter King equalised after 4 minutes and we went wild, unfortunately too much for the Metropolitan Police who were standing right behind us and me, Pogs, my old school friend and one other were taken to cells under the ground. Didn't they realise how bad we were in those days? Of course we were excited! They dealt with us separately and decided to throw us out the ground. I was told I would be arrested if I was seen in the away end again. I was excited and keen to see if we would take the game by storm so decided to pay again, this time going in the Paddock on the South Africa Road side of the ground. I wasn't too chuffed; even in 1983 London match prices were expensive. Pogs cheekily went back into the away end without being apprehended. Alternatively, I stood near the dug out and politely clapped 7 other goals for Q.P.R.! I think it was poor Smith's last game in goals for The "Alex".

In 2000 I went on the official coach that surprisingly left at the late time of 10 o'clock. Arriving relaxed and in plenty of time seemed unlikely. Low and behold the driver ignored the 'congestion on the M42 signs' and drove right into the traffic. The only bright spot in the jam was on Radio Leicester where an advert played De-lilah by Tom Jones and then went on to talk about an 'Icelandic Karaoke team.' I guess the advertisers have missed the irony of the comments that could refer to our friends in the Potteries. After a rushed service station stop we were in sight of the ground about 2.20pm. However, the driver took a wrong turn and we found ourselves going away from the BBC and the ground. Talk about the 'Magical Mystery Tour.' We arrived at 2.40pm, a little frustrated although it did give us the chance to see the individual 1930's style houses and flats that were quite unusual and interesting surrounding the ground.

After past experiences I was a little apprehensive about standing up and chanting. The stewards seemed friendly enough and I wasn't told to sit down during the exciting bits. Mind you the "Alex" fans were so quiet that I wasn't going to have to pay twice today. The "Alex" played spiritedly, especially Jack and Street, but we were a bit lacking in the middle and up front.

Thankfully, the drive home was smoother and me and Pete Johnson arrived back just after 8.30pm for a few beers down the Golden Mile of Nantwich Road. Some things don't change in 17 years. Mind you I was painting and planning my second wedding the next day, so some things had changed although the devotion for the "Alex" was still there.

Reading

I was 13 when I visited Elm Park in 1977 and not really aware of the punk scene that was going to influence my life so much. By all accounts the ground didn't change until they moved to the outskirts of the City.

I have never been a big fan of open ends and there were two here. I have got wet too many times and felt frustrated by the lack of atmosphere generally. Today, it didn't rain but the atmosphere was lacking in our end. It reminded me a little of Twerton Park, Bath.

I went to this ground without my Dad, he let me go on my own because it wasn't Stockport, Northampton or Tranmere and it would be apparently be safe (although recent press and friend reports about Reading fans suggest he was being naïve). Still, there was no trouble that day.

My biggest fear of the day came at the service station stop somewhere near Newbury. The coach was surprisingly full and we parked in the middle of 6 Bolton coaches on their way to Southampton. Now they seemed more pleased to see us than we were. They surrounded the coach and made gestures for us to join them. Only the elderly and the coach driver got off. This has been the only time I have ever feared violence at a service station. We certainly needed the toilet when they sped off.

My nomadic friend Phil lived in Reading for a year and said that it was enough, describing it as a traffic jam! However, he stayed long enough for his daughter Willow to be born there.

I will try to get to the Madejski sometime in the future, Royal Way roll on the republic!

Rochdale

This was always a ground that The "Alex" travelled to, even when half empty coaches were commonplace. Perhaps it was because in the 70's we were always competing for bottom spot. Maybe we thought they were not as fearsome as the Stockport's of this world and it was pretty local.

On my first trip in the late 1970's, I remember being stuck at red traffic lights on the coach and being confronted by a mob that rushed out of the pub and threw beer. The year after the coach was bricked so it was a bit of a mystery why we travelled in larger numbers than usual to Rochdale.

I always liked the ground, a little run down but with plenty of cover it was usually a good atmosphere.

However, they used to have this ridiculous system where the club made money through potential crowd trouble. You could pay to get in the side terrace and the Rochdale End, which often used to end in skirmishes and the bringing of fans back to where they were at the start. A good ploy in the 1970's when you get less than 2,000, Thatcher would have been proud!

My visit on the first day of the 83/4 season was a bit of a turning point for me with regards to hooliganism. It has always fascinated me. But this day made me re-examine my views.

I went to Rochdale with about 6 others, Brian from Alsager being one who I had got to know through away trips. Changing in Manchester was fun and we drank in Rochdale having a' belter' of a day. The pub by the station was friendly and I remember their town hall being a magnificent building.   As we left another pub we came to some traffic lights, aware of an older and bigger mob behind us. A charge predictably came from behind us and a couple of us got jumped, Brian got a really bad kickin', as did Wilkie. I thought I had got away before the rest of us were confronted by the same mob that had obviously taken a short cut. It was by some traffic lights not far from the ground. Some other Rochdale fans charged from behind and I ran forward into a punch by this big guy in front of me. Suddenly, as often happens when you are punched, your hearing goes all numb and you become disorientated which was superbly portrayed in the first 10 minutes of the film 'Saving Private Ryan'. Luckily, I stayed on my feet and managed to get away. I ended up hiding in somebody's garden in a quiet street. My eye was swelling, but I realised I had been lucky. I remember asking a girl if she could spot a gang up ahead. I was alone and frightened.   After 10 minutes I headed back to the ground, the mob were hanging around on a wall by their ground, this time they were just happy to laugh and point out at my swelling face.

Once in the ground we swapped stories and compared injuries. We sang with real emotion that we hated Rochdale.   Most of us decided to try and get the coach or a lift back rather than risk the train. After some of them approached me again, pushing and kicking me, warning me about trying to take Rochdale. I became separated again before luckily bumping into Garf Kent who thankfully had room in the car he was travelling in. A bit of a joker he took my mind off the situation with some light hearted chat, and we agreed to go together to the 'Up yer Tower' punk festival at the end of the month in Blackpool.

Now I had to think of the implications of a black eye. Thankfully my Mum and Dad were on holiday, they would have gone bonkers. My younger sister Heidi would keep quiet about the situation and I would play it down. The worst teasing came at work, and some of it was nasty. I was slowly getting a reputation for being a soccer lout and not the only one at the Post Office. Some sympathised over my arrest at a home match believing my not guilty plea, but this confirmed I must have asked for it, maybe I did? I didn't like it, football seemed to bring the worst out of me, music the best, maybe I needed to concentrate on this more, they were both big loves of mine.

At the Burnley game my shiner was still apparent and was attracting attention and doorways were opening if I wanted to go down the hooligan route. Something I had occasionally fantasised about, no longer seemed as attractive.

Mind you I still attended away games, but I think I had learned some lessons that were severely tested by the first round draw of the cup, yes you guessed it Rochdale away. This competition always attracts every nutter in the town and some were talking about revenge for the earlier game.

I went on a mini bus to the game with some P.O. lads, Danny ran the minibus and was sensible, although that cannot be said for everyone on board. We drank in Crewe and Heywood and although we were drunk and dying to go to the toilet, the banter was all good natured (although punching somebody on the cock when he's desperate to go the loo is a bit stretching it!)

When we arrived in Rochdale we heard that it had kicked off by the cemetery and when we walked along the side of the ground by the club "Alex" fans were running amok, chairs were being thrown it was something like the O.K Coral! I could have tried some revenge, we were ubiquitous but somehow it didn't appeal. I took a back seat, happy we had gained some respect but content just to sing and shout, that is what I love doing but I was now aware that in certain circumstances it could get you in trouble. I think I grew a little that day, although I still found somebody stealing the Rochdale goalkeeper's gloves funny!

It seemed like a life time ago when I returned in 2010. I went with my sister's lad Rob and his mate Robbie who both go to my school. On approaching the ground I looked out for memories but it was a bit hazy. On arrival we wandered around, and the lads treated themselves in the newsagents with some sweets and a drink. On our way back to the ground we popped in the Church Inn for a drink. It is a lovely pub with lots of different rooms and character and ideally suited for away fans being situated on the away side of the ground along the same street as the pub.

Spotland is still compact and covered although it has now been modernised throughout. It wasn't a great match from our point of view, but it was nice to return with my nephew who I was becoming increasingly close to. I think he is getting as obsessed as I used to be!

Rotherham United

This was a Boxing Day fixture in the 1989/9 season, our big promotion year. I was home for Christmas in my second year at University and tho trip to South Yorkshire was going to be a must, student life meant trips to the "Alex" were mainly confined to holidays, and Boxing Day games are always special.

I managed to get loan of the Talbot Horizon and efficiently managed to escape the family cluster for the day. I was able to recruit the Johnson brothers, Garf and PGCE Bolton student Pete Wraith for the trip.

Garf was the usual navigator in the front; we had been on this route several times before. Pete had done his degree in Sheffield and I had visited him for several excellent weekends. Garf and I had also travelled this way to see The Subhumans and Chumbuwamba at The Leadmill in the early eighties. Chumbawamba performed with just underpants and square box televisions on their heads! It was on the way back where I nearly drove the 'spaceship' (Maxi car) over a precipice near Buxton. Garf re-told the story as we approached Macclesfield, already well into his whisky, he was his boisterous self with nobody willing to share a tipple at such an early hour. Garf took pleasure in ridiculing walkers who were out in large numbers on this early morn. Naturally we had to stop for a piss somewhere; it was near the Cat and Fiddle in the middle of the bleak district!

We arrived in Rotherham in time to have a couple of excellent beers in a friendly boozer a bit away from the ground. As tradition would have it, the pub was heaving with happy people pleased to escape the claustrophobia of the home.

The walk to the visitor's end is a memorable one, with a walkway surrounded by high walls - I wouldn't fancy walking down there on a cold winter's night, but excellent for a good sing song after a couple of beers. Once in the ground you are in a homely covered end with 3 other covered areas that generate an excellent atmosphere. It immediately grew on me; with compact, individual sides and a Boxing Day treat with your mates I was going to enjoy this ground. Well, Mark Gardner helped with a superb individual bending free kick and it was greeted with vociferous chanting of 'Jingle Bells, Jingle Bells ...The "Alex" win away'. A 2-1 over our promotion rivals in front of 7,000 meant we left the ground on cloud nine.

The winding route back over the hills looked glorious as we travelled back westwards triumphantly. We knew Boxing Day was an excellent night out in Crewe as we longed for this happy day to continue. Boxing Day meant St Trinian's night at Gregory's in Nantwich and although none of us were going tonight the prospect of glancing at some stocking tops and suspenders would finish the day nicely.

I went to their temporary home in Sheffield in 2011/12. Kev drove to the game and I joined him with his lad Rob. We arrived and parked in an industrial area near to the ground. It was absolutely pouring down and I was glad I had come prepared with my Docs on. As we approached the ground, the athletics stadium reminded me of some of the French grounds with its open ends and canopy stands and boy the rain was going to test the canopy today. I bumped in to Steve Shone at the game, a mate from the past that now lives in Leeds; it was nice to catch up. We were all cramped into a corner section with the Rotherham fans alongside us, with the other three sides empty. We played awfully, the atmosphere wasn't great but there was something about being under the canopy that was different. Maybe I just liked watching the rain dripping in different directions, but I didn't think the ground was as bad as everybody else did. Perhaps the game was better because you couldn't see how badly we played?

I had the opportunity to go to the New York stadium in January 2011. The American styled named ground didn't arouse me too much, but as with any new ground I was keen to explore it and maybe be pleasantly surprised. It was going to be the last entry before looking for a writing publisher and I had decided this was going to be the cut off point, knowing that I couldn't visit any other new grounds this season with only a relegation battle to look forward to. I had intended on taking the lads but financial issues led to Jak saying don't take the lads as it will be too expensive. I genuinely enjoy taking the lads and do not find it burdensome, even if it often a little less relaxing. We had all enjoyed a recent trip to Molineux, but I guess the New York stadium will probably remain through all of our lives and the opportunity to visit Rotherham is likely to be fairly prevalent as we seem to have been at similar levels and leagues over recent years.

The cheapest route seemed to be the official coach, as the unofficial coaches tend to turn into a more expensive bleary eyed day and the train route is not very direct. In January your thoughts often turn to the year ahead on and off the field. On the pitch it was going to be a fight to stay up which tends to make every game even more important than usual. On the job front I had been doing more health care shifts at Leighton Hospital over the Christmas school holidays and had just returned back at school. The dilemma of choosing between two different careers, both with very different pay scales and pressures remains one that could rear its head this year. This is likely to be complicated with my daughter saving for her first car, expected budget cuts at school, the deteriorating health of my parents and concerns about the constant rise in the cost of living.

On the coach I ended up sitting next to Ian Jones, a guy I had known before from other coach trips. I knew he was a keen follower of new grounds like me. He informed me that he has recently visited the new Brighton ground by going on a Nottingham Forest coach, driving to Nottingham for 8 o'clock in the morning. Now that is a dedicated fan, he had also done similar trips to Newport, Swansea and Cardiff to notch off new grounds, although he was keen to tell me that he would return to the ground if the "Alex" returned there.

We went via Stockport and then the minor roads across the Pennines, passing as ever a multitude of weather, sun, mist and icy tops and some breathtaking views of lakes and unpopulated scenery. A text came from the hospital bank as we drifted towards civilisation on the other side of the Pennines and I was able to book an early shift on Monday morning on Ward 15.

When we got to the outskirts of Rotherham at 12.15, one of the women stewards said that we were going to stop at the Meadow Hall Shopping Centre in Sheffield as it was early. I was devastated as I was going to meet a mate for a drink. I coaxed the woman into changing her mind, bigging up Rotherham town centre which was stone's throw from the ground.

So as we arrived in Rotherham it became apparent that New York was an area of Rotherham and perhaps I had maligned them unnecessarily with the Americanised name. New York Pub, the New York Tyres etc did justify the name, although the club do exploit it with Sinatra songs and cheer leaders?.

The coach offered anyone a chance to get off in the town centre or to carry on to the ground. I got off and made my way towards the Bridge Pub opposite the Railway Station. In there I met Newton and son that seemed football friendly with a variety of scarves, football food and some decent beer. There were quite a few other Crewe fans in there like the Newton's who had made the trip on the train. Included in this there were about 25 young lads who were immediately chanting in an aggressive manner and were clearly looking for trouble. This is an increasing issue recently although for a non-local game, I was a little surprised at the turnout. Accordingly we thought we would try some where else just in case it turned ugly.

We headed into the town and as I had left my butties in the fridge, I looked for some cheap food while the Newton's got the drinks in at the Rhino Pub in town. I found a pastry shop that did two cheese and onion pasties cheaper than Greggs. I sat down on the bench in the January sunshine eating the pasty, listening to the religious preacher and looking at the impressive church in front of me. The surrounding town was pleasant with very few empty shops which is fairly impressive in the winter of 2014.

There were a few other Alex fans in the Rhino like Mick Gill and Adi Dobson - dedicated fans who love to make a day of it on the train. The cheap prices had meant a busy and lively pub with a good friendly atmosphere.

On reaching the ground I was very impressed. Not only was it very near the old ground which I liked, but it was in the middle of the town and I immediately placed it in one of my best new ground categories. The badge on the side and the colour on the side of the ground is something that Gresty Road sadly lacks. This is even more impressive after dark when it is all lit up.

We were situated behind the goals and I met up with some top ex students I knew like Dan Robinson and Scott Morris. The "Alex" started lively and took the lead and the atmosphere was surprisingly good in our section with the fans really behind them. This was swelled by a group of 50 young lads who seemed keen to cause trouble and the first half saw 3 flares being set off. It was only after the third flare had gone off that the liberal G4 stewards took any action, which I don't think would have happened at most grounds. Maybe Rotherham were as surprised as me as the number of lads today who seemed up for trouble. The use of flares shows that fans are now taking a more global view of the game, although I'm not convinced that it is the most positive thing that the British football fans could be taking on board. There is quite of lot of friction between some of the older fans at the moment, many who were/are not angels themselves and the younger lads. Did older people think the same of us when we were younger lads? Were they any worse than younger lads 20, 30 and 40 years ago? It's an interesting sociological debate for discussion.

The game was turned on its head by us missing a penalty and Rotherham breaking away and scoring a third, and eventually beating us 4-2. The game had been entertaining with two penalties that probably were not, but it was an entertaining game and superior finishing was the deciding factor on the day. This was not helped by Hitchcock moving on loan from Crewe to Rotherham this week and he being involved in the controversial penalty decision, such as football life is.

Steve Davies was still being backed at the end, despite the relegation threat which was positive and rare in 2014. As we left on the coach, we left the impressive ground behind us. Our view had been good and the stands were quite steep, the ground had no drafty corners so we got on to the coach not as cold as you sometimes are in the winter.

On the way back I arranged to arrange to pick up some chips on the way home for Jak and the kids. It had been a good day out. Ian's interesting conversation on the coach kept my mind off the stresses of work, football is an excellent escapism. Ian surprised me with his fascinating tales of following the England cricket team to India, Pakistan, Bangladesh, Australia, Barbados, South Africa and New Zealand. It must have cost him a fortune but he had clearly loved visiting the different continents and made some great friends on the way. Now that would be an adventure that could be a ground for divorce.

Runcorn

My mate was keen to come to this second round FA Cup encounter, especially after enjoying the two first round Crewe games. Mick had this idea of trying to go to every round but he didn't make this ambition. After seeing this one he saw Sutton beat Coventry (on the day the "Alex" nearly beat Villa, David Platt scoring for us before throwing away a 2-0 lead at half time to lose 3-2) in the 3rd round and seeing Everton beat Plymouth 4-0 in the 4th round before bowing out of the idea.

This was a morning kick off in 1988. I lived in Garston at the time and Mick was going out with Rita who lived in our shared house (I lived with 5 women actually!) I thought they would be well suited both being good Catholics, but it isn't always as simple as that. I think this was near the end of their relationship at the time because the night I met Kate in the Rainbow Pub Liverpool in February, Mick also copped off with Julie a mate of Kate's.

We lived a minute from Garston Station and got the train to Hunts Cross before going to Runcorn. It was a fairly comfortable victory with the goals being met by some friendly pitch invasions. The ground was far more 'non league' than Stafford in the previous round making pitch invasions very easy. The two ends were both very small open ends - I think everybody thought Runcorn could have been a potential flashpoint for trouble on the day but I saw no hostility from them. There were plenty of belligerent Crewe fans who marched through the town centre after the game towards the railway station; Rita was quite shocked and excited at the same time. Many had made the journey on the train and there was a huge police presence at the station.

Rita, Mick and I were still waiting for the Liverpool train when the Crewe train pulled in. The police had been checking tickets harshly that day, and some "Alex" fans were not let on the platform. As the train pulled away, a handful of fans ran from the far end of the platform as mates held the non electric doors for them, jumping on the train before the train picked up too much speed. It was lucky that they all made it on the train safely. It was the Crewe fans who were the handful today. It was strange not going back to Crewe with the rest of the fans, but we had all settled and loved Merseyside and the Runcorn Bridge was synonymous with going back to the 'Pool.'
Both Mick and I were soon to be in new relationships but for the moment it was the FA Cup and the 3rd round draw that was of immediate importance.

Scarborough

In the 1977/78 season we had surprisingly won at Bradford and gained a home draw with ambitious non-league Scarborough. Such a draw attracted large numbers from the coast including many who wanted mither and there were many who were prepared to give it to them. Ian P boasted at school on Monday morning how he practiced his Kung-Fu kicks on various opposing fans as we listened in awe. He was the cock of the year and we had seen him in action. He had a moustache in year 7 and went around with older kids and we had no reason to doubt it. The 0-0 draw was made more entertaining by running battles in the Gresty End where the dust was flying around like a cowboy film.

My Dad and I decided to make the trek to Scarborough on December 21st. Being a Dad now, I can't believe he was prepared to go to the seaside just before Christmas. In those days he was not the football obsessive he is now. Perhaps the school holidays were longer then? Maybe he wanted to just escape the Christmas stress? Either way it was a wrong choice.

We were surprised to find the one coach full, Brian Johnson a classmate who used to be in my class and his Grandad were on board - "Alex" stalwarts even today. We should have stayed in making a Christmas list.

We stood on an open terrace and there was a biting wind. Everybody was spread out and there was nothing to cheer us up. We were losing and 'Boro fans were intimidating some "Alex" fans without guardians by us. Surrounded, they were being spat out, cigarette stubs were being thrown; sporadic kicks were aimed in "Alex" fans backs. We felt helpless, humiliated, frozen and embarrassed on and off the pitch. The lights of warm houses surrounded the end, rooms we would have longed to have been in. This is probably my worse "Alex" experience. The coach journey back seemed an eternity, but at least we were warm. Young Alex fans take note, "misery" - you don't know the meaning! The romantic road to Wembley was complete.

I returned to Scarborough in August 1992 with my wife and Gareth and Gill. Taking advantage of the school summer holidays and Gareth's unemployment we set off to Scarborough in my Talbot Horizon on the Friday Morning. As we got past York, we noticed how many pigs there seemed to be. I have travelled all over the country and this is the only area that you see visible pigs in fields. Garf and I joked about greeting the Scarborough team with pig grunts.

When we got there we split up briefly. I dropped Gareth and Gill at a campsite on the outskirts. They didn't have much money and Kate and I were not the camping types being far too vain for that. Glastonbury has been my only time for camping and that's the way it has generally remained apart from the odd night with the kids.

Kate and I found a cosy bed and breakfast opposite the railway station .I picked the others up later and we explored Scarborough. This time I fell in love with the place. There were many old-fashioned seaside cafes that were reminiscent of the 1960's, some beautiful Victorian tearooms with some striking black and white tiles where you could imagine the wealthy dancing and some great pubs that sold my favourite beer Old Peculiar. A great night was had with the beer flowing, games of pool and money spent on punk classics on the jukebox.

The next day we explored again, this time the castle that gives you the most amazing views being perched so near the coastline. The weather was even good, putting us in the mood for more beers as we made our way in land to the ground that is in the middle of an estate. I think the girls went to the game as well; it had been a good session!

The ground seemed different to before; in daylight you didn't have the lights from the hills surrounding the ground. Both ends were still open; I think we were in the opposite end this time although I couldn't swear on it. We lost but we didn't let it spoil our weekend. Garf went back to the campsite and after a kip we went to an alternative/rock night in a big club. We danced and drunk and even got talking to one of the locals who seemed to be far more interested in me than Kate. Kate is one of the biggest flirts going, so this was a surprise for both of us. Maybe the "Alex" could have scored in Scarborough that day!

Garf liked the story and kept us amused on the nightclub incident on the way home. It had had been one of my best "Alex" away trips making my two trips to Scarborough poles apart. This is one of my favourite resorts; I'd have never thought this was possible on that bleak December evening many years ago.

I returned here on a family holiday and the place still holds a place in my heart. We explored nearby Bridlington and Whitby, as well as tracking down the ground. The ground was still there but all boarded up. I got talking to a local who said they have reformed with one team playing in Bridlington and one playing at the McCain Chip Factory sports ground. I feel gutted for their fans and I hope they can get back to Seamer Road or somewhere nearer in the future.

Scunthorpe United

I never made it to the Old Show Ground and unfortunately missed the trip to Glanford Park in the playoffs in 1991/2. In my first disastrous year teaching in Birmingham, the game coincided with a teaching parents evening. I only had 4 parents coming but I couldn't really miss it. I didn't really bond with the staff, the kids were giving me the run around and the Head didn't like me.

I was trying to move schools and was in need of a good reference so the "Alex" would have to do without me. I remember the disappointment as I heard the score on the radio, hoping I had misheard. I had been there for the first leg, leaving the ground knowing we had probably thrown it away, but still feeling guilty for not being there.

My other main memory of Scunthorpe was getting them in the 2nd round of the FA Cup in 1981, it was a rare year to have progressed so well and the 3rd beckoned with a home tie. A lucrative tie was a possibility and Leeds played Scunthorpe in the 3rd round. To make matters worse my mate from the Post Office was on a real bender, sharing a bottle of whisky that had been acquired. He paid his money, walked through the turnstile and fell over laughing obviously worse for wear. When the police went over they took the opportunity to get an easy arrest and he ended up charged with drunk and incapable. It was a sorry afternoon for us both.

I did make it to Glanford Park in the 2008/9 season. This was a ground that had eluded me and this was the year I was definitely going. (Un)fortunately the "Alex" had had a bit of a run in the League Cup and had drawn Liverpool away on the Tuesday after the trip to Scunthorpe. The midweek was a busy one with school and my own kids and I was under pressure from Jak to choose one of the fixtures. I had been to Anfield on numerous occasions and although lots more people I knew were going and very few to Scunthorpe I chose Glanford Park. Choose life, choose Scunthorpe! I didn't want to regret not going to Scunthorpe again, I didn't want it to turn into another Exeter (I still haven't been). Well I did go to Scunthorpe in the end, although I didn't really see Scunthorpe. We didn't travel through the town and went to the retail park which is in the countryside somewhere near Scunthorpe. The ground is reminiscent of Chester and Walsall, but neat enough in a characterless way. We were behind the goal and the hardcore made a lot of noise that day despite a poor defeat. The only positive was a new young signing in the name of Brayford who had a promising debut. I convinced myself on the long journey home that I had made the right decision and I was a loyal fan and not a glory fan. I believe it was a pretty good effort and atmosphere at Anfield!

Sheffield United

The name Sheffield United will always remind me of my brush with the law. Was I guilty? Did it do me good? Are the police corrupt? Did it stop me getting in to further trouble? Did I get a kick at being the only "Alex" fan arrested on a day when 5,000 Blades invaded Crewe in 1982? Was I a naive 17 year old? (See Crewe chapter for details)

15 years later I returned as a 33 year old teacher just going through a divorce. Seeing less of my daughter meant the possibility of new grounds easier, some compensation for an upsetting mess.

We managed to get a drink in the friendly and busy Cricketer's Pub outside the away end. It was a cold, fairly dull game played in a quieter atmosphere than the one in the excellent film 'When Saturday Comes.'

I met an old friend at half time who now resides in Sheffield; Mick was the singer and songwriter of the under-rated and tuneful punk band Two Fingered Approach. Mick had a melodic voice and was responsible for excellent songs like 'My first world album'. He certainly had a better voice than my mate Strainy who was thrown out for turning up to practices drunk or not at all. I was certainly shocked to see him at the game; he was always a music fan more than football. Maybe football was more fashionable than the early 80's? Perhaps moving out of Crewe makes some identify more with the town?

I returned to Bramhall Lane for the August Bank Holiday Monday Sky clash in the 1999/00 season. Wanting to please my fiancée Jackie and see the game was a problem that I had to solve. I managed to coax Jackie to leave a sunny Crewe for a day in Buxton, followed by a trip over the Peak District to Sheffield in the evening.

The lovely weather in Crewe disappeared as we approached Macclesfield and when we arrived in Buxton it was cloudy at best. I tried to appease Jak with an up-market tea and scone near the pavilion before walking around this lovely Victorian town. At least it wasn't too hot to walk around. After a really pleasant day we headed off to Sheffield, parking on some grass near a nearby pub. We treated ourselves to some chips before having a pint in the Cricketer's again. It was packed and Jackie felt a bit claustrophobic, so we didn't stay long and walked around the ground - that was impressive and had a big club feel to it. Sky games are notorious for having conversations with fans before the games and the introvert Jackie made long diversions to avoid the cameras. I would have loved such an opportunity, but knew I would be pushing her too much on her best ever Bank Holiday!

I met my mate Pete Johnson at the game who was equally surprised to see Jak there. I think she would have preferred to have watched the game in the pub, if at all. Bramhall Lane is a great ground which with lots of variety, the two tiered end where we were was impressive, as is the huge Kop that faced us. We did witness a special Rodney Jack goal and a rare "Alex" sending off. Jackie wasn't completely put off by defeat and does voluntarily attend the odd game.

Sheffield Wednesday

My first trips to Sheffield Wednesday coincided with my friend going to Sheffield Polytechnic. Pete Wraith was studying Business Studies while I was a 17 year old postman. He stayed in Halls of Residence around Broomhall, and both weekend visits saw Wednesday play at home.

We set off on Friday evening, on both occasions taking the slow, winding, dark journey past the Cat and Fiddle, which was arguably the quickest route in those days. I had only recently passed my test and my friend Strainy winced as I drove atrociously through the Peak Disrict, fearing for his life. This fear became worse as we entered Sheffield; my Maxi's exhaust dragging along the floor. Luckily we were near enough to Pete's place for it not to be too serious. The friendly caretaker in the Halls of Residence gave us some rope and directions to a Kwik Fit fitter the next morning.

That night was spent at a local pub with some joints when we returned - my first experience of drugs, which by today's standards would probably be seen as extremely late. I think I was too drunk to analyse any of its effects. It could have been anything for all I knew; such was my naivety and the drug education in the late 70's.

On arriving near Hillsborough and trying to park I couldn't believe how steep the streets were, which didn't help when trying to squeeze into a parking place. The streets were nearly vertical. Wednesday was in the old 2nd division (1982/3) at the time and that year we saw them draw with Carlisle and beat Brighton. Both times we stood on the big, open, Kop in freezing conditions. The view from the top of the end was amazing with countryside and industries so near each other. On both occasions the away fans were vociferous, but we adopted Wednesday for the day.

On one of the Saturday nights, we were drinking in the Limit club in the West Street area and on the other we went to the John Peel Road Show at the Octagon Centre at the University. I was and still am a fan of Peel and was delighted when he played Teenage Kicks for some lads from Crewe. (I still love the Undertones). On another visit we saw Peter and the Test Tube Babies at the Bier Keller. Not long before I left my school in Bilston I took my school chess club to a national competition at the Sheffield Octagon Centre where it was a little more sedate! At lunch time I gave the lads a break from chess and took them to see some great football ground photographs in a football ground exhibition at a nearby museum.

I returned to Hillsborough in the 1995/6 season for the 2nd leg league cup-tie. I left my school in Bilston in the West Midlands early and arrived in Sheffield earlier than I thought. I got some grub and parked on the flatter side of the ground this time. I walked some way to meet Phil Connor in a pub that had been recommended by his sister who lived in Sheffield. He was late as usual and it ended up being bit of a rush to get to the ground, not for the first time. It's funny how you tolerate your friends bad habits time after time.

Going towards the entrance to the Leppings Lane End, I couldn't help feeling sad as images of the pictures we have seen many times on TV came flooding back. Similarly I found myself looking all around both tiers of the end during parts of the entertaining 5-2 defeat. I was a student in Liverpool at the time of the disaster and spoke to some about their experiences. Their tales had more impact then any media reporting, a description of a young boy who had shit his pants before dying will remain rooted in my mind forever.

The "Alex" took a good following, but were quiet that day, largely because we were spread over both tiers, friends were separated and the noise was through little pockets. The "Alex" had scored 4 goals against Premiership opposition over 2 legs and showed they were capable of playing with more superior opposition. The trip back to Kidderminster completed the long day. As a rule such a trip tends to tire me on the second day, you tend to be still on a high the next day. However, with my daughter Becky now being aged 2, the day after at school was a nightmare, especially with Year 10 who gave me some stick about the flattering result.

It was as equal partners that we met at the end of the year 2000/01 season. Austin Jones, a friend from the Post Office, took me in his car for this meaningless and celebratory game. Few would have expected us to be going into this game safe, but thanks to goals from Ashton and Hulse and some good defending in the latter half of the season we were. Hulse was superb on the day and the "Alex" fans in the upper tier of the Leppings Lane never shut up - it was fantastic!

We sneaked a quick drink in a home only pub at the bottom of Halifax Road after we parked at the side of a garage at the bottom of Leppings Lane. Mind you, we only managed the one we were waiting 25 minutes to get served! Steve Shone, who I met at half time in the loos, seemed to have been more successful judging by his demeanour and time at the urinals. We took the M1 and A500 going back on this visit where we enthusiastically talked about the coming season. Imminent fatherhood again will mean following many games on the radio.

Thinking about my visits to Hillsborough I haven't had to bite my nails too much being a neutral twice. A cup upset would have been a pleasant surprise but wasn't expected and 2001 was a Mardi Gras. I even remember watching an 8-1 defeat by Wednesday in a friendly at Gresty Road, sitting on the terraces in lovely sunshine thinking we'd win if it mattered. I wonder if I will always be so lucky at Hillsborough.

Shrewsbury Town

My memories of Shrewsbury are clearer from recent day trips on the train than my visits to Gay Meadow. I drove on my first trip there for a night game in 1986 for a dull 0-0; the country drink on the way home was more memorable, with a beautiful bar maid. I remember some of those exciting Shrewsbury cup games against top opposition in the 70's that I watched on the television and this was completely different with regards to excitement and atmosphere. The ground was still similar, the away end with its quaint cow shed cover although the Riverside Terrace at the side seemed deserted and lacked the atmosphere of the past.

I returned to Shropshire in the 1995/6 season travelling from Kidderminster, a similar car time journey to the one from Crewe. I drove past the school by the ground going into the car park thinking how wonderful it must be to teach there if you are a mad Shrewsbury fan. On a similar subject the geography teachers in Crewe must do better after a number of "Alex" fans started singing, "Eng-er-land" in an aggressive manner. Many others and I found the incident quite embarrassing, although I guess the idea was to make it seem if Shrewsbury are Welsh. The Shrews have a mob that follows England, so I bet that pleased them. Well I suppose Shrewsbury is not far away but so is Crewe!

I have recently spent summer Saturdays on train trips to Shrewsbury which is so quick, easy and picturesque I don't know why I had driven before. It is a lovely town, has an interesting Museum and Abbey and some great pubs, parks and shops. I actually took Jackie for a walk right around the ground, walking through some wild weeds around the river and found some really old "Alex" graffiti on the wall by the Riverside Terrace. They don't make spray paint like that anymore! The gates were open and we took a quick look around the stadium. I'm not sure if it was on her agenda for the day, but for somebody who is obsessed with grounds, you take any opportunity to, even though it might be a ground for divorce.

I returned to the new Meadow in 2009/10. I went on the train with my nephew Rob and his mate Robbie. The new Meadow wasn't as convenient as the old one, but as it was a very warm September day we decided to walk it, not sure how long it was going to take. We walked up the hill before turning left and walking down the hill, not far away from the old ground. Unfortunately, there was a long way to go and after crossing the impressive bridge over the River Severn, the walk becomes less interesting. After a garage on the left, most of the walk involves walking along grass verges along ring roads. I wish I had brought my bike it would have been a lot quicker. We certainly got warm in the heat and I was pleased I had put a hat on, better to be careful at my age and with my lack of hair. The lads were struggling more than me; I think they are used to being ferried everywhere. At the end of the journey we followed some others and we seemed to be taking a short cut over a golf course. This could only happen at a new ground!

In the ground we were behind the goal with the Shrewsbury singers to our right. There were banners all over the end ahead of us and to the side which gave the new ground a little more colour. The young lads seemed to spend a bit on food and drink, as you do when you're young; perhaps they were worried about their energy for the return walk. The lads did make it back to the station after the game with a couple of stops to prevent dehydration as it was still pretty warm. The walk is an hour to the railway station, something I may consider again, depending on who I was with.

The next season we played them on January 3rd and I took Dylan and Reuben on the train. Garf came with us and when we got there we decided to have a drink in a boozer near the bus station. We all got a drink in the quiet friendly pub and waited for the Red Bus Double Decker that took fans to the ground. The bus was a mixture of home and away fans, but wasn't that crowded. We got to the ground about 2.30 and Garf ordered a red wine, it is was about a third of a bottle in a small bottle and he insisted that this was the best value for alcohol content at the bar in the ground and I have no doubt he was right. I think he may have had a couple of others at half time to see in the New Year. The second half saw temperatures really dip and my youngest Reuben was struggling and Garf put him on his lap and bounced him up and down to keep warm. It was brilliant of him, Reuben can be a handful some times and this consoled him. We also had a 1-0 victory and a jump around to get the blood flowing again.

On the way back we got the bus again, which was a bit more crowded. Not long after setting off the bus broke down on the Ring Road, now this was probably the highlight of the day for the kids. We all trudged off the bus, most waited on the grass verge while a few decided to walk. The bus was causing traffic chaos but surprisingly a replacement bus arrived in ten minutes. As a result we were able to make the train back as planned and Garf even managed a sneaky pint before getting on the train.

In August we were back here again and I brought the lads again and this time Pete Johnson joined us. We got the same double decker bus and this time it was less dramatic with a smooth journey to and from the ground. The "Alex" was on a dreadful run and the fans were very quiet and turned restless when losing to Shrewsbury, with Dario taking much of the brunt for the bad results. The game was out of reach when young Nicky Powell was sent off and the "Alex" was heading for the foot of the table. It was the season when Dario left in a manner not fitting for what he had done for the club, but it was the right decision as Steve Davis took over and led the club to promotion at Wembley. On that day this seemed impossible.

Southampton

This visit to The Dell was memorable for an obscure postponement and moving house. Kate and I were going through a bad patch and were living with extended family. We thought this set up could be the source of our problems, so we decided to move out and buy our own house. A few months later I found out that the extended family was not the problem but our own. Perhaps living in an extended family lengthened our marriage; the added freedom and time to ourselves seemed to exasperate the situation.

Anyway, things weren't helped by the exciting 4th round 1995/6 FA Cup draw at a new ground. Living in Kidderminster meant it was fairly accessible, but it clashed with moving house. We were moving into a new house because they were paying our deposit. We were about to move on the Friday before the game and I was desperate to go to the game. Could I leave my wife and 2-year-old daughter to unpack? We were moving house to get a fresh start, of course I couldn't. I knew I wouldn't be very relaxed on that Saturday afternoon, and then I was given a lifeline. The builders of the new house came up with problems beyond their responsibilities, for once I was absolutely delighted with their excuses and I was on the way to the Dell. We were due to move the following Friday.

I diligently helped pack some things from early morning, gave Kate a lie in, clothed, fed and played with Becky before leaving for the Dell. It had been an icy morning and I listened carefully to the radio for postponements as I drove down the M5. The game was on as I came off the motorway and headed through some idyllic villages in Wiltshire. I was thinking how lucky everything had gone when I entered Marlborough when Five Live announced the game was postponed. Apparently the pipes in the toilets were frozen and unusable. The pitch was playable but the game was off. I carried on to Southampton for a couple of miles thinking I must have misheard, not wanting to believe what I clearly had heard. Eventually, I rationalised my thoughts and turned around to drive home.

I gathered my thoughts and considered turning around and going to the ground just to say I had been. Going to Southampton would be too much on a mid week day with a busy time at school and moving house. Then while on the M5 I had a brain wave, my father and brother-in-law were helping us move and there were numerous things that could be done the next week. So I decided to take 2 half days off for moving house, the first on the day of moving and the one on the afternoon of the re-arranged game at Southampton. I helped unpack, played with Becky and sorted out the new TV license before taking the same journey.

I arrived in good time and parked up in a fairly affluent area that is quite unusual for a football ground. I found a pub not far from the away end that was full of Crewe fans. I wondered how many sick days had been taken in Crewe that day. I bumped into Andrew Steele an old mate from old "Alex" and punk days and the atmosphere was fantastic, better than your average pub on New Year's Eve at 12 o'clock. This continued in the ground where I was seated in the lower tier of the East Stand. The Dell is a compact ground that appealed to me. The Archer Road End reminded me of the present Gresty End, while the slanted other end reminded me of the Cow Shed end at Tranmere. It's the kind of sized capacity that would suit The "Alex" if we reach the zenith of our dreams, although it may sadly not be enough for the premiership of the future. The equalising Saints goal brought the East Stand to our left alive, but it was us who faced a long and happy journey home after a commendable performance. It was a shame that the time in the new house was not as joyous, I had moved out during Euro 96, returning to live in Crewe.

I returned to Southampton in 2005/6 for the August fixture. By now Saints had moved to St Mary's and it was a great opportunity to visit the new ground. It was at the end of August when teachers start to think about school when you wake up in the night so this was going to be a nice distraction. I went on the coach with Pete and we arrived in the City fairly early. I again thought that it seemed quite an affluent City, despite knowing that like everywhere there are riches and poverty wherever you travel.

Tony G joined us for a drink near the ground, we were in a room up the stairs and we enjoyed a couple of bevvies before going back to have a look at the ground in the sunshine. I liked the ground - it was in the City and had some character. It was equally impressive inside; we were in a ground that had good cover and acoustics. We were in the end with singing Saints to our right and a few giving us some stick to our left. We were not good enough on the day, but I enjoyed the atmosphere and a 'me' day before going 'back to school on Monday'.

Southend United

This game came less than a month after my first marriage to Kate. It was like a second honeymoon, the first being a weekend in a caravan in Anglesey. We were still students before I hear you cry 'paupers'.

We drove down from Kidderminster in September sunshine arriving just before kick off. Kate made her way into town and I went to the ground. Housing behind it boxed in the open end. The entrance was near the corner flag and I met Pete Wraith who had travelled up from Surrey, Garf Kent who had travelled from Nottingham, and Pete Johnson from Crewe. There were 2 stands at the sides and a covered terrace end that I liked. The racist chants at this game by "Alex" fans stood out as a real low point for me. We responded with a chant of 'There ain't no brains in a racist twat' to there chant of 'There ain't no black in the union jack' that may have been effective because it wasn't repeated in song at this or any other game to my knowledge. Hopefully, it made a few think, I won't dwell on it any further, I'll just finish by saying it angered me enough to write to the Chronicle, I enclose the article below.

An entertaining 3-2 defeat did not spoil our mood; Pete and I drove with our partners to find a bed and breakfast. We found one which had a lovely corner bath, and after a freshen-up and some food we went to explore 'Soufffend.'for those who have not been there it is similar to Blackpool, but not as commercial and its clientele is Londoners rather than Northerners, Brummies and Scots.

We met up with Garf and one or two other "Alex" fans that were checking out the pubs on the front. Garf seemed particularly worse for wear and amazed us all by finishing off a jar of prawns and then gulping down all the excess vinegar in one go. Mind you, you know what bitter in the South tastes like! I think Pete's girlfriend was horrified and thought it was a little uncouth.

It was great weekend and it's strange how football takes you to the places most Northerners would never go to. Mind you it's a long way to travel to spread racist shit.

Southport

I was in my first year at school in Ruskin Road in 1975 when the trip to Southport seemed to capture the youth. The Friday evening game seemed to be a trip where the "Alex" was going to have a bit more of a following than usual.

I persuaded my Dad to take Tony Ralphs, Rob Kelsall and Brian Johnson to take us in the car.

We didn't see the sea (well you don't even from the beach as I found out on numerous train, day trips from my student days in Liverpool) and took our position in the covered end with the other 150 "Alex" fans. There was no segregation in those days, but this was clearly the end favoured by the home fans. There was a modern, large stand to our left, a small open end and a covered terrace to our right. Trouble was in the air that night as we stood fascinated as "Alex" fans ran around to the side terrace to chase Southport youths who fled towards the open terrace. However, as the game continued there seemed to be less Southport fans running off and re-grouping. By half –time, it was the Southport fans that were now encroaching to take their end back, this being the focal point of violence in the 1970's. Taking an end was a measurement of hardness. Eventually it was the "Alex" fans that were fleeing, apart from a several brave ones who put up a heroic fight. It was even more exciting than the charismatic tales told by Mr Bradshaw in history.

My Dad said he wasn't moving, so we stood near the front of the wall for the rest of the match. We stood in relative ease apart from a few mouthy 13 year olds who occasionally taunted us.

On Monday morning it was the running battles that our schoolmates were keen to hear about, the 2-2 draw coming a second best in our exaggerated reporting of the trouble.

Stafford Rangers

Sixteen years after watching Rangers in my first Alex game (See Crewe chapter) I travelled to Marston Road 1988 for another FA Cup first round game. I went there with my newish mate Mick from Coventry. It wasn't until the end of the first year that I seemed to really click with male mates at Uni, and Mick was one of these who was a footy fanatic. I would go to some Cov games, especially against the Merseyside clubs and he would come to the odd "Alex" game with me.

We got the train to Crewe and he met my folks before Kev drove us to Marston Road. My Dad also came and we all got on like a house on fire. After a brief drink, we went to the ground. I think we were on terracing at the side and opposite us there was a small stand.

Mick was used to the big time following Coventry! However, it was the immediacy and intimacies of the non-league experience that Mick warmed to. He was intrigued by the small floodlights and the fact that you could move around parts of the ground, even on a big day like this! We also had another friend Phil who was a Macclesfield fan, this trip to Marston Road led to Mick flirting again with the non league scene. Unfortunately these type of romantic grounds have become a new reality for Coventry in recent years.

Rangers came back from being 2-0 down to claw back a replay. Surprisingly, Mick was keen to attend the replay, I rarely attended home games while at Uni, but I admired Mick's enthusiasm so we got the train down for the night. We took another Phil, a Newcastle fan who decided to join us to see the "Alex" squeeze into the second round. I was unaware at the time that he used to occasionally sleep with my soon to be partner Kate. This was one of the first of several relationship issues that lay ahead of me.

Stevenage

Being in the lower divisions has its advantages when attempting to do the new grounds; you are more likely to be able to do them than if you are a Chelsea fan. Relegation to the fifth division nowadays also means that you are likely have done many grounds in that league and beyond.

Pete Johnson and I went to this one on the official coach in September 2010. I had started to take the lads to the odd local away game, but the longer journeys were a no go at this age. These journeys pretty much take up the whole day and as you get older and more family orientated they can cause tensions at home and guilt at the freedom of your day - although we all need these days to keep us fresh from time to time. Accordingly, I read the Guardian in peace with a vague awareness that there are chart hits in the background, many that I don't recognise, apart from the odd one like' You've Got The Love' by Florence and the Machine.

When we arrived at Stevenage, the coach parked on the other side of a busy road and we took the underpass to where the Broadhall Way Ground was. There didn't appear to be an obvious pub nearby so we ended up having a drink in their club. It was friendly and we got chatting to some local fans.

We were situated behind the goal, in a covered end with seats and a decent view. There was a smaller covered terrace end opposite us. A few hundred had made the trip a few old faces were mixed in with new faces. I met up with Kev's mate Roy who teaches in East London, and Jonathan - a lad who I used to teach and now lives in London after living in Manchester. I was again impressed by the noise coming out of the covered terrace to our right. Thoughts were drawn towards thinking how the fans who are so pleased to be in the football league are still really enjoying their time in the higher league and creating some great vocal support.

The game was memorable in that the "Alex" played in a Stevenage kit. The Stevenage kit clashed with our home and away kit and the home team had to help us out to avoid a similarity of colour.

Stockport County

Whenever I see this name, I automatically think of football violence. In particularly for the 40 plus somethings, these were real local rivals who would always cause trouble at Gresty Road. I believe from older fans like Pete Johnson that this has been the case since the 1960's. This is probably exaggerated due to the close proximity of Crewe, especially by train, but for those who have read Kevin Sampson's 'Away days' on Tranmere thugs in the 80's, County have always excelled in hooliganism in areas much further afield.

It was due to this reputation and reality that I never went to Edgeley Park until the 1987/8 season. My Dad went to one game where they ran amok all over the ground and forbade such a trip. The "Alex" has given as much back on some occasions, but they have always been larger in number and more organised. Some of their boys were rumoured to work at the P.O and follow England. They always infiltrated our end in the bad old days and even did so in 2001, which shows what they are capable of off the field in the more civilised era. I remember being punched in the face in the corner of the Pop side when Stockport fans attacked a small group of us. On a trip to Edgeley Park, Garf Kent was hit, had his money stolen and train ticket ripped up.

I drove to Stockport tentatively for a very low-key game in 1987/8 standing in the open end that remains the same today. It was quiet and uneventful. Ironically after all I have said, the following promotion year the "Alex" went on mass on the train and gave them some of their own medicine at their place. It was also the first night of our song Blue Moon being sung; as the moon shone brightly on a cold winter's night it was successfully and amusingly sung and adopted as our own. City fans present at the game may have copied it.

I returned in the late 1990's to see a defeat and view the new impressive stand that dwarfs the rest of the subbuteo ground as it does at Gresty Road. Maybe it is these similarities that add to the rivalry, we were both strugglers for much of the 1970's, and for a while we both punched above our stations in terms of social class. Whatever the reason, it is the local game that has always had an edge for me.

I returned to Edgeley Park in the 2008/9 season. Initially the game was going to be on a Saturday but was moved to a Friday night. On the Friday night I had already bought a ticket to see The Levellers at Victoria Hall Hanley, Stoke. The venue is a real cracker but sadly underused, and I had looked forward to this as The Levellers always put a good show on. However, time was running out for the "Alex" to avoid the drop and the last but one game at County was the last chance to stay up. We had to win both games to stand any chance, and the last game was against the champions Leicester City. The fourth tier loomed, but I felt I had to be there, a massive game against our rivals. It was a footy/music dilemma, this time the "Alex" took priority I had to be there, I felt the lads needed me more than ever and if we were to win or lose it would it would be awful to have missed it. I wouldn't have been able to relax at the gig and luckily I found someone who took the ticket off my hands.

So on the warm Friday night I went on the train with Rob, my nephew, his mate Robbie and his Dad. We walked from Stockport Station - walking through the pedestrianised area of Edgeley where there was a large police presence. In the away end, the end kept getting fuller, and in the end it was probably over capacity - the flat bit at the back was heaving and many stood in the aisles. The game had caught the imagination of the "Alex" fans only for hearts to be broken. The "Alex" were being beaten 4-1, and although we brought it back to 4-3, awful defending had cost us and we were down.

On the way back to the station there were little skirmishes all around and on the station "Alex" and County fans taunted each other about relegation and financial difficulties. County went into administration later that week and if they hadn't have won, they would have been relegated with having ten points deducted. We mistakably thought that they had nothing to play for and it explains why both teams played like it was a cup tie.

I returned in 2011 on the train with Bruce from Nantwich Library which made a nice change. Stockport is a brilliant ground to go to on the train with so many trains that are quick from Crewe. It was another exciting game that ended in a 3-3 draw. I met up with Steve Brereton on the day, which was nice, although it was his negativity about Dario and the "Alex" that dominated conversation rather than our nostalgic, music and education chats that are usually more entertaining.

It has been the "Alex" who has continued to have some success and financial security, while Stockport have fallen and fallen. There was a time I might have taken pleasure in that, but now I feel so sorry for their loyal fans. When looking on the red button they are one of the first teams I look to see how they are doing in the Conference North. Maybe it's because I fear that we might suffer a similar fate sometime in the future or you don't like your rivals but you demand the right to be playing them. I hope I make the trip on the train soon with County in a better state.

Stoke City

When I was young a trip to the Victoria Ground would be an ideal opportunity to see top-flight football. The "Alex" were marooned in the Fourth Division and people would make the odd short trip to see some of the stars that you collected in football cards. Of course most people supported a top-flight team and the "Alex" and I took the opportunity to see my other team Everton.

In those days the away end was the open Stoke End. It was a fairly big end that backed down on to alleyways and terraced housing. The Boothen End was a huge end with a cover, a great end where you could imagine friends have had their own place for years. In those days it was a dangerous place to visit, although ironically Stoke has probably become a more dangerous place to visit in more peaceful times. I believe this often happens when a team slides down the leagues; it gives the fans a strange sort of pride. I remember going with a cousin from down South to a Tottenham game which turned into a free for all afterwards outside the open end.

The Stoke End was developed later and I stood in the new covered terrace that had a big stand behind it. The game was memorable in that my Dad encouraged me to wear my glasses for the first time. I was terribly shortsighted but never wore my glasses out of the house: "You're so vain". The transformation was amazing; a fairly ordinary game became brilliant. When standing behind the goal previously, the far end was just a blur; no wonder the nearby hooliganism had been so interesting. At the "Alex" in the 1970's, you changed ends so I had always had a clear end of the attacking but for how much of the game was that! That was the day that I became determined to have contact lenses, in the 1980's the price was starting to come down.

My trips to the Potteries are occasional but often enjoyable; Waterworld, Cineworld, Concerts at Victoria Hall, and the Wheatsheaf, trips to see Garf who lives in Fenton, Chicos and The Void. However, I never went to the old ground again which was a shame because it was one of my favourite dilapidated stadiums.

I find the new stadium rather grey and ugly, characterless by the ring road - but call me a dinosaur; I know conditions had to move on. When I went with the "Alex" as equals in 1997, the situation was unique as we were meeting a team that aged 30 some things would have dreamt of in the 1970's. We were now playing in the same league and a decent league at that. The game obviously captured the imagination of the town with 3,000 plus making the trip. Many chose the safer coach option; the one I went on went to Junction 15 and then North to the ground! The Shaun Smith free kick will be one of the great "Alex" moments in the history of the club, thundering into the onion bag. A 2-0-win was the icing on the cake. For many it meant a great victory against the 'clayhead scum', the demise of Chester and not playing Wrexham anymore had made this a good opportunity to gloat one of our new rivals. We all savoured the momentous moment, but I for one am a bit bored with this petty rivalry, I'd rather concentrate on how far we have come.

This was to be one of several visits in the noughties; on other occasions we usually met up with Garf and had a drink in his Fenton local the Angel or occasionally the Duke of Wellington. There would often be a mixture of adults and children and the local lads made us welcome, they probably all thought we drank as much as Garf! We were always met with friendliness and often admiration for the Alex which made me feel strange knowing that many hated Stoke and for most it wasn't reciprocal. We would walk to the ground from there which didn't take long because of Garf's local knowledge. The children used to enjoy walking over the bridge that crossed the ring road and waving at the cars going past.

Becky went with me for a couple of the Stoke games and also made the trip to the Britannia stadium for the Love Music, Hate Racism gig in 2009. The gig was in Stoke deliberately as the BNP had some success at local elections in the noughties. The May gig was enhanced by some really hot weather which will surprise a lot of fans reading this. It has been the only gig that I have been with my daughter which is disappointing as I am a big music fan. The gig was very cheap and had enough bands on to please us both. I believe N Dubz were big at the time and appealed to her and Mick Jones out of the Clash, Reverend and the Makers ,the Beautiful South and Pete Doherty were some that appealed to me on the day. It was great because we were allowed on the pitch to watch the bands with the stage behind the one goal. We were also allowed to sit in any of the three ends and sides which were great as it gave you different perspectives of the bands and fans. There was also a clothes market outside and lots of stickers and balloons being given out promoting the excellent cause. The gig was a mixture of young music and footy fans, political activists and families. The atmosphere was uplifting despite some upsetting truths being told; it was fantastic to see some hard young lads proudly putting anti-racism stickers on their faces. It is this type of event that can educate and help prevent ignorance; the messages given were great in that they gave an alternative to the lies peddled by the right.

It was one of my favourite days with my daughter, the weather was perfect and the message was great. Pete Doherty not only spoke with great emotion and sense but musically was brilliant. I'm not a great fan, I'm probably a bit old for that but he was superb on the day and I could definitely see his appeal to his cult group of loyal fans. Well done to the club for hosting and putting the event on.

Sunderland

I never went to Roker Park and given my views on new stadiums I went to the Stadium of Light with negative expectations.

This was an official coach trip with Phil Connor; Pete Johnson was on another coach so we kept passing each other with a range of faces and gesticulations.
It was Easter 98 and Phil and I caught up on gossip. He talked about the merits of dance culture, about a possible career in teaching and how we had been so fortunate in being able to travel to so many new grounds this year. I talked about the fun I was experiencing now I had got over my divorce.

I immediately liked the new stadium because it was not stuck on a ring road or trading estate. It was near pubs, shops and people although the stewards were a little over zealous reprimanding fans about standing up. Inside it is totally enclosed with a great view and The "Alex" fans tested the acoustics of the stadium successfully getting behind the team in a game we were unlucky to lose. Charnock scored from a difficult angle in front of the biggest league crowd we have ever played with over 40,000 in the ground. This was the day I was tempted to say progress in football stadiums has been good! Welcome to the 21st century Sav.

Swansea City

My first trip to Swansea was going to be in the 1994/5 season. I drove down from Kidderminster to Cardiff to see Phil. I was going to his flat in Roath and from there we were going on to the Vetch. However, the rain was terrible driving down and my worst fears were confirmed when I arrived in Cardiff, the game had been called off.

Sarah, Phil and I decided to spend the afternoon at the cinema and we chose to go and see Interview 'With A Vampire' at the City centre cinema. I have never been into the horror genre and this confirmed my opinions although they both really enjoyed it. Still we all had a great night out in Cardiff afterwards and I returned home on Sunday morning.

The next year we were more successful with the game being in sunny May. I picked Phil up in Cardiff and we parked near the Marina and County Hall that was in stark contrast to the industrial terminals that you pass on the way. The Marina reminded me of the Swansea I had visited as a child although the excellent 'TwinTown' gives another side to the town and also reminds us that football is just as important as rugby (the bath scene).

Swansea have a bit of a reputation, so we approached the ground with some fear before we were greeted with a strange sound – "Alex" songs coming out of a pub near the ground. This was very brave as no pubs were recommended in the

Football fan's guide. Anyway it was 2.45, so we went straight to the ground, a ground that has been one of my favourites on the TV. It didn't disappoint my strange obsession for the older stadium. This had the added bonus of every side being completely different, some would say this looks a mess, and I say it is unique and interesting.

It was the last game of the season and we were already in the play offs, but several hundred had made the long journey down. The away end still has 80's style fences and they were adorned with numerous flags, we even added our small play off final banner that looked a bit sorry compared to the rest. I loved the end we were in, it reminded me a little of the old North Bank at Wolves I stood in when I was a small child. To our left was a covered terrace where Swansea were extremely vocal, considering they had been relegated. They were also optimistic; a banner displayed said 'Swansea 1996/7 Division Three Champions.' I couldn't imagine seeing that at Crewe in a relegation year.

At the opposite end was an impressive terrace and seating with an unusual white stand to our right. I loved the ground, it didn't disappoint. The atmosphere was cracking, with some good-hearted banter about Cardiff and a 2-1 defeat of no significance.

After the game, we were sent towards the Marina and had a hassle free trip home. I remember having major problems finding any football scores on the radio on the way home, the radio had never been so west before and was extremely distorted. I remember listening to the excellent number one smasher 'Spaceman' on the way home; this was some comfort for not getting the scores until we were nearly in Cardiff.

It was another night on the beer with Phil and Sarah's friends in Cardiff. It was nice to talk and flirt with Janice again. The new house hadn't helped my relationship with Kate one bit, so it was a change to be talking to someone who seemed to like talking to me. On the journey home, I wondered how long I could tolerate my marriages failings. The summer would be a big time for reflection and decisions. It was.

I have since found a new wife but, as yet, not the new Liberty stadium.

Swindon Town

I made my first trip to the County Ground in the 1995/6 season. I spent the morning with Becky before making the small car trip from Kidderminster. I found the ground early and parked on a retail park nearby. This was a big game for both, first versus second in the old 3rd division, watched by 12,000 with about 1,000 "Alex" fans enjoying the October sunshine in the open end. The game didn't disappoint and we were treated by a rare touch of brilliance from Steve Garvey, he scored after an enigmatic run and I clearly remember going wild with everybody else. The benches were made to be danced and jumped upon; the thump of adrenalin produced by the goal gave way to elation and a rush of energy with thoughts of bigger stadiums in the old Second Division going through our heads. We eventually lost, but I remember walking past the park thinking we had performed admirably.

I returned to the ground in the 1999/00 season when we were both struggling in the old Second Division. Swindon were miles behind everyone and seemed doomed and we were looking increasingly vulnerable to the drop.

I travelled on the official coach from Crewe at 8.30am with Austin and Connie. I was increasingly getting friendly with the Post Office worker, years after disliking him when I worked there. "People are strange…"

We arrived in Swindon at 11.45. Was Swindon getting nearer? Our roads better? Were the official coaches encouraging drinking before the game?

We had a drink in a pub very near the ground by the car park before walking further a field and finding an Irish pub on the Manchester Road. This was an older area with more of a community feeling (which I hadn't seen on my previous visit where I had only seen the retail side of the town which looks so uniform you could be in any town in Britain). It was nice to drink leisurely in a pub that was not heaving. Steven Foden, an old school colleague and ex-Evertonian music fan who now works at the Post Office, joined us. Conversation and beer flowed well, allowing me to relax and enjoy the atmosphere of the pub, the smoky atmosphere and the banter between friends at the bar. When we left, I was immediately struck by the brightness, something, which is familiar with dinnertime drinking and however many times you have done it, the feeling when you hit the fresh air, is unforgettable.

The first half was awful, but the beer helped us get behind the lads. The Swindon fans were fantastic in the Intel stand, getting behind a poor side clearly going down. We were located in the corner of the North Stand adjacent to the Stratton Bank and were delirious when the winner went in; I personally think this was the turning point of our season, in which we survived relegation. I certainly enjoyed my sarnies and juice when I got back on the coach after a fantastic day. I love Saturdays like this when it is easy to forget the stresses of work.

I returned to the County ground in Easter 2009. The "Alex" were struggling near the bottom of the third tier. This kind of underdog situation often encourages my passion and it was this that pulled me South. It also helped that my brother-in-law and the two Robs were driving there and had offered me a lift. We had a quick stroll around the ground before going in to the North Stand at the side. There was a good 700 who had made the trip and were in good voice despite the fairly dismal season. To our right, a long haired lad in a full tracksuit with his girlfriend kept gesticulating at the "Alex" fans. He was met with "tracksuit from Matalan" which was quite amusing for the younger "Alex" fans that often prefer to be aggressive in their songs rather than funny. We ended up with a 0-0 and we were fairly pleased at the time, only to find later in the month that it should have been better if we were going to stay up.

Tamworth

I thought Tamworth away was a great draw in the FA Cup. It was a new ground and with good rail and Midland connections I was elated. An old student called David went to play for Tamworth when I taught in Bilston which added even more spice to the fixture. I am also a big fan of Julian Cope. However, the cup also coincided with my lad Dylan's birthday and this year Jak's sister from Spain was coming over for the occasion. There was going to be a big family meal on the Saturday, the day of the Tamworth game. To say I was gutted would be an understatement, but it was my son's birthday and to miss the party would have been selfish and grounds for divorce. On the day, I still couldn't properly settle until the game had started, knowing then I wasn't going for definite.

We did visit Tamworth Castle on a mini caravan break to Staffordshire and we were suitably impressed with the old castle and the modern tower blocks nearby. We had a great day in the town, spending the whole day there and I will hopefully return to visit the Lamb ground sometime in the future.

Torquay United

My only visit to Plainmoor was in the 1992/3 season.

Phil Connor was a student in Derby and made his way to Kidderminster. I left my pregnant wife to make the trip down to Torquay. We made the journey surprisingly quick listening to the excellent Manic Street Preachers and were surprised by the mild February weather. Not only was it mild, but also bright and sunny - it made you glad to be alive. We ate some chips and talked about wives, girlfriends, grounds and growing up. This really was the English Riviera, as we looked across the bay; I spotted the excellent Rock Garden club where Kate and I had spent many an hour a couple of summers previously. There were no dress restrictions in the club, with disco music on one floor and rock on the other. I also spotted an Indian we had visited which was on the first floor giving a great view of the bay.

After a couple of beers, we got back in the car before setting off to Plainmoor. We parked up in a pleasant suburban area and made our way to the ground. The away end gives the impression of a quiet, rural, station platform with its small amount of steps with a flat open top. It gave a great view of nearby gardens.

The opposite end was covered with seating and I felt it looked quite impressive and original. Luckily it remained a lovely day and we remained dry and victorious.

We arrived back in Kidderminster in time for a few jars, Kate taking us to Dusties in Kidderminster to round off a good day.

Tottenham Hotspur

It was an amazing draw in the League Cup, one that I did and didn't want. A new ground would be great, but not on a Wednesday night in the busiest term. It wasn't ideal, but of course I was going. It was going to be a night for me, not for school or anybody else, but me.

I was fortunate to get a 24 pound ticket, much cheaper than the 28 pound in the upper tier. Fans were justifiably moaning, but I had to go. It was surely a once in a lifetime trip, even in the lofty season of 1999.

Getting there was going to be the main problem. The coaches from Crewe were setting off too early and a train from Wolverhampton might be difficult coming back with the last train not being very late! With extra time and penalties on the first game, I didn't want to miss the last train (I thought optimistically ignoring the fact that our record defeat, 13-2, was against Spurs).

A solution had loomed at the Tranmere Rovers game, Becky's first to Gresty Road (Permission was given; Kate had mellowed since her second baby). Chris Kelsall, a friend a couple of years older than me was driving and worked in Rugeley and offered to give me a lift from Hilton Park service station. This was brilliant, less driving, good company and less stress, until I got a call on Sunday cancelling due to the high price. Oh well, as the Levellers said "There's only one way of life and it's your own". So driving on my own it was.

After a bad day at school, the trip to Tottenham was a tiring but exciting prospect. After a quick change, I took a leisurely ride to White Hart Lane, a lovely named ground. I'd save thrashing the car (which is more tiring) for the way back. The directions in the Football Fans Guide book were as good as ever, practically a straight drive from Bilston, M6, M25, A10 and turn left. London driving had never been easier! I parked near Middlesex University making sure I was turned around for a quick getaway. It seemed a safe place to park and it turned out to be that way. I walked past the Railway Pub and White Hart Lane Railway Station arriving on the Tottenham High Road, which I loved being a real bustling community with the ground, houses, pubs and takeaways. People were milling around eating drinking and chatting. I bumped in to my old mate from primary school Clive Jackson in the chippy, of whom is now part of the Nantwich Town set up. It's a small world. I waited patiently for a pay phone to ring Jak and soaked up the atmosphere.

On entering the ground I met up with Pete Johnson, Austin and Connie. The game was an exciting and mouth watering prospect which was slightly dampened by the lower numbers of both home and away fans. When walking up the steps to see the inside of the ground, it gives a "ground fanatic" a real buzz - and this didn't disappoint. The side where the TV cameras go is often where my eyes are first averted because it's the side that is less familiar to you; the old Shelf had unfortunately disappeared. The ground was substantial and impressive, more cosy and intimate than some of the bigger grounds. It was nice to see Tottenham shops on the High Street making the whole experience between fan and community seem closer.

My seat was not with Pete and Austin in the first half, but I luckily bumped into an old acquaintance I hadn't seen for several years. Steve used to live at the Wells Green Post Office. Steve was into the Neph musically, cars and rally bikes but was an "Alex" fan from my late teens. We had lots of nostalgic chat and for the first half the football was similar to background music. Steve was settled down now in the Potteries, he was still an "Alex" fan with an indefatigable memory for "Alex" details and was very critical of Dario. He was also from our era where fan behaviour was always a consideration. His refusal to sing and remain cool, his insistence that Tottenham wouldn't sing on, to them a mundane fixture, reminded me of the 1980's days. I always loved singing even in the pretentious 1980's and enjoyed it being back in vogue in the 1990's, but today I had to curtail it due to being with Steve. Maybe I should have joined a choir!

The game was entertaining and seeing some of Ginola's touches almost justified the overpriced entrance. He was predictably mocked by many "Alex" fans. It is those magical touches that do excite fans and I suppose the hostile words are a form of flattery to the player.

A 3-1 defeat, their third goal in the 89th minute suggested that it was a decent performance. I left in injury time, very unusual for me, and ran towards the car for a quick getaway. I got carried away and missed my turn, only realising when I got to an unfamiliar Safeway. I reached my car and quickly joined the dash Northward, I reached my Nan's house in Cannock at 12.15, car whizz kid Steve would have been proud of my velocity

Tranmere Rovers

I shall take this opportunity to praise Kevin Sampson's 'Awaydays' because he describes the visits of away supporters to Prenton Park in the late 1970's and early 80's in a realistic way that summarised the period. I never went there until the later 1980's, but the intimidation given out sounds similar to the tales of friends. Many describe being spat at and taunted in the paddock below the main stand.

Home games were always lively affairs with a Boxing Day fixture and a Tuesday night fixture standing out. Ironically, with their boys being renowned for using Stanley knives, it was a Tranmere fan that was horribly slashed by a Crewe fan on Crewe station after one game.

I first went to Tranmere in the 1987/8 season during my first year at college in Liverpool. I dragged my newfound football fanatic from Coventry to this meaningless end of season encounter. We got the train from nearby St Michael's Station in Liverpool to Rock Ferry, and from there tentatively walked to the ground. I was still fearful of their reputation so we didn't ask anyone the way to the ground, following anyone we thought were football fans. We arrived at the ground and took our place on the open terrace in the corner with about 50 diehard fans. It was a warm, end of April evening and I liked the ground with an impressive main stand to our left and a big floodlight in the middle of our corner. The atmosphere was terrible, although the game was quite entertaining, enough for Mick to make The "Alex" his 4th division team!

The next year, Mick must have thought he had gone to a different ground. This time he was sharing a magical moment in our history, the fixture a crucial end of season game, a draw could be enough to put both of us up.

Garf Kent came over for the weekend and we started off drinking near my new student abode in Garston near the station. My brother-in-law and Mick joined us. We got a lift over the Mersey and what a change, 15,000 instead of nearly 3,000 fans?. In our away corner 3,000 squeezed into the corner, with many clambering up the floodlights for air and a better view. The atmosphere was pulsating in a carnival spirit with a plastic rhino being thrown around throughout the game to the amusement of the crowd. This was the year when there seemed to be less trouble, but a defeat by one of us would have tested this theory. The delayed kick off due to congestion meant a draw was enough for both us, something that the players seem to be aware of - accordingly both players and fans relaxed and enjoyed. Tranmere fans covered the pitch at the end and "Alex" fans followed celebrating in unison. Readers of 'Away Days' would be amazed by the contrast of behaviour in the eighties. The partying went on in Crewe and Nantwich all night, and I wish I had been part of it. However, we had our own little promotion party in Liverpool city centre where my new girlfriend Kate joined me.

The next visits were always going to be an anti-climax; the next year Mick and I were joined by another scouse Crewey, Phil Connor who was on a community project in Liverpool for a year. He told of his new love for a girl from Kirkby on our journey across the water. The "Alex" did take quite a few and made a bit of noise, but the result and atmosphere could never live up to the previous season. Still, I had got a marriage to look forward to later that year.

When I returned in 1998/9, things were very different. I had moved back to Crewe, now divorced and now seeing Jackie. I was no longer a student and teaching practices in Kirkby, Huyton and Allerton had prepared me for my teaching career. Dramatic changes had also taken place at Prenton Park. The old away end was now a huge covered end with away fans being seated on the left. The end gave an excellent view of the nearby area. I had to get a 'flier' from school in Wolverhampton to Crewe where I was catching a coach to the game. My Dad had got the ticket for me, I thought the game was on Saturday, Friday was a bit of a rush and I probably wouldn't have bothered going normally, but the ground changes and a nostalgic trip to Merseyside were not to be missed.

Living in Liverpool for 4 years has made me defend its people, visit the town for shopping and nights out and even got me into the Beatles.

I returned the following year after just getting engaged to Jackie. We had just returned from a short break in Stratford where we came back with the pleasing news. On return, Austin rang and offered me a place in his car for the Tranmere match. I declined the offer, but after telling Jackie she told me to go. What a love!

We went into the friendly Mersey Clipper before the game. I have been there on recent visits and have always enjoyed the atmosphere, although it seems to be more of a home pub on recent visits. The end has got a great atmosphere with the fans seated in close proximity to each other. The banter aimed at some of the ugly and badly dressed Crewe fans was quite funny and kept me amused in the duller parts of the defeat. The obsession of looks was a recurring theme in 'Awaydays'. I hate the constant moronic, predictable, Scouse songs aimed at Tranmere who largely claim to their own identity although I think the "He had a shell suit for Christmas" song is quite amusing if not predictable for Tranmere fans.

At half time I met an old friend from Crewe and spoke to him through the caged gate near the tea bar and toilets in the Tranmere end. Apparently he was working in Liverpool for a while and had gone to the game with a Tranmere fan. It reminded me of two people from East and West Germany talking over the Berlin Wall in a bizarre dream. A steward looked on suspiciously confused at our friendship.

I have visited Prenton Park more recently where the away fans are now positioned in the old home Cow Shed end. On two of the occasions I went with Bruce and Andy. Andy is a big Tranmere fan and lived in Nantwich. I used to play footy with some lads on a Sunday night and I got to know

Andy through this. Not only was I impressed that he claimed to sit near Nigel out of Half Man Half Biscuit, who I love, but he was also a decent guy. Andy was matey with the kit man at Tranmere who lived in a flat in one of the leafy streets near to the ground. Andy used to park in his drive and we would go around to his house after the game, have a brew and chat and wait until the traffic had disappeared before we drove home. It was good to chat with Rovers fans and get a different perspective on the game. Andy has recently emigrated to New Zealand, a fair way from the Wirral!

In one game the "Alex" was on a terrible run with Steve Holland, who is now a successful No2 at Chelsea. We were awful and well beaten before half time and the "Holland out" chants had begun before the game. It was all nasty and angry and doesn't really make for a pleasurable experience. However awful a job a manager might be doing, I don't get the pleasure some seem to take from helping to oust somebody. On the other hand, such fans are often passionate and care for the club. I guess some people are just more fickle than others.

On Boxing Day 2012, I went with Craw's mate in the car. Alan is a top bloke but drives far too fast; we were certainly ready for a drink to calm our nerves. We went in the Mersey Clipper again where there was a superb atmosphere as usual. We met up with some "Alex" fans by the ground that had been on some drinking coaches. They had been in Camel Laird Social Club since

11 o'clock. This was the name of an excellent Half Man Half Biscuit album and seemed a very appropriate drinking place for "Alex" HMHB fans. At least Pete Newton appreciated the significance of the trip being a fellow Biscuit fan.

It was a good trip out, one good thing is that there is often fans you don't always see at Christmas fixtures and it was great to see ex-students Craig Parker and Chris Lines, as well as the usual ex-students like Sam Proctor and Amber who usually go.

I have fond memories of this ground, thanks to our 1989 promotion side, Kevin Sampson (one of my favourite writers) and Half Man Half Biscuit. When I go to each Tranny game, I always have this thought that I might bump into Nigel from the band at home or away games. It's quite embarrassing to admit. Sometimes I like to wear my HMHB t shirt, but I also think this would be really embarrassing if I saw Nigel. I wouldn't want to chat to him as he would probably be with his mates and so I wouldn't want to impose. Would a "hi" or a nod be appropriate? This fixture has changed with my obsession with the band, I would love Nigel to read this, but I am worried that he would hate it? That is what happens when you become obsessed with the best band in the world!

Walsall

I was born in Bloxwich in the Borough of Walsall, so there is always some added interest to this game. I lived in Great Wyrley and have relatives in Cheslyn Hay and Pelsall. I have taught in Bilston for 10 years and many of our students came under the Walsall authority.

I visited Fellows Park on a handful of occasions before moving to Crewe when I was eight. I remember standing by the wall at the covered end of the ground, a game against Torquay stood out as my Dad and a Torquay fan that he worked with went with me. I remember the Laundry End being talked about fondly. I probably went to a handful of games when I was young that are a bit of a blur. My Grandad took me to Hednesford Town when I was young and this memory merges with some of my hazy images of Fellows Park. I returned on Boxing Day in 1989/90 with the "Alex". I took Kate with me on the way to visiting Midlands relatives. This time we stood on the covered terracing at the side of the ground.

At senior school, I clearly still had some affiliation of the club, I recently found an old school folder with some Walsall graffiti amongst my Everton and the "Alex". However, when we met in the play-offs in the 1992/3 season, I was desperate for "Alex" success and delighted with Ashley Ward and Tony Naylor's contribution in annihilating them in both legs. Walsall had now moved to Bescot, a new compact fairly characterless stadium with a good view.

Walsall fans were not too pleased as some of our fans invaded the pitch to celebrate our first trip to Wembley as they chased us back into the seats. They have taunted us with chants of "runaways" ever since, although I witnessed some of our older 'boys' after the game who were anything but that.

In fact, the play-off defeat seems to have made increased the rivalry between the two clubs and Walsall has caused some trouble at recent games at Gresty Road. Mind you the Saddlers got some revenge with two late goals to beat us in 1995/6 at the Bescot on what was one of one of the coldest nights ever!

On some of my trips to the Bescot, I have had really friendly chats in their huge Social Club and genuinely believe that midlands people are the friendliest people in the country. I remember bumping into Chris, a Walsall fan from my school in Bilston and going for a drink with him and his Dad after one game; these were encounters that were part of the true friendly spirit that can come out of football.

When Becky was living with me, I went to this fixture and dropped Becky with her Mum at the IKEA car park nearby. We were due to meet there at 6 o'clock after having a quick drink after the game. While at the game her Mum informed me that we would have to pick her up from Kidderminster. I was not too impressed, but I didn't have much choice, so I drove over there with Pete and Garf in tow. Of course they were in a pub and that is where we picked them up. Garf decided to have a pint or two and catch up with Kate so the short stop became a longer one. I wouldn't have minded him catching up with Kate, but I was in a mood and Kate had pissed me off, not for the first time; and there is nothing worse when you are fed up and sober and Garf and Kate were not. At least picking Becky up distracted my bad mood.

On another trip to the Bescot, I had arranged to meet a relative of mine. When my Uncle John split up with his wife Phyllis, I found that I lost contact with the in-law side of the family, as can often happen in such cases. Yes blood is often thicker than water. I was also very close to John and his new partner Joan, and it was easier in the early days to just keep in touch with them: the years sometimes vanish quickly when your own life is so busy which I know is no excuse. After not seeing Phyllis for ten years, I thought I ought to get in touch. I was very fond of her, and when Becky was born I thought it might be an opportunity to get in touch again, albeit a bit late, as she hadn't taken the split well. It was quite a nerve wrecking experience, but after the initial shock we caught up and the visit went really well. She was now with a new partner who supported the Saddlers. My Uncle was a Wolves season ticket holder.

The next season we met with Phyllis and Vic in their Social Club which was nice. I was so glad that we had got back in touch, as not long after meeting up Phyllis died at too early an age. More recently I have also caught up with the Higgs family, Paul, Joan and Steve who I have known since I was very little. They are big Saddlers fans and we have recently met up for the "Alex" games. They have a dry sense of humour which makes for some good banter. It is the only time we see each other, but it also shows that despite the hostility that football can and dooo bring, it can more often than not bring families and friends together.

Watford

This was a new ground that I didn't want to miss in the 1996/7 season.

The game clashed with a period over Easter that I had Becky. Should I miss it? Should I take Becky? Should I tell Kate if I do? It was less than a year since we had split up and this period was our most acrimonious with regards to finance and access. She was seeing an English lad from Gibraltar and I was having a good time.

I decided to take Becky on the coach and not tell Kate until afterwards. Becky was nearly 4 and we prepared for the trip: balloons, a plastic drum, crisps and sweets. On the coach we sat near Pete Johnson and Wigan Claire from the club shop who gave Becky lots of attention - she hardly had time to do any colouring in. She enjoyed the stop at the service station; we had our photo taken at one of the booths before returning to the coach.

We got to Vicarage Road and Becky was let in for nothing, we explored around the Stanley Rous stand at the side before taking our seat for the match. I kept thinking about my first trips to grounds, where the reaction of the crowd and the towering stands were far more interesting than the game. We let off balloons when the teams came out and banged the drum when we were singing. We stayed in the same seat for 70 minutes; we went down the front near the end.

I didn't get much of a chance to quietly reflect on the ground, but it looked colourful, was a bit mix and match - which I like. I loved the little stand amongst bits of terracing; it was also Becky's first game with a rare Gareth Whalley goal and a crucial away win We got back to the coach easily and she had a bit of a nap on the way back in between getting a lot of attention off many people sitting on the coach.

I arrived back happy; we had both had a lovely day, explored and travelled to another part of the country. I informed Kate of where we had been and she went absolutely ballistic. I was accused of putting her life in danger and being obsessed by football. She was going to malign me to her friends and family about the kind of father I was. She was going to take Becky to Gibraltar to live (she didn't, but it worried me for a long time). If the game had been 12 years ago I would have agreed with her. Watford are a reputed family club despite the impressions given by Doug Brimson, yes we all have some 'nutters' but they don't come out for an "Alex"/ Watford game in 1997(yes I know the game was stopped at the fixture at Gresty Road in 1978 for running battles that spilled on to the pitch)

I am allowed to take Becky now! Watford will always remind of a great day with her and a polarisation of relations with Kate. Oh and that Mr Taylor.

Wembley

I suppose for many fans a trip to Wembley is the ultimate football ground experience. It is a name that is associated with so many football songs and the word itself is magical around the world. Despite agreeing with all this, for me it isn't necessarily one of my favourite grounds, despite having some wonderful moments there.

My first experience was for an England under18 fixture. There was a special train from Crewe and kids from all the schools in the area made the journey to Wembley Central in the mid 1970's. A young prodigy, Peter Coyne who played for the "Alex" scored on the day, although he didn't go on to fulfil his potential at the highest level.

I returned to Wembley in 1977 to watch the league cup final between Everton and Aston Villa. This was the first success my boyhood heroes and had since I had supported them. I managed to get a ticket by being an "Alex" season ticket holder and some bartering by my Dad. On the day, my Dad and I were in the tunnel end with the Evertonians and my sister and Mum were in the seats near the Villa fans. The game was famous for not going to extra time; I think that it was changed not long after that. I remember a long haired Villa fan spitting on an Everton scarf at the tube station on the way home, something that enticed more passion than the 0-0 draw on the pitch.

In 1993, the "Alex" made the trip in the play-offs in 1993 to play York City. We were driven by Johny

Clarke, a great saxophone player who made a career in music after leaving Crewe Works. He lived in Manchester and picked us up in his Peugeot 405. We were also joined by Phil and Faz. On arriving at Wembley, we had a drink in a pub where the York fans out sung us and it was them who had more to sing about at the end after they won a penalty shoot out after a dull game with extra time. We were seated at the side where the medals and cup were collected from the Royal Box.

We returned in 1997, and this time a place in the second tier of the league was up for grabs. I went on a coach and arrived in London during a glorious period of hot weather. I went to a different pub this year, which like most of the pubs was dominated by Brentford - the West London fans out numbered us 2-1 on the day. I was again at the side of the ground that day and this time the "Alex" finished 1-0 winners with Shaun Smith getting the winner, a lad who had a good scoring record for a left back. The win made for some appetising fixtures the next season and the town was buzzing when we arrived back in Crewe. I remember being outside the Brunswick on Nantwich Road singing with many others as cars kept passing with horns blaring and scarves flying from the windows. It was a euphoric bank holiday weekend with even better days ahead.

In 2012, nobody expected to be going to Wembley in the play offs. In November the legend Dario Gradi departed after a dip in form that saw us languishing near the bottom of the fourth tier of football. Like Tony Blair and Brian Clough, he made the mistake of staying on a little too long. Steve Davis took over the top job having being groomed to eventually take the post. Steve steadied the ship and topped it off with a terrific run at the end of the season to sneak into the play offs.

My mate Craw had decided to run a coach to the game and it was on this double decker that Dylan and I caught the bus. We were at the last pick up and as a result Dylan and I were not sitting next to each other, which was not ideal. Despite this, there was some good company on there including my sister Heidi and Craw himself, my Chameleons buddy who loves the "Alex" and teaching!

The coach from Leicestershire stopped en route at the service station which was awash with "Alex" fans. There was a real buzz as you bumped into ex-students and old friends. We also stopped at Bushey in Hertfordshire for a drink, it was the hottest day of an awful summer and most people made extensive use of the beer garden. It was at this pub that Dylan started to get a bit of a phobia for going to the toilet brought on through the excitement and heat of the day. This continued at Wembley, I remember getting to know the toilets pretty well. The only saving grace with this was that it was the coolest place on the day. We were behind the goals near the front in the cheap seats where you were exposed to some scorching sun. It was possibly too hot. (Are we ever happy?) The game against Cheltenham Town was memorable for the wonder strike by Nicky Powell, a strike that paved the way to Old Trafford. It was great to celebrate with my friends Peter and Phil who I hadn't seen for a while. Dylan often hums the song 'Paradise' as a result of the generic songs that are played for the winning fans, so despite his stomach problems, he seemed to enjoy it. The journey back was a long and sticky one, but nobody was complaining, it was a season where the agony had turned to ecstasy.

Unbelievably we returned again in 2013 in the Johnstone Paint Final against Southend United. I travelled on Craw's coach again, this time Dylan took his friend Robert, but Reuben, despite going to most matches, decided not to go and watch the game at Grandad Don's house. It was much more relaxed this time, Dylan knew what to expect and was more relaxed being a year older. Faz and his son made the trip on the coach and I decided to wear a fake sheepskin coat I had picked up from a charity shop. The game kicked off early, and this year we decided to wander around the Bobby Moore statue talking and soaking up the atmosphere.

Southend fans outnumbered us on their first visit to Wembley, which made for a much larger attendance than the year before.
In the ground, we were in a very similar position behind the goal. The weather was decent but not tropical this time. The "Alex" had another great day on the pitch with Luke Murphy's strike relaxing us early on. A second goal in the second half led to a fairly comfortable win. I enjoyed it far more this year, maybe there is less at stake in the cup, maybe it was because Dylan was more relaxed or I am getting less fazed by the place. The two kids were taking photos of everything, which was great

because I am useless at that type of thing. On the way back we stopped at the service station when we were joined by the team coach. The kids were elated and manage to get some autographs and their photo taken with the JPT trophy. There were even some Japanese holiday makers who got in on the act, so hopefully the "Alex" message has crossed several continents.

In conclusion, the buzz of visiting and getting to Wembley is magical and I hope it continues to be through all the cups. On the day I think there is a bit of snobbery amongst loyal fans and the ones who rarely go which sticks in the mind of the fans who go to Hartlepool on a Tuesday night! However, if we only took 4,000 to Wembley I would be annoyed so I suppose you can't have it both ways. I should chill out, fly my flag and enjoy the moment because the gloomy trips are never too far away.

WEM-BER-LEY..................

West Bromwich Albion

This was the first ground that I ever went to. I was 5 and remember very little. I was in a seat that was at the side near the corner flag. My eyes were at ground level; the score was 2-2 and was either against Man Utd or Liverpool. I'd never seen so many people in my life.

I quite like the Albion; their badge is the best in the land. The throstle is magnificent; it was my favourite badge in my Esso badge collection in the 1970's.

I never returned to the Hawthorns until we joined the old 2nd division in 1997. I parked under the bridge by the Moat house near Junction 1 of the M5. I have parked in exactly the same place every year since then. It's a bit of a walk, but not too bad for getting away after. It is also has a friendly bar where I have got talking to some friendly Albion fans. I took Jackie that year as we were going on the piss in Wolverhampton afterwards, staying the night at Graham Collins' house. It is one of my favourite grounds, a good view, decent cover and a pulsating atmosphere. It was a cold day, but a happy one, I met Phil at the game and The "Alex" won the first game that Jackie and I had attended together. We were not as fortunate the next year I took her but we had a great night drinking in Wolverhampton again.

I was there for the Easter Monday 5-1 massacre of the Baggies. I had just dropped off Becky at Kidderminster, this being quite fortuitous as it was one of those games that you will never forget. David Wright scored from a great distance and much more. The Albion fans were furious but didn't vent their anger on us but at the players and directors. Some fans ran on the pitch and tore their season tickets up.

The next year, I took my favourite parking place again, walking past my favourite badge on the way to an entertaining 2-2 draw. I had just had some lovely days with Becky and was flying to Amsterdam the next day with Jackie. Life didn't get much better than this, especially with an OFSTED inspection after half term. The calm before the storm!

West Ham United

The opportunity to attend Upton Park came as a result of an excellent cup run in 1990 /91.

I was fortunate, as it coincided with a reading week during my PGCE in Liverpool! I travelled on a supporter's coach to the capital and had a quick look around the ground before taking my seat in the corner of the upper tier of the stand by the police box. There was a lot of "Alex" fans in the end to our right in the corner of the terracing behind the goal that was segregated .The "Alex" fans had filled both areas and were extremely vociferous. "Alex" fans had apparently dared to go and sing in local pubs and West Ham boys were responding to us in the section right by the seats and terraces. As country bumpkins we had taken the piss too much (especially the politically incorrect "Where's your caravan" aimed at the talented Ian Bishop) and were due some intimidation. Someone told me we were voted the best away supporters at Upton Park in their fanzine that year.

Before the game, I spoke to my old Government and Politics lecturer that I had had a bit of a fling with. I had forgotten that the London woman was a West Ham fan and had made the trip from Crewe. It was good to speak to her, I hadn't seen her for ages and we didn't leave each other in the best of circumstances, so it was nice that she was still speaking to me. The game was a belter and we were so unlucky to lose in the last few minutes.

I had just gone teaching part-time in 2012 when we drew West Ham away in the League Cup. I was just adjusting to the lack of money and never made it. There was going to be some games I was going to have to sacrifice and it wasn't easy adjusting to a more austere lifestyle.

Wigan Athletic

I went to Springfield Park in the 1989/9 season. It was a Sherpa Van Northern quarter final; this is the point where a meaningless cup becomes interesting when the twin towers become more than a dream.

My brother-in-law and mate Kevin was working in Liverpool that day, fancied the game and picked Michael and myself up. Mick was a football fanatic and jumped at the chance to go to the game. He picked us up from Christ and Notre Dame College in Childwall and we made our way to Wigan. We were running late and got a bit lost in Wigan. We asked the way and were given some good directions - only to find ourselves at the rugby ground.

We got to the ground and missed the kick off. We found a gap on the open bank with several hundred "Alex" fans, cup fever had reached us and the fans were in a good mood. Some rolled down the grass bank and we went home happy with a 1-0 win. The ground reminded me of Doncaster's Belle View with 2 open ends, a similar stand and covered terracing. In the toilets at half time I met an old friend who I hadn't seen for ages; Brendon Tapley was a joiner and was off to work in Europe. I haven't seen him since, but I don't think he has come back to Crewe.

We were going to get the train back to Liverpool, but Kev is a hell of a bloke and insisted on taking us back to Liverpool. He took us back to the halls of residence and I went to Kate's room that I had just started seeing. I left Mick and commented on how he might

becoming a lucky mascot; he was certainly enjoying his "Alex" games, would supporting Coventry ever be the same?

I returned to Wigan to go to the new JJB Stadium in the early noughties. I use the train a lot more nowadays and can't believe I didn't travel on the train this day as you are there in only thirty minutes. I went on the coach that got there early enough to wander around and go for a drink. In the pub there was quite a lot of younger Crewe fans. Towards the end of my first pint the Crewe fans burst into a rendition of 'No Surrender'. As somebody who is on the left of politics and its association with racist groups I was very shocked and surprised, Crewe has never been a hotspot for right wing activities. I was pretty disgusted and depressed to hear it and when a couple of Wigan fans started to be a bit mouthy to the Crewe fans, I decided to make a sharp exit. The incident didn't make me feel great and clouded the afternoon for me, despite bumping into a couple of people I hadn't seen for a while.

At the time the away fans were in the side where the TV cameras are. The game was ruined by the sending off of favourite Efe Sodje, famous for his colourful bandanas and erratic defending!. The "Alex" never recovered and ending up losing.

I ended up leaving the ground not feeling brilliant. I had left Jackie with a young Dylan and I hadn't really had an uplifting experience, despite thinking that the ground was one of the more impressive newer grounds, and importantly for me, being situated fairly close to the town centre and the station.

Willenhall

In the 1981/2 my Midland connections haunted me again in the year of the classic "Ghost Town" by the Specials. This first round FA Cup draw took me back to a childhood I had left behind, but flickered on and off through visits to relatives in the area.

I went on an official coach to the ground, although many went on the train, as is the attraction of the cup in the lower divisions. Postmen who had arrived on the train told many tales of trouble. Some had met with trouble on Wolverhampton station, others in Willenhall. Tinny, a mate of a postman friend, had been arrested in the vicinity of the ground. He had been seen jumping over car roofs in an attempt to escape arrest. Generally, the ground was open terraces with a small stand and like a lot of non-league games in that period there were rumours that some big clubs fans, in this case Wolves, were out for trouble. Well we scraped a 1-0 victory and got back to the coach safely. I remember the coach being parked on some grass; a few trees and gangs of lads hanging around.

I used to pass the ground when the traffic was busy on my route to school in nearby Bilston. It enabled you to miss out the horrendously busy Neachells Lane. Nowadays there seems to be less trees and more industrial units in the area, perhaps it was just a few bushes, maybe my mind is playing tricks with me. The front of the ground is smarter and certainly more impressive than I remember. We take many students from Willenhall; some of those hanging around on that day are probably parents of students that I teach. It's strange how life turns out sometimes, if you had told me in 1981 that I would be teaching near Willenhall, I'd have laughod.

Wimbledon

It was one of those games that you shouldn't really go to but you do. January midweek cup game, get a life! However, what if you won at a Premier League ground and you were not there? What if you never got the chance to go to Selhurst Park again? It's easy to be retrospective writing in 2001.

I set off from Bilston in the dark, tackled the M25 and called for Pete Wraith who lives in Sutton. I said a quick hello to Monica and Jasmine before Pete gave me a rest from driving, drove us to his wife's families place of work, where we parked up. We walked for 10 minutes before spotting the strange sign that showed that 2 sides played there, something I wouldn't like to see at my club. We paid our money and was incredibly surprised by the amount of "Alex" fans had made the trip, at least 1,500 others. We gave a spirited display to less than 5,000 people who were seated on 2 sides of the ground. We had the whole of the side while the Dons fans were all in the Holmesdale Road end. At various home and away games, Wimbledon have always made quite a noise for their small numbers. Tonight they were easily out sung by the "Alex", much of it directed at Dean Holdsworth who had recently hit the tabloids for playing away from home.

I was back at my Nan's house in Cannock for 1am, trying to rationalise the trip that was going to knacker me for the rest of the week. As I had my sherry nightcap in the bath, I knew it was worth it, the result could have been very different and at least I would have been able to say I had been there.

I never went to Plough Lane and missed the opportunity to visit their current home due to it clashing with a wedding. I am intrigued that they play at a ground called the Cherry Red Records ground. It was the excellent label that the fabulous Dead Kennedys used to be on. I am keen to get to Kingston on Thames soon, but would love them to get back to their London Borough - if at all possible.

Wolverhampton Wanderers

This is a special ground and key fixture for so many reasons. Living in Great Wyrley in the early 1970's, practically everybody supported The Wolves - my best friend, Ian Pearce, my elder sister and my influential Uncle John. Of course I have always been an awkward bastard and supported Everton from the age of 5 because I loved the letter E.

It was my Uncle John who took me on my first trips to Molineux. He would have loved me to support Wolves, he had no kids of his own at the time and was and still is a Wolves fanatic. He even took me in the old North Bank with my Everton scarf on. I remember him picking me up in his orange Capri. He wore a sheepskin coat and had sideburns. He smoked coolly, had the radio on and was brusque.

I remember the route into the industrial town, the flats and the black faces. It was exciting and we would park in the same place by some closed businesses on the Cannock Road. Sometimes my Grandad would sit in the car while we were at the game, partly for security, mainly to listen to the horses on the radio in peace away from his wife. We would walk past a pub and go under the bridge and the brewery, I think it said Brew XI on it. At the junction we would cross by another pub, before crossing the busy road and cutting through the flats. I used to be fascinated by these flats, I now know they are student flats. When I see them, I automatically think of the walk to the ground.

John would stop at a corner shop and get his fags and a Mars bar for me. This shop was now where Asda is.

It was 15p to get in the North Bank. When I went later I thought it was smaller than on my first visits. I loved the singing and the shouting. At one game Slade came on the pitch at half time. We all sang "Super Slade". We both loved them. I loved the clock on top of the stand to our left. Wagstaffe and the 'Doug' were familiar names. He bought me a programme.

When I returned years later, I realised that the South Bank was far bigger than the North Bank. I came with Everton and we nearly always lost. There were police lined down the middle before the fences. Both fans would make attempts to burst through the line. I remember one wintry season, when the terraces were covered with snow, snowballs were thrown at each other all through the game - some of them hurt, especially the ones with stones in them. That year we were caught up in running battles outside the ground as we made our way from the exit to the infamous subway. Everton fought back, but came out worst that day. This was rare with Everton.

Then came the demise of Wolves. I was true Crewe and we were in the same league. 1986 at home, John came up for that one. He hated playing us; it showed how far they had fallen. Peter Bodak got a hat trick in one away victory. Then Bull, the saviour arrived. We missed the Bull and Mutch show on January 2nd 1988 - my sister Heidi married Kev. The Midlands clan were up for it. John was first to the car radio to inform us of the score. He enjoyed that. He was optimistic again.

Wolves moved up the leagues and I got older. John was still part of our family and a big influence, but it was different. I was not an awestruck child anymore. My Dad was a bigger influence now.

I went to Molineux a couple of times while living in Kidderminster, with Kate's friend's boyfriend, Lee Perry. I stood on the South Bank a couple of times when the present ground was half built. A 5-1 defeat in the old Second Division stood out nearly as much as the old memories. We drank in the Goal Post. He lived in Stourport and was cocky and likeable.

I was then teaching in Bilston and surprised by the lack of Wolves fans at the school. It wasn't like that in the 1970's. Man Utd were not as much of a multi-national company. The ground had now been fully modernised and I loved the glimpses of it on fantastic work nights out in Wolverhampton which were part of the post Kate era: The Varsity, The Hog's Head, Blast Off, Moon Under the Water, Kings, Cheeky Monkey, The Canal, The Light house, Picassos, It's a Scream and Yam Yams.

In 1997, we joined the old Second Division and John hated it. Like most Wolves fans they hate playing any small clubs, thinking they can automatically roll over anybody who hasn't got tradition or money.

Teaching in Bilston has put me in the spotlight and I have felt pressured going to Wolves/Crewe games. Will they play terrible? Will we take many fans? Will we make any noise? On each occasion at Molineux at least one of the above has applied. I had 'higged' the "Alex" so much and had a red face so many times; Graham Collins my mate from work has loved it.

My stag day was the exception in 2000. Many from work came up for the game and we had a 7 a side game beforehand, Wolves v's Crewe. I played for the work team, and we beat the Crewies. However, after a massive session in the Brunswick, the "Alex" finally performed superbly, for the first time since working in Bilston. The non-Midland Wolves fans joined us for a sing song in the Gresty and did we play well and sing?

I have returned on other trips with the "Alex" and for gigs. Wolverhampton is a brilliant venue for gigs and is very easy to get back from on the train. The Robin Hood, the Little Civic and the Wulfren are all fantastic venues with more springing up all the time, like the new one on Broad Street which used to be a night club that I had been to many years ago.

At Molineux, we played really well when we were relegated from the championship. The few that made the trip celebrated our point like we were being promoted. It is strange for me, because with my friends and family still supporting Wolves, they have almost become my second team - they are certainly one of the first results I look out for. I bet my Uncle John wish I'd said that all those years ago.

I am looking forward to taking my children for the first time on Boxing Day for the "Alex" game. That is going to be a strange one, bringing back for me, many nostalgic memories of being a child. I am hoping to meet up with my uncle again, still a season ticket holder in the North Bank.

The Molineux ground will always be special for me, even though I am not teaching in Bilston any more. The ground may have changed, but you can't erase childhood memories.

Wrexham

When I lived in the Great Wyrley in the Midlands, Ian Pearce was my best friend. He was older than me, had a snotty nose and was a charismatic commentator during Subbuteo matches. Not long after I moved to Crewe his second parent died and he went to live with his sister and husband in Rossett, 6 miles from Wrexham. I used to go up and see him one weekend every couple of months, before we started growing up and eventually drifted apart.

On a couple of occasions his sister dropped us off at the Racecourse for matches. Wrexham were now his team, Wolves still his big team. I remember him talking about the Tech End that was an open visitors terrace in those days. We used to stand on the Kop at the other end. In those days there was a miniature stand in the middle of the terrace. I'm not sure if it was even open half the time, but it gave the singers a place to gather and increase their volume. I remember Burton Albion trying to take the end before one FA cup game. I also recollect being there for a promotion celebration against Peterborough. Wrexham were already promoted to the old 2nd Division and some Preston fans turned up because the result was crucial to them. The ground was full with celebrating fans.

In the 1980's, Wrexham's fortunes took a nosedive and a new derby was created. I went there in 1983/4. Steve Brereton took us in the car, Pete Johnson and Tony Farrell joined us. We stopped at country pubs on the way near Peckforton, one being full of Crewe fans in a friendly and lively mood. Some "Alex" fans were on bikes - fantastic.

We were stood behind the goal with the large stand behind us. 5 minutes into the game, all the Wrexham fans in the Kop spilled over to the Mold Road side of the town to taunt a mob of Crewe fans that had travelled by train and gone into town. According to a PO colleague they'd been putting it about. I remember talking to Phil Connor through a mutual friend we knew through the alternative night out at the Cheshire Cat. I liked him and decided I wanted to see more of him as a mate. Dave Pullar scored a brave diving header to give us the points, injuring himself in the process.

After the game, Steve drove into Wrexham rather than going straight home. Steve was a mad driver at the best of times but speeding up and nearly hitting one of their mobs took me by surprise. They started to give chase, but we had no worries the big mob wouldn't catch Steve's car. Then, there was a red light round the corner. Their quickest runners started to kick the car; when he went over the red light. I thought the car and passengers were 'gonners', we laughed our heads off in relief with my heart still beating rapidly.

The game was a real crunch derby home and away, Wrexham fans took our Social Club roof one year and hostilities still remain today, even though we haven't played them for years.

I returned in the 1988/9 with my Coventry friend Mick. We travelled on the train from Liverpool changing at Bidston. The route is brilliantly described in the first chapter of 'Awaydays' by Kevin Sampson. This was the year some "Alex" fans refused to go in until the club lowered the prices - Marxist football fans shock horror! I suppose they gave in as the police didn't want loads of "Alex" fans milling around the town. I had my black hooded army combat coat on when we met Garf, it was cheap to buy because it had this stain on the front. Gareth called it my elephant spunk coat! The police were trying to improve tense relations and one kindly asked if I had a cold, he thought it was snot. The 3 of us were laughing our heads off about it all through the game.

Mick and I went back to Liverpool that night where there was a Hall of Residence party. I copped off with one of Mick's girlfriend's mates that night. Mick's girlfriend came from Bilston where I now teach, small world. Her friend was a scouser, my first student scouser cop off. I was chuffed; it had been a great day.

Wycombe Wanderers

I went to Wycombe in 1993/4. Phil came down to Kidderminster and met Becky who was was nearly 5 months old. We were both keen to go to Adams Park for the first time, neither of us had been to many games that year and we were looking forward to it.

While driving down the M40 with my foot firmly on the accelerator, the power suddenly disappeared and we managed to pull onto the hard shoulder safely. I am hopeless with cars, as was Phil. I think both of us feared the worst, missing an opportunity to 'do' a new ground. Luckily, we were parked near a phone and waited for Green Flag to save the day. Our scarf was hanging out of the window and an "Alex" fan stopped to see if there was anything he could do to help. He couldn't do anything, but it was very philanthropic of him which was very refreshing.

The Green Flag came within the hour and it was the accelerator cable that had broken. He tied it together, which was sufficient temporarily if we drove carefully, although it did need fixing in the short term.

We continued our journey quickly and carefully! We pulled into the car park at 3.30 and found the away end. It was interesting listening to the crowd and wondering what was happening. The stewards would not let us in until half time, so we waited with about 10 other Crewe fans who were also late. We were eventually let in for nothing and found Strainy and Pete Johnson who informed us of the 1-1 score. I managed to see the two Wycombe goals in the second half. The ground was compact and there was a good atmosphere. We were standing up behind the goal with a small amount of space for us at the side as well. The ground has trees on a high bank above the stands; they looked impressive in the twilight of that late, November afternoon. The trees have a season ticket for nothing!

The car park traffic looked terrible so we had a leisurely drink in their Social Club before heading back to Kidderminster. Thankfully the car made it back without any problems, which was a relief. We stayed in that night and watched 'Match Of The Day' with a couple of beers and forgot the car problems that day.

Yeovil Town

This is an appallingly long journey; I travelled by car because I was picking up my daughter Becky in Kidderminster en route to the game in the 2006/7 season. Tony from the Post Office travelled with us, he was now living in my street and he is a guy who likes to tick off new grounds so he was happy to come along.

We finally arrived in a sunny Yeovil and went for a drink in the marquee next to the ground where a very relaxing drink was had after the long journey.

We were situated in the open end, which was lovely today due to the sunshine. I chatted to Bricky, a student of mine, who for several years never missed an away game, but like many of us cannot sustain this for ever, even if we wanted to.

The game was fairly uneventful; my main memory of Yeovil is that my lad Dylan was mascot for the home game that season and the commemorative picture is still proudly on his wardrobe. Ben Rix was his favourite player and we have photographic evidence to prove this, something that 99% of Crewe fans would find incredible (He was often a target, rightly and wrongly for abuse).

Becky was up for a few days, but I had to quickly drop her off before going to Austin's birthday bash. He still looked incredibly good for his age and was celebrating the night by partly 'djing' his own Northern Soul night. He was a serious fan so I was unlikely to get my commercial favourite 'Ghost in my House' tonight. It was nice to meet up with some old friends from the Post Office at the end of a very long day.

York City

I went to York in the 1981/2 season. I was a postal cadet and finished work at 3.30pm. I got changed, enthusiastic and excited, and went to meet ST and a couple of "Alex" fans in the Royal, 2 minutes walk from work and the "Alex". ST was older and a real snappy casual dresser and I was flattered that he was going to the game with me. We had a few beers before catching the coach to York. I think it was full, which was quite rare at the time. I remember getting off the coach and being surprised to see lots of bed and breakfasts down the street, not the norm for most grounds.

At the start of the game we noticed a bit of an affray in their open end, and some Sandbach Reds were supposed to have been responsible. We were also in an open end and it became clear that on the pitch we were in for a stuffing. ST decided to make his own entertainment and proceeded to the Tea Bar in the corner by the Main Stand where a stunning young woman was working. He spent the second half sweet-talking the desirable Yorkshire lass who enjoyed the attention. He got it right, The "Alex" lost 6-0. He left her at the end to mouth off to a couple of York fans before returning to the coach.

I returned to York with Jackie in 1999 for a short break on the train. I returned to Bootham Crescent to get a cheap B&B. We had a great couple of days sightseeing, eating and drinking and I asked Jackie if I could move in with her. We were very drunk after some daytime drinking but she still seemed cautious. Accordingly, the next day I thought what the hell, lets go to the ground, the more romantic strategies seemed to have failed. We tried to get into the ground, but to no avail, so I looked through holes in fences to be nostalgic. I could see that the home end was now covered and visiting the ground kind of made up for yesterdays disappointment. Later that day Jackie surprised me by saying she would be glad for me to move in, explaining how she was very cautious because of a bad experience and because she's so "bloody indecisive." I have always wondered if that walk around Bootham Crescent and peeping through holes swung it!

I did return to Bootham Crescent in 2001 for a Tuesday night encounter in the League Cup. We decided to make a day of it, Jackie who was now 6 months pregnant and my daughter Becky who was 8 at the time. We decided to drive and strangely we met Shaun Smith, the "Alex" legend in a car park as we were parking up - being a Yorkshire lad he had decided to make a day of it too.

We wandered into town and in glorious sunshine visited the small castle that is York Castle. After a few photo opportunities, we headed up to the river for a bit of a picnic. I imagined some of the pictures on the news when the river has burst its banks there, but was no chance of that today. Later we sauntered back into town and visited the Viking Centre. The tour round was quick and interesting, and the authentic smells stood out as being very realistic. That was enough culture for the day, so we wandered around a few shops before having something to eat in a pub. Jackie was getting a bit tired, so we took a leisurely walk to the ground. We decided to go into the open terrace, it was a lovely night and the two girls sat on the dry terrace, while I did what I like best - which is to stand up and watch football.

Unfortunately, the girls were getting a bit fed up and when the game went into extra time, so I decided that we would call it a day and make our way home. I often tease Dylan by saying that was his first away ground, even if he missed the extra time.

I would love to return to Boothan Crescent as I have become matey with Ali, who is a York City fan, at my school in Nantwich and I'd love to make a day of it again in the future.

Thanks

I would like to thank my Mum first of all who is an avid reader and encouraged me in the past time, this has helped inspire me to take this project on.

My Dad remains forever enthusiastic in supporting everything I do and I hope that at least some of his enthusiasm has rubbed off on me. I am envious of his continued zest for life.

I thank Jak for being patient when I have been writing this and as ever for her technological help without which I would be lost. The kids have been taking little snippets of chapters in and I hope they will enjoy and understand the book in time.

Michael Keane from Coventry has been an inspiration for me and has helped especially in the final stages. Cheers mate.

I would also like to thank Ash's wife Nikki for her help and advice. Nicola Ashton is a brilliant chick lit writer.

I would also like to thank my mate from Malbank, Shep, who is a proper author, has been really supportive and who is responsible for the excellent name of the book.

I appreciate the gallant efforts of Hayley who bravely took the role of proof reading and giving me some sound advice.

I would also like to thank James for helping with IT and social media communication and for helping this book to happen.

I hope I have not offended anybody in the book and stress that it is just my opinion and that my memory may sometimes have played tricks on me. I have tried to be honest and sincere throughout.

Printed in Great Britain
by Amazon